Barnes & Noble Critical Studies

General Editor: Anne Smith

Anthony Trollope

ANTHONY TROLLOPE

edited by

Tony Bareham

WITHDRAWN

BOOKS

10 East 53d St. New York 10022
(a division of Harper & Row Publishers, Inc.)

BARNES & NOBLE

Barnes & Noble Books
81 Adams Drive
Totowa
N.J. 07512

ISBN 0–389–20027–1

First published in the U.S.A. 1980
ⓒ 1980 by Vision Press, London

Printed and bound in Great Britain
MCMLXXX

Contents

Editorial Note

Walter Allen's essay is published by permission of David Higham Associates Ltd.

The Editor thanks Rosemary Gilmore of the English Department, the New University of Ulster, for invaluable assistance with the typing of this book.

There is no standard edition of Trollope's complete works. This makes uniformity of citation for chapters and pages of books impossible to achieve in a collection of essays covering a number of different novels. Contributors have endeavoured to quote from texts which may be available to readers; by giving chapter as well as page references an attempt has been made to facilitate the process of consulting alternative texts.

Introduction

by TONY BAREHAM

1982 will mark the centenary of Trollope's death. The intervening years have seen curious shifts in his popularity and in assessments of his place among the Victorian novelists. The essays in this volume offer new evidence on the range and scope of his achievement, often through consideration of novels which the contributors believe to be unjustly neglected.

Trollope wrote nearly fifty novels, ranging from the gentle *commedia* of *The Warden*, through studies of intellectual alienation such as *He Knew He Was Right*, and the social satire of *The Way We Live Now*, to Wellsian science fiction in *The Fixed Period*. For many years this intensely prolific author was an active civil servant at the Post Office, and in his heyday he combined all this with regular hunting, frequent afternoons of bridge, and travel books on his journeys to Iceland, America, the Caribbean, South Africa, the Middle East, and Australia. His output both of energy and words was phenomenal. Taken with his outward façade of bluff normalcy, his apparently unintellectual advocacy of the values of mid-Victorian respectability, he has proved difficult to assess. He compounded the bewilderment by leaving to posterity a frank yet curiously partial account of himself in *An Autobiography*, which has too often been taken at face value.

By the time he wrote *Doctor Thorne* in 1859 Trollope was being hailed as a potential rival to Thackeray and Dickens. The critics awaited the development which would confirm the promise of *The Warden* and *Barchester Towers*. Yet though his output continued unabated through to 1882, no one single novel seemed to offer complete confirmation of his excellence. As Robin Gilmour points out in his essay for this volume, Trollope never wrote a *Middlemarch* or a *Vanity Fair* to be hailed as his pre-eminent masterpiece.

As they awaited the anticipated *magnum opus* the critics grew uneasy then exasperated; the note of praise in reviews of Trollope becomes somewhat querulous through the later 1860s, and then downright carping. The feeling grows that his art is 'mechanical.' He cannot 'refrain from striking off more copies of an idea than the plate will bear' complained the *Westminster Review* (vol. XXVIII, July 1865), and the notion of Trollope as merely a photographic recorder of actuality is thus given currency, whilst the *Saturday Review* (vol. XVI, 1863) condescendingly likened *Rachael Ray* to 'a brick without straw . . . a very good saleable brick of its kind'.

This suggestion of mechanical output and mercenary motive grew into the claim that Trollope lacked imagination. Four principal charges were laid against him; he lacked any religious message, was deficient as a social prophet, wrote without sense of poetical concentration, and suffered a deficiency of critical self awareness. Henry James's argument that Trollope was a moral coward, afraid to follow to conclusions the problems he raised, coincided with a general distaste for mid-Victorian values and further depressed Trollope's stock. Though not planned as a specific rebuttal of such charges, the essays in this volume suggest that contemporary critics are willing to re-assess the case.

The first real attempt at a revival came with Michael Sadleir's *Trollope, A Commentary* in 1927. As bibliographer and as critic Sadleir drew attention to the whole range of Trollope's work and thought, and subsequent critics have leaned heavily on him. If the writers in this collection sometimes take issue with Sadleir's conclusions, they do so whilst acknowledging his achievement and through a desire to develop rather than contradict.

Large doses of pseudo-Palliser on television have undoubtedly stimulated a new interest in Trollope. The spectacle of these lavishly costumed productions, and the sense of reassurance offered by their evocation of a comfortable affluent world are part of what Trollope intended. Anthony Cockshut and John Halperin have both written books which offer excellent reasons for appreciating the 'political' novels on a far more sophisticated level, and both add to that view in their essays here. Mr. Cockshut analyses 'Trollope's Liberalism', a curiously complex and sometimes apparently self-contradictory sense of values which permeates not only the Palliser novels, but virtually everything Trollope wrote. Professor Halperin looks at the political undertow in *The Eustace Diamonds*, to which he attaches a fresh importance. Both writers suggest that consciousness of the issues of justice, equality, and social balance is never far from Trollope's mind and art.

The emphasis on politics was no sudden eruption, though it may have been given new direction and impetus by Trollope's unsuccessful attempt as Liberal candidate at the Beverley bye-election in 1868. From his early years in Ireland he could draw on first hand experience of schism, dissension, and social violence. The ten years Trollope spent in Ireland were personally happy and fulfilled. They were lived against a background of turbulence, however, which certainly impinged upon the young writer, and he returned to Irish characters and events long after he had left the country. In 'Anthony Trollope and the Matter of Ireland' John Cronin investigates Trollope's Irish background and the work which stemmed from it. Though Trollope may have gradually lost touch with the realities of the situation, and produced the consequent failure of *The Landleaguers*, Dr. Cronin suggests that the two earliest novels—*The Kellys and the O'Kellys*, and *The Macdermots of Ballycloran* are fine achievements, and worth far greater praise than they have received.

These essays on Trollope's political and social thinking add a new strand to the general approach to his work. Other aspects are equally open to reappraisal. Outside the Palliser and Barchester books there exists a vast gallery of finely observed characters. These are depicted with delicate moral sensibility, yet with massive good sense and humour. There is a surprising diversity of tone and method too.

Sadleir observed that Trollope's fiction embraces a conflict between individual decencies and social disingenuities. This is often achieved by drawing a distinction of actions motivated by the heart and those springing from the head. Taking *The Three Clerks* as his starting point Tony Bareham shows how Trollope invariably valued the benignity of the heart above the calculation of the head. *The Three Clerks* embodies this pattern in a complicated web of allusions and metaphors; the novel emerges as 'Dickensian' in its use of symbolism to ramify message.

Simon Gatrell takes us a step further towards a reappraisal of Trollope's art. He argues that *He Knew He Was Right*, with its emphasis on love, mastery, jealousy and madness offers a reminder of the subtle analyses Trollope was capable of making concerning the depths of the human psyche, and that it couples this with a series of deliberate analogies with *Othello*, thus using structure to emphasise meaning.

Robin Gilmour investigates quite different territory. He looks at *The Way We Live Now* in context of the old assertion that Trollope is 'a lesser Thackeray'. In this book Trollope turned upon all the comfortable premises of the mid-Victorian world he inhabited and supposedly upheld. Though he may have lacked some of the remoteness necessary in a great satirist, Trollope's account of society is a grim one. Here at least Trollope refutes the criticism that he accepted too readily the social and literary conventions of his day.

Diversity, ability to surprise, and willingness to experiment thus emerge as attributes of Trollope's work. John Sutherland, in studying Trollope's contributions to the writing and editing of the *St. Paul's Magazine*, offers a further reminder of the man's sheer capacity for literary labour. As well as supplying several suggestions for hitherto unattributed articles, Dr. Sutherland is able to revalue Trollope's own account of his dealings with Virtue in the management of the journal. *St. Paul's* was not a success; 'I was too anxious to be good, and did not enough think of what would be lucrative' was Trollope's claim—an assertion which may surprise readers who know only the Trollope of the Barsetshire novels, seemingly so careful to cater for the public taste.

In the last resort it is these Barsetshire chronicles which have given Trollope his popularity. There is both comfort and assurance in this self contained world of broad acres; genial and affluent, ruffled only by the storms of drawing room fracas and ecclesiastical prejudice, 'hewn out of the earth and put under a glass case, with all its inhabitants going about their daily business . . .' as Nathaniel Hawthorne described it, Trollope's complete new English shire is a marvellous creation. Yet its very success may make that creation seem to be achieved without much art. Joseph Wiesenfarth, in 'Dialects in Barchester Towers' demonstrates that this sense of reassuring detail—Trollope's 'mechanical realism'—is controlled by a sharp sense of order and pattern. He is also able to show Trollope's frequent sympathy with people who live outside the pale of middle-class conformity. If Mr. Arabin is the hero the reader expects, then Bertie Stanhope, his sister Madeline, and old Mr. Harding are the characters Trollope may have most admired in his private capacity as artist.

Discerning the author's true standpoint is frequently a problem. Several of the contributors to this volume find themselves talking of 'the narrator' rather than 'the author'. Trollope contrived to have several voices speaking from outside the story itself, sometimes adding an ironic commentary, sometimes presenting an alternative to the actions and wishes of his *dramatis personae.* As with Professor Wiesenfarth's conclusions on *Barchester Towers* this delicate inter-mixing of narratorial registers can lead to surprises. Walter Allen discusses another Trollopian surprise in his essay on *The Last Chronicle of Barset.* This is assuredly among the half dozen finest novels Trollope wrote. Professor Allen praises the observation of men and manners, the beautifully circumstantial detail of the Barsetshire *mise en scène*, and the comic masterpiece Trollope produced in Mrs. Proudie. All these are surpassed, however, by the study of Mr. Crawley, the perpetual curate of Hogglestock. This analysis of wilfulness, pride, near derangement and heroic fortitude has a capacity to remind us of King Lear: 'with Mr. Crawley . . . Trollope transcends himself'.

Hence, whilst these essays urge the rewards of a broader and more adventurous reading of Trollope, they never repudiate the assured centre of his achievement. His 'sweetness of mind, his sanity and charity' irradiate all, as Professor Allen says.

1

Trollope and the Matter of Ireland

by JOHN CRONIN

To anyone with even a little knowledge of Irish history it must be a source of astonishment that Trollope found his arrival in the country in the year 1841 a liberating and highly enjoyable experience. Yet that it was so is very clear from his forthright account in the *Autobiography*. At twenty-six he put behind him the miseries of his childhood and adolescence, as well as the more recent memories of his seven years of dreary clerking in London, and embarked upon life in his new country with cheerful vigour:

> Ireland accomplished a transformation in him hardly less dramatic than that which characterizes the life-cycles of insects. Hitherto, his state had been dark and larval, or chrysalid at best, and his days had been spent in obscurity and lonely poverty. 'From the day on which I set foot in Ireland,' he wrote, 'all these evils fell away from me. Since that time who has had a happier life than mine?' The essence of the Irish magic was that for the first time he found himself among people who liked him, who did not regard him as a shameful and useless encumbrance.[1]

Yet, the Ireland of 1841 was, in truth, a sombre place enough and one on which the ultimate horror of the Great Famine of 1845–47 was shortly to descend. Daniel O'Connell was still the giant of the political scene and achieved a notable personal triumph in the very year of Trollope's arrival by becoming Lord Mayor of Dublin, the first Catholic to hold the office since the time of James II. Despite this, however, his great career was nearing its end. The accession of a Tory government in 1841 had closed the door to the reforms he had been seeking from Melbourne's administration and had forced him to resume an active campaign for the Repeal

of the Union. Ireland had lost a notable public servant with the
death of Mulgrave's hard-working and devoted under-secretary,
Thomas Drummond, in 1840 and the wretched Tithe War had
been but poorly patched up by the Act of 1838 which had extended the English work-house system to Ireland, contrary to the
recommendations of Whateley's commission. The country at large
was deeply troubled and, during the decade preceding Trollope's
arrival, agrarian secret societies, which had been inactive during
the excitement and enthusiasm of O'Connell's famous Emancipation campaign, once more revived and expanded to an extent
which alarmed the government into the introduction of stringent
Coercion Acts. As O'Connell's Repeal campaign swelled to a
climax which seemed to be bringing the country to the brink of
civil war, the lord lieutenant, De Grey, advised Peel to stand firm
against O'Connell's demands. Extra troops were drafted into Ireland and, in October 1843, a proclamation was issued declaring
O'Connell's monster meeting at Clontarf an illegal assembly.
O'Connell, ever a constitutionalist and no revolutionary, can-
celled the meeting and his personal prestige never really recovered
from this defeat. A prosecution was instituted against him, charg-
ing him with conspiracy to incite disaffection. He was found
guilty and sentenced to imprisonment but the Lords quashed the
conviction on appeal. It is with this conspiracy trial that Trollope
opens his second Irish novel, *The Kellys and the O'Kellys*, though
he soon abandons the political theme in favour of an elaborate
double love plot.

By the time the newly appointed Deputy Postal Surveyor published his first novel, *The Macdermots of Ballycloran*, in 1847, the
country had been devastated by the national cataclysm which was
to become known as the Great Hunger and most of the Irish
novelists had long since fallen silent. The best known of them all,
Maria Edgeworth, had published her last novel on an Irish theme,
Ormond, as long ago as 1817 and in 1834 she wrote to her step-
brother Michael Pakenham Edgeworth, proclaiming her inability
to cope any more in fiction with the grim realities of an Ireland
which was rapidly moving beyond her ladylike ken:

> It is impossible to draw Ireland as she now is in the book of
> fiction—realities are too strong, party passions too violent, to
> bear to see, or care to look at their faces in a looking glass. The

people would only break the glass, and curse the fool who held the mirror up to nature—distorted nature, in a fever. We are in too perilous a case to laugh, humour would be out of season, worse than bad taste.[2]

Her younger contemporary, Gerald Griffin, whose celebrated romantic melodrama, *The Collegians*, had made his name in 1829, had gone on to portray the troubled Ireland of his time in grim tales such as *Tracy's Ambition* (1829) but gradually became oppressed by a ruinous scrupulosity and a conviction of the essential irrelevancy of the writer's trade to the realities of Irish life. He burned his manuscripts, entered a religious teaching Order and died in 1840 of typhus at the early age of thirty six. Griffin's great friend, John Banim, the Kilkenny novelist who had come to Griffin's assistance during his first lonely years in London, had vividly portrayed the turbulence of Irish affairs in the *Tales by the O'Hara Family* which he published, in collaboration with his brother Michael, in 1825 and 1826. But Banim also died young. He fell victim to a cruelly chronic ailment which crippled him while he was still a young man, so that he spent his later years in a wheel-chair and died in Kilkenny in 1842. Charles Lever, of whom Trollope was later to speak with warm affection, left Ireland for the Continent early in 1845. Thus, by the time Trollope turned to the craft of fiction and the matter of Ireland, the only notable figure left from the ranks of the Irish writers was William Carleton. His *Traits and Stories of the Irish Peasantry*, the work by which his considerable reputation principally endures, had appeared in the early 1830's and in the following decade he turned to the writing of fierce political satires such as *Valentine McClutchy* (1845) or elegiac novels like *The Emigrants of Ahadarra* (1847). His bleak and powerful 'Famine' novel, *The Black Prophet*, ran as a serial in the *Dublin University Magazine* throughout 1846 and went into book form the following year, contemporary with Trollope's first novel.

In his choice of material for his first novel and also in his approach to that material, Trollope would seem to have been powerfully influenced both by the Ascendancy fiction of Maria Edgeworth and the grimmer social analyses of such novelists as John Banim and Gerald Griffin. Sadleir credits him with having read 'all the principal novels of Irish life which had appeared during the preceding thirty years':

He read Banim's *O'Hara Tales* and *The Collegians* by Griffin; he read Lady Morgan, Maturin and the early books of Mrs. Hall; he read Maria Edgeworth; most effectually and eagerly of all he read and re-read the works of William Carleton. Then, at Sir William Gregory's house, Coole Park, whither he had gone to exchange Harrow memories with his old schoolfellow, he met Charles Lever.[3]

Bradford Booth is a little more cautious, but agrees that Trollope had some knowledge of the principal Irish novelists:

It is difficult to determine precisely what Trollope had read in Irish fiction when, probably on long evenings in back-country inns, he began *The Macdermots of Ballycloran*. Not a great deal, I think. No doubt he knew *Castle Rackrent* and *The Absentee* through his mother's interest in Maria Edgeworth. And having met Charles Lever at the house of a Harrovian friend, William Gregory, he had surely read *Harry Lorequer* and *Charles O'Malley*; but the picaresque tradition of Irish high-jinks was of little importance for him. What we should like to be able to establish is that he had read Lady Morgan, John and Michael Banim, William Carleton, Gerald Griffin, and Mrs. S. C. Hall. His library catalogue is not very helpful. He owned no book by Carleton, the Banims or Mrs. Hall. Of books by Lady Morgan he had only the *Journal in Italy*, and of a set of Griffin's works only volumes one and eight: a biography and *Poems*. Yet it is unthinkable that an aspiring novelist living in Ireland should not know the work of the leading writers. No doubt as a young man paying off a large debt he chose to borrow books rather than to buy them. We have it on the authority of Escot that he read and admired Carleton. *Fardorougha the Miser* he thought a "really stimulating story," and *Tales of Ireland* he always compared with Dean Ramsay's *Reminiscences of Scottish Life and Character*. It is reasonable to believe that although his reading was not extensive, he had a bowing acquaintance with the chief Irish novelists.[4]

In his first novel, Trollope was indebted to some extent to the 'Big-House' tradition inaugurated by Maria Edgeworth in *Castle Rackrent*. His general framework, relating as it does to the decline of the family whose house gives the novel its title, cannot fail to recall the crazy doings of the Rackrent squires in their creaky castle. There are, however, important distinctions to be made between Trollope's use of this convention and Edgeworth's. Most importantly, Trollope chooses as his hero the doomed son of a Catholic family. It is much more common for the nineteenth-century Irish novelists, from the Edgeworth of *Castle Rackrent* (1800) to the Somerville and Ross of *The Real Charlotte* (1894), to employ the 'Big-House' genre for the exploration of a declining Protestant Ascendancy. Edgeworth brilliantly had the best of both worlds by choosing as her narrator in *Castle Rackrent* the Catholic servitor, Thady Quirke, around whom critical discussion of that novel has continued to revolve. While Trollope does not match the complex insights which the earlier novelist achieved through the choice of a peasant narrator of dubious allegiances, his decision to explore the decline of a well-to-do Catholic family was an important one in that it gives his novel an inwardness in relation to the political stresses of the time which it might otherwise have lacked. For, in the detail of his work, Trollope is much closer to the grim realism of Banim and Griffin than to the Ascendancy manner of Edgeworth. Sometimes the echoes are startlingly precise, as in the hideously brutal account of the savage attack on Hyacinth Keegan in Ch. XXV of *The Macdermots*. In its gruesome detail, one feels, this clearly recalls the equally unpleasant scene in Banim's *Crohoore of the Billhook* in which Peery Clancy savagely cuts the ears off the tithe-proctor who has been buried to the neck to facilitate the dreadful surgery. Both horrific incidents effectively embody the brutal cruelty engendered by the frustrating injustices of the period. In his genuine appreciation of the source of such dreadful behaviour Trollope is much closer to Griffin and Banim than to Edgeworth and Lever. It was an inwardness which Trollope was to display in this one alone of his Irish novels. In *The Kellys and the O'Kellys* and, to a large extent, in *Castle Richmond* he abandons social realism in favour of the novel of manners, and in his last novel of all, *The Landleaguers*, published in an unfinished form in the year after his death, Trollope abandons all attempt to understand the sources of Ireland's violence and, apparently appalled by the Phoenix Park assassinations of 1882, simply mounts an all-out partisan attack on the Land League's agitation against the Irish landlords. This move from sympathetic insight to jingoistic diatribe has been remarked recently by a perceptive American critic:

> The gradual blurring of his vision of Irish experience is reflected in the form of each succeeding Irish novel. The series begins with

17

a fine tragedy, *The Macdermots*. His second and third Irish works are in the tradition of the novel of manners; but because they set their plots against the grim background of 19th-century Irish life without ever being more than superficially touched by that background, they appear either imperceptive or disunified, very unlike Trollope's usual probing and realistic fiction. His last and weakest Irish novel, *The Landleaguers*, is in fact a melodrama, a form that corresponds to the distorted view of Ireland it embodies. . . . *The Macdermots* is Trollope's only Irish novel to succeed as a work of fiction.[5]

Trollope himself appears to have sensed some special quality in *The Macdermots* in spite of his rather dismissive account of its reception, in the *Autobiography*. Many years later, in a letter to Mary Holmes, he comments:

> *The Macdermots* had its merits—truth, freshness, and a certain tragic earnestness being the best of them. The execution was *very bad*.[6]

The mature novelist is here recording both his later dissatisfaction with the novel's technique and his abiding impression that his first novel had in it something in the way of imaginative discernment and real power. It is a judgement with which it is easy to concur. Trollope succeeds in enlisting our genuine sympathies for the unhappy predicament of his hero, Thady Macdermot, around whom he weaves a convincing network of cruel circumstance. What Trollope displays very clearly in this first novel is his precise understanding of the dangerously corrupt methods employed by the authorities to repress a restless subject nation. The society he depicts is one already made familiar in the earlier works of Banim and Griffin. Ribbonism is ever at hand to tempt those who have been alienated from the law by the high-handed and corrupt behaviour of the law's officers. Myles Ussher, a domineering revenue policeman from the north of Ireland, is a handsome and ruthless bully who cares little whether he arrests the innocent with the guilty in the course of his swoops on illicit stills. His seduction of the unfortunate Feemy, Thady's beautiful but ill-educated sister, is equally arrogant and insolent. Trollope handles very well the depiction, of small-town Irish people, fundamentally good-hearted and peaceable but driven to violence by a hard-hearted and corrupt administration in the hands of overbearing Gauleiters like Ussher. Trollope roundly condemns the methods employed by the police to secure convictions:

> It is true, that by paid spies and informers, real criminals may not unfrequently be brought to justice; but those who have observed the working of the system must admit, that the treachery which it creates—the feeling of suspicion which it generates—but, above all, the villainies to which it gives, and has given rise, in allowing informers, by the prospect of blood-money, to give false information, and to entrap the unwary into crimes—are by no means atoned for by the occasional detection and punishment of a criminal.[7]

The novel abounds in examples of precise observation of both groups and individuals. Thady is shuttled backwards and forwards between the moral extremes represented on the one hand by his good friend, Fr. John, and on the other by the local Ribbon organisation. His crazy father, Larry Macdermot, one of the novel's more memorable achievements, hides himself away at home and declines ever further into alcoholism and senility as he neurotically tries to evade the process servers. Thady can look for no comfort from him. Indeed, Larry regularly abuses his son, dementedly accusing him of all sorts of greedy designs. Feemy sits in her parlour across the hall, in sleazy deshabille, deep in romantic novelettes and her dreams of the swaggering Ussher. Thady is left alone to try to stave off the financial ruin which impends and becomes fair game for his scheming rent-collector, Pat Brady, and the embittered Joe Reynolds, and their dangerous associates. The scene in Mrs. Mulready's shebeen at Mohill, in which the Ribbonmen plan the assassination of Ussher, is splendidly convincing in its almost casual horror. The would-be murderers, many of whom can scarcely afford the price of a drink, reach their dangerous decisions by a sort of semi-drunken concensus. One feels the ring of truth here. This, we readily believe, is just how it might have been. Later, at the crowded wedding-scene in Ch. XII, Trollope once again displays considerable power to combine effective comedy with a constant undertone of dangerous menace. He is at his best throughout when he is furthering the central issues of his novel, those which have to do with Thady Macdermot and the cruel inevitability of his eventual doom. When Trollope momentarily abandons his hold on this central issue, the novel lapses into a pattern of rollicking knock-about which is sometimes remi-

19

niscent of the early Lever novels and, indeed, at times almost recalls that quintessentially 'stage-Irish' farrago, Samuel Lover's *Handy Andy*, which had been published the year after Trollope arrived in Ireland. There is, thus, little real excuse for the extended account in Ch. XVII of the 'auction' of the race-horses. Trollope seems here to be offering conventional entertainment to an English public which expects an Irish novel to be full of horses and farces and knock-about fun. In the *Autobiography* he was to be engagingly frank about his tendency to fit in a hunting scene into his novels whatever the consequences:

> I have written on very many subjects, and on most of them with pleasure; but on no subject with such delight as that of hunting. I have dragged it into many novels,—into too many no doubt,—but I have always felt myself deprived of a legitimate joy when the nature of the tale has not allowed me a hunting chapter.[8]

In *The Macdermots*, in the main, he manages to keep the true 'nature of the tale' in mind for most of the time. Thady's accidental killing of Ussher is contrived with economy and fair credibility. It is an act which places Thady at the mercy of the law and causes him to flee for assistance to the very Ribbonmen whose dangerous clutches he has been trying all along to avoid. More cruelly, however, the killing of Ussher earns him the hatred of the sister whom he was trying to protect. Poor Feemy, deprived of her lover, cannot easily forgive his killer and Thady enters on his final ordeal deprived of his crazed father's love and also unsupported by the ruined Feemy. We are made to feel that Thady ought not to hang for his killing of Ussher but the inevitability of his execution is well charted by the novelist, who produces a splendidly Trollopian account of Sir Michael Gibson, one of the three magistrates who are to decide Thady's fate:

> Sir Michael was by far the richest, and would, therefore, naturally have had the greatest number of followers, had it not been that it was usually extremely difficult to find out what his opinion was. He was neither a bad nor a good landlord—that is to say, his land was seldom let for more than double its value; and his agent did not eject his tenants as long as they contrived not to increase the arrears which they owed, when he undertook the management of the property; but Sir Michael himself neither

looked after their welfare, or took the slightest care to see that they were comfortable.

On the bench, by attempting to agree with both his colleagues, he very generally managed to express an opinion different from either of them, and as he was, of course, the chairman, the decisions of the bench were in consequence frequently of a rather singular nature. . . .[9]

To make matters worse, the Ribbonmen's brutal assault on Thady's chief foe, the attorney Hyacinth Keegan, makes Keegan even more embittered against Thady and more determined to contrive his death. The trial scene is very well handled in the novel's closing chapters. Defence counsel's difficulties in the cross-examination of the slippery Pat Brady would suggest that Trollope had read Griffin's celebrated novel, *The Collegians*, and had relished Griffin's corresponding account of the cross-examination of the equally devious witnesses at the climax of the earlier novel. At the end we are left with a profound sense of horror at the fundamental injustice of Thady's death sentence but the novelist's charting of Thady's path to that doom is altogether convincing. The victim's dreadful loneliness is what is most cogently impressed upon us. There is a particularly memorable evocation of his desperation in the chapter which shows him fleeing to the Ribbonmen's cottage on the mountain of Aughacashel, before he decides to give himself up to the law. His only companion during the time he spends at the cottage is a silent old man, Andy McEvoy, whose dreadful presence acquires for Thady an ominously ghoulish quality:

> There he sat on the bed, quite imperturbable,—he hadn't spoken ten words since Thady had got up, and seemed quite satisfied in sitting there enjoying the warmth of the fire, and having nothing to do—how Thady envied his quiescence. Then he began reflecting what had been this man's life—had he always been content to sit thus tranquil, and find his comfort in idleness. At last he got almost alarmed at this old man, why didn't he speak to him? why did he sit there so quiet? doing nothing—saying nothing—looking at nothing—and apparently thinking of nothing; it was as sitting with a dead body, or a ghost, as sitting there with that lifeless, but yet breathing creature.[10]

Trollope's imaginatively sympathetic response to the frustrating tensions of Thady's situation in a society teetering on the brink of dissolution finds a suitable symbolic embodiment in this near-Beckettian confrontation between the hunted Thady and this speechless and senile ancient who somehow, without undue authorial insistence, seems to embody the sterility of the terrorists' hopeless cause. It seems entirely logical that Thady should decide to give himself up, caught as he is between the circumstances of Ussher's murder and the futilities of the Ribbonmen's flouting of all authority. His dreadful isolation finds its appropriate climax in a brutal death on the scaffold and, as he waits his fate in prison, his nihilistic broodings imply the novelist's firm moral condemnation of a society which could thus destroy so inoffensive a person :

> Could he be but once quiet in his grave, and have done with it all—be rid of the care, turmoil, and uneasiness, he would have been content. Could he have been again unborn—uncreated! He had once replied to father John, that existence had been for him a necesary evil; and though checked by the priest for the impiety of the thought, was it odd, if he often thought, that he was one of those, for whom it would have been better had they never been born.[11]

Trollope was never again to sound so sombrely perceptive a note on Irish affairs. This fine novel abounds in genuine insights into the dreadful state of the Irish poor and is throughout informed by a feeling for the root causes of Ireland's troubled state. James Pope Hennessy, while aware of the novel's occasional slackness of form, is alive to its considerable virtues also:

> In form, The Macdermots of Ballycloran is an inchoate work, and, naturally enough in a lengthy first novel, it lacks discipline. But then it deals with a society in conditions of disruption—that chronic Irish state of disruption which had always persisted through the long centuries of British rule, and which has only ceased in the Irish Republic in the last fifty years. There is already much evidence of what Henry James called Trollope's 'good ear'. The speech and the behaviour of the Irish characters swarming through the novel is admirably and meticulously reproduced; but there is far too much of both. It is as though everything that Anthony Trollope had seen and heard in his three years of Irish living had been stored up in a mental reservoir which, as he began to write his novel, burst its banks and became a torrent or a flood.[12]

Trollope's own account of the book's reception has puzzled critics:

> I can with truth declare that I expected nothing. And I got nothing. Nor did I expect fame, or even acknowledgement. I was sure that the book would fail, and it did fail most absolutely. I never heard of a person reading it in those days. If there was any notice taken of it by any critic of the day, I did not see it.[18]

That the novel was noticed by the critics and, in general, favourably received, has been made entirely clear by recent critical investigation.[14] Apart from any more strictly literary considerations, his mother's huge reputation would have ensured that any work by a Trollope would be unlikely to be altogether ignored. His own bravely dismissive account of the reception accorded to both *The Macdermots* and its successor, *The Kellys and the O'Kellys*, barely conceals the wounds inflicted on his sensibility by the blatant surprise manifested by the family at Anthony's turning author. He cared enough about his first novel to revise it extensively for reissue at a later stage, though he was usually adamant in his refusal to cut his work. The extent of his revisions has been charted by R. C. Terry in a valuable article which also commends the novel's successful fusion of public and private themes:

> The great merit of the book is the way in which Trollope integrated an impressive social theme with an engrossing domestic drama, centering on a personal tragedy involving the weak but well-intentioned Thady. Nowhere in Trollope is there more assured harmony of public and personal themes; *Orley Farm*, for example, fails in this respect by a certain discord between the sensational elements of the Lady Mason plot and the attack on the commercial spirit which is the book's main theme. In *The Macdermots* the unity is absolute.[15]

A writer like Trollope, who was in his maturity to display so nice a sense of his public's taste in fiction would, one feels, have been unlikely to fail to sense the English public's growing distaste for Irish novels of a certain kind. It is clear that, by the 1840's, people were weary of reading about Ireland's tedious and apparently incurable woes. The *Athenaeum's* review of *The Macdermots* made the point pretty bluntly:

> . . . an Irish novel has become to us something like the haunted chest in the corner of Merchant Abudah's apartment, which even

when closed he knew to contain a shape of Terror and a voice of Woe! Nor will *The Macdermots of Ballycloran* disenchant anyone from a reluctance engendered like our own. . . .[16]

Trollope's mother and his publishers were quick to point out to him the unpopularity of Irish stories, applying their strictures equally to both the first novel and its immediate successor, *The Kellys and the O'Kellys*, which appeared in 1848. In fact, a perceptive reader would surely have noted the significant change of stance adopted by Trollope in the second work. Indeed, the fact that the second novel was to prove much more popular in England, going into a cheap edition before *The Macdermots* and always remaining easier to procure even up to the present day, indicates that Trollope's second Irish novel contained fewer of those troublesome Irish ingredients which tended to discourage the average English reader. In fact, *The Kellys and the O'Kellys* is as different from *The Macdermots* as Lever's *Harry Lorrequer* is from Carleton's *Fardorougha the Miser*. In his second novel, Trollope completely abandons his earlier involvement in the tragic resonances of the Irish scene and embarks instead on a loosely linked double plot involving two pairs of lovers whose complicated doings occasionally scratch the surface of Irish comedy but never at any stage probe into any more troublous matters. It is true that the novel opens with the conspiracy trial in Dublin of Daniel O'Connell and his Repeal associates but this is simply made the occasion for bringing together the two young men whose complicated amours will subsequently form the twin strands of the novel. These are young Martin Keefe who is to be the wooer of Anty Lynch and Frank O'Kelly, Viscount Ballindine, who eventually weds the wealthy heiress, Fanny Wyndham, niece of the Earl of Cashel.

Michael Sadleir, to whom belongs the credit of resurrecting Trollope's reputation in modern times, is severe on the early Irish novels. He calls *The Macdermots* 'a false dawn', insists that *The Warden* is 'the first Trollopian novel', and sees Trollope's Irish fiction as something from which he was fortunate to escape into more congenial subjects which came to him when he fell 'beneath the slow, wise, soothing spell of rural England':

Ireland produced the man; but it was left to England to inspire the novelist. Indeed one may go further. Ireland, having by

24

friendliness, sport and open air saved Trollope from himself, all but choked the very genius that she had vitalised by her insane absorption in her own wrongs and thwarted hopes.[17]

Sadleir isolates the Irish novels firmly from the rest of the Trollopian *oeuvre* and sees John Murray's rejection of Trollope's guide-book to Ireland as a blessing in disguise. The Irish experience is seen as physically therapeutic but fictionally insignificant:

> Thanks to Ireland he becomes a personality; then a political personality. Nearly he hardens in this mould—so nearly that it leaves its trace on every handling of an Irish theme. His mother takes a hand at reformation. On her advice he tries romantic comedy, but shackles himself with fetters of dramatic form. Fortunately a candid friend is found to disabuse him of complacency. The play is locked into a drawer, and Trollope drifts again to tabulation of Irish actuality. He becomes the fortunate (though angry) victim of a publisher's indolence. He hesitates. Perhaps he has no bent to authorship? And at this vital moment the third and happiest chance of all befalls him; the Irish influence—once a stimulus, now an induration—is withdrawn.[18]

How neat it sounds! But it won't do. Sadleir's demarcation of the Irish fiction is an oversimplification which leaves out of account both the detail of the novels themselves and the gap of over a decade which intervenes between the writing of *The Kellys and the O'Kellys* (1848) and the third Irish novel, *Castle Richmond* (1860). In between, Trollope wrote *The Warden, The New Zealander, Barchester Towers, The Three Clerks, Doctor Thorne* and *The Bertrams*, while the writing of *Framley Parsonage* overlaps that of *Castle Richmond*. Thus, the latter has to be viewed as some sort of sad lapse, if Sadleir's forthright summary of the Irish fiction is to be justified. Indeed, this is how Sadleir views it:

> If *The Bertrams* is Trollope of poor quality, *Castle Richmond* is not in the classic sense Trollope at all . . . *Castle Richmond* must claim the attention of readers of Trollope for its 'Irishism' and not for its fictional significance. It is a document, not a work of art; its appeal is to nationalist enthusiasm, not to the literary appreciation that knows no nationality.[19]

Without in the least wanting to insist that either *The Kellys* or *Castle Richmond* is a neglected masterpiece, one can still feel that Sadleir's views on this are both unhistorical in relation to the

sequence of the published work and, more important, heedless of
the many ways in which both novels abound in distinctively Trollopian characters and effects. One might add that Sadleir is somewhat wide of the mark in thinking that *Castle Richmond* can have
had any sort of 'appeal to nationalist enthusiasm'. Its tiresome
reiteration of Trollope's curious conviction that the Famine was
some sort of divine judgement on the land would be unlikely to
produce the effect Sadleir appears to envisage.

Critics have not been slow to reject Sadleir's strictures on the
Irish novels and the reasons seem fairly obvious. Even in *The
Macdermots* which has, as indicated earlier, a tragic purpose lacking in the rest, one can already see Trollope's capacity for evok-
ing a sense of bustling community life. Mrs. Mulready's shebeen,
the meeting-place of the local Ribbonmen, springs to vivid life.
Denis McGovery's wedding is a memorable combination of rustic
comedy with sombre menace. The assizes at Carrick-on-Shannon
have the ring of actuality—one can almost smell the damp frieze
coats. In *The Kellys and the O'Kellys* Trollope does not allow the
darker side of Irish life to intrude and is free to exercise his talent
for urbane comedy. Anyone with an eye to see will recognise quite
a number of characteristic Trollopian figures in this second work.
The Earl of Cashel is as fully realised and as morally convincing
as any of the principal figures in the Palliser novels. Trollope
shows us a man who is willing to attempt the financial rescue of
his scapegrace son, Lord Kilcullen, through a contrived marriage
with his ward, Fanny Wyndham. If he succeeds he will do so at
the expense of Fanny's real lover, Frank O'Kelly, but Trollope is
already well able to generate for us his distinctive blend of social
comedy, moral insight and that comforting confidence that in the
end everything will work out for the best or, at any rate, for the
better. The teasing malice of our introduction to Lord Cashel is
surely vintage Trollope:

> He had been an Earl with a large income, for thirty years; and
> in that time he had learned to look collected, even when his
> ideas were confused; to keep his eye steady, and to make a few
> words go a long way. He had never been intemperate, and was,
> therefore, strong and hale for his years: he had not done many
> glaringly foolish things, and, therefore, had a character for wis-
> dom and judgement. He had run away with no man's wife, and,
> since his marriage, had seduced no man's daughter; he was,

therefore, considered a moral man. He wasn't so deeply in debt as to have his affairs known to every one; and hence was though prudent; and as he lived in his own house, with his own wife, paid his servants and labourers their wages regularly, and nodded in church for two hours every Sunday, he was thought a good man.[20]

In the feline undulations of that passage, with its momentary unsheathing of the moral claws followed by the reassuring purr of conventional approval, we surely have a foretaste of the mature Trollope of the Barsetshire novels. The Earl's daughter, the Lady Selina, is another triumph of gentle satire:

Lady Selina was always useful, but with a solid, slow activity, a dignified intensity of heavy perseverance, which made her perhaps more intolerable than her father. She was like some old coaches which we remember, very sure, very respectable, but so tedious, so monotonous, so heavy in their motion, that a man with a spark of mercury in his composition would prefer any danger from a faster vehicle to their horrid, weary, murderous, slow security.[21]

The early account of the idiotic royal sinecures occupied by the second Viscount Ballindine is a fine example of the novelist's talent for delicate derision of the pomposities of English public life:

His whole long life was passed in hovering about the English Court: from the time of his father's death, he had never put his foot in Ireland. He had been appointed, at different times from his youth upwards, Page, Gentleman in Waiting, Usher of the Black Rod, Deputy Groom of the Stole, Chief Equerry to the Princess Royal (which appointment only lasted till the Princess was five years old) Lord Gold Stick, Keeper of the Royal Robes, till at last, he had culminated for ten halcyon years in a Lord of the Bedchamber.[22]

This mocking catalogue is, of course, being applied to an Irish absentee landlord whose unfortunate tenants suffer the dire consequences of his neglect, but the moral is not tediously stressed in what is essentially a comedy of manners rather than a study of Irish actuality. There is a faint foretaste here of Trollope's account of his best-known Irishman, Phineas Finn. When Phineas goes to the Commons (and when, later, he returns there in *Phineas Redux*)

27

he will fret and fume as he waits to see whether he will be
granted office of some kind in the government, and Trollope will
apply the same gentle mockery in his depiction of the arcane
gamesmanship of the best club in the world.

In a valuable article on the early novels, Robert A. Donovan
has gone so far as to reverse Sadleir's judgement and contends
that *The Kellys and the O'Kellys* is more typically Trollopian than
The Warden.[23] He sees the second of the Irish novels as a fully
characteristic treatment by Trollope of two sets of lovers who are
subjected to complicated social pressures before a resolution is
reached. The interest lies, he argues, not in the inner, emotional
life of the characters but in the careful exploration by the novelist
of the 'unwritten laws of social propriety, operating at two quite
distinct social levels'. Donovan's study is particularly interesting
in that it opens up for consideration the theoretical issue exposed
by Sadleir's rejection of the Irish fiction as unrepresentative.
Donovan shows how this view can only survive in the context of
a somewhat oversimplified view of what constitutes the essential
Trollope. He considers Sadleir's contention that 'fiction of the
highest type must exclude both an author's private prejudices and
recognisable contemporary events' and comments:

> . . . he is probably correct in assuming that Trollope' best and
> most characteristic work does exclude, if not always his private
> prejudices, at least a distracting concern with contemporary
> events and problems. In other words, *Doctor Thorne* is purer
> Trollope than *The Way We Live Now*.[24]

Donovan then proceeds to place *The Kellys* firmly among that
group of novels to which Sadleir attached the label 'Novels, of
manners, convention, and social dilemma'. He astutely indicates
how a number of characteristic Trollopian fictional practices are
to be seen already fully developed in *The Kellys*. He adverts, for
example, to Trollope's habit, which proved irritating to Henry
James and others, of interfering omnipotently in the affairs of his
characters to remind the reader that what he is perusing is, after
all, only make-believe. He also points to Trollope's regular deter-
mination to explode his own mysteries, his refusal to attempt to
surprise the reader. This habit of the novelist is evidenced in
Castle Richmond by his exposure of the precise significance to
Lady Fitzgerald of the villainous Molletts, a point earlier noted

by Sadleir also.[25] Donovan further asserts that 'Castle Richmond (1860), with its grim and artistically irrelevant pictures of the famine of 1847, substantiates Sadleir's thesis much better than either of the earlier Irish novels'. An early review had commented on the divided nature of Castle Richmond soon after its first appearance:

> Perhaps the most curious part of the book is that which relates to the Irish famine. It is impossible not to feel that that was the part of it about which Mr. Trollope really cared, but that, as he had to get a novel out of it, he was in duty bound to mix up a hash of Desmonds and Fitzgeralds with the Indian meal on which his mind was fixed as he wrote . . . the milk and the water really should be in separate pails.[26]

Although this anonymous commentator differs from Donovan in rating the Famine as Trollope's real subject in the novel, both agree that Trollope's combination of the thesis novel with a novel of manners makes for an uneasy work. Castle Richmond is not really sufficiently effective in either of the areas with which it concerns itself to enable the reader to decide which of his topics was closer to Trollope's heart at the time of writing. The romantic plot concerning Lady Fitzgerald's matrimonial secrets topples over into melodrama in the presence of two such cardboard villains as the Molletts, while the Famine passages, some of which are effective enough in themselves, have the air of being tacked on rather than meaningfully integrated into the fabric of the story. Once again, only a few minor characters survive in the memory to justify the work. The proselytising Aunt Letty, with her horror, of 'Puseyites' is an entertaining creation. Most interesting of all, perhaps, is Lady Desmond who, in her hopeless desire for her daughter's lover, Owen Fitzgerald, seems to be a clear forerunner of Lady Laura Kennedy and her equally hopeless love for Phineas Finn. In view of Trollope's clear announcement, in the opening lines of the novel, of his awareness of the unpopularity of Irish stories, it is not easy to see why he turned to this kind of material at the point where Framley Parsonage was running in the Cornhill but the pattern of his interest in Irish material in the first three Irish novels seems, broadly speaking, clear enough. The Macdermots shows him evincing a genuinely sympathetic interest in the fundamental tensions of the troubled

Ireland of pre-Famine days. The fact that he chose to set it in the 1830's is a clear avowal that he is probing into causes and roots of subsequent unrest and unease. He is consciously placing himself, in this work, in that part of the tradition of the Irish novel which is earlier represented by Griffin and Banim, and, during Trollope's Irish period, most notably by William Carleton. He follows this first novel immediately with one which is altogether different both in its central concerns and in its structural tactics. *The Kellys* is, as Robert Donovan cogently demonstrates, a novel which anticipates in many respects Trollope's later ventures into the exploration of manners, convention and social dilemmas. When, over a decade later, he returns to Irish material in the knowledge that Irish stories are unpopular with both publishers and public, he seems to fall between two stools and produces a near-melodrama with a top-dressing of famine commentary. The troubled Ireland of the nineteenth century, which led so many novelists into the writing of propaganda and social history rather than fiction, was eventually to prove unmanageable for Trollope also and it is no accident that his best-known Irish character of all is one who shakes the dust of his native land from his feet and hies him to the larger island, there to partake in the delicious business of governing an empire. Trollope uses Phineas Finn as Maria Edgeworth had used Lord Colambre in *The Absentee*. Finn is the innocent but totally fascinated neophyte who provides his creator with an invaluable point of entry into the established order of his new country. Through him, Trollope is able, literally, to discover as though they were new all the engaging eccentricities of mid-Victorian England, just as Colambre enabled his creator to discover post-Union Ireland to her readers. The handsome Phineas, amiable, adaptable, not *too* bright, provides Trollope with just the right blend of involvement and detachment for his distinctive kind of social satire. The only time Trollope puts a foot wrong with Phineas is when he allows him to return to Ireland at the end of the first of his novels, to wed the utterly unconvincing Mary Flood Jones. This uncharacteristic gesture by Phineas serves the purpose of bringing the novel to an end but it does so quite unconvincingly. For Phineas to get a conscience about Irish Tenant Right at that stage is about as probable as if Barrington Erle were to enter a Trappist monastery. It is a great relief when, at the beginning of *Phineas Redux*, we find that Mary

Flood Jones has had the fictional decency to die in childbirth, thereby leaving our hero free once more to return to the scene of his earlier parliamentary triumphs. Yet, in a curious way, what Trollope seems ultimately to demonstrate through his handling of the character of Phineas Finn is the unsuitability of a certain type of Irishman for English public life. In the end, Phineas seems as incapable of accommodating himself to the stresses of England as poor Thady Macdermot was of adapting to his lamentable Irish situation. As he explores the gorgeously detailed tapestry of the English ruling classes so brilliantly unfolded for us by Trollope, Phineas is always an odd-man-out. His good looks and general amiability combine with the support given him by Lady Laura Standish to launch him on what seems to be a successful career but his is an uneasy progress at best and, indeed, he finds himself in the climax of his public career under the shadow of the gallows, as does Thady at the end of his story. Even when he has been freed from gaol and resumes public life he finds he lacks the suppleness of conscience required by holders of government offices. The Irish landowner, Laurence Fitzgibbon, is happy to perform any *volte-face* required of him by his governmental superiors but the moneyless Irish Catholic, Phineas Finn, finds such goings-on unpalatable. When Madame Max Goesler asks him whether he thinks public life is altogether a mistake, Phineas replies simply 'For a poor man, I think that it is, in this country'. Thady Macdermot dies cruelly on the gallows, while Phineas ends up in the warm embrace of the beautiful and wealthy Madame Max but, in their inability to accommodate themselves finally to their Anglicised environments, the pair have more in common, perhaps, than their different fates might suggest.

By 1882, the year of his death, when Trollope tackled his last novel of all, *The Landleaguers*, he had moved a very long way from the imaginative penetration of Ireland's problems which he had displayed in his first novel. In the interval, Ireland had seen two attempts at insurrection, in the abortive efforts of 1848 and the Fenian Rising of 1867, and Trollope, never a radical, seems to have moved more and more to a High Tory establishment stance on Ireland. James Pope Hennessy has rightly pointed out that the horrific Phoenix Park murders of Lord Frederick Cavendish, Chief Secretary for Ireland and his Under-Secretary, Mr. Burke, were not the actual occasion of Trollope's last novel.[27]

31

Various letters make it quite clear that he had already begun the book before the assassinations took place. In a letter to his son, Harry, on 19 February 1882 he announces his intention of 'taking a run over to Ireland in reference to a book I am thinking of writing'[28] and he wrote to George Bentley, editor of the periodical *Temple Bar* on 30 March following that he intended going to Ireland and 'shall bring out a novel as to the condition of the country—which you will agree with me is lamentable enough.'[29] All the same, the Phoenix Park murders, which took place on 6 May, must have horrified Trollope as they did everyone else. In Ireland, as his letters make clear, his contacts were all with 'men, who are informed and thoroughly loyal.'[30] He stayed with or called on judicial commissioners, bank directors, resident magistrates and, inevitably, senior officials of the Post Office such as Baron Emly, a former Postmaster General. He was unlikely to hear much radical discussion in these circles, and in a letter to his wife he voiced a strongly anti-Parnell line:

> My own idea is that we ought to see the Parnell set put down. We should try it out with them and see whether we cannot conquer them. I do not doubt but that we could, them and the American host at their back.[31]

He returned to England in June but, evidently feeling the need for further researches, he went to Ireland again in August and stayed until September. The novel which occasioned all this travelling at a time when Trollope's health was failing badly, remained unfinished at his death and was published in 1883 with a brief Postscript by his son, Henry, indicating how Trollope had meant to develop some of the relationships in the novel. Although *The Landleaguers* is unfinished, he had completed over three hundred pages before his death and there is enough of it to enable one to see the nature of his broad design. It is a vehement but disjointed attack on the Land-League and its efforts to undermine the power of the Irish landlords. There is no pretence whatever of political objectivity. The attitude to the Land-League agitators is even more openly antagonistic than that displayed in Somerville and Ross's novel, *Naboth's Vineyard* (1891). Conscious, perhaps, of the continuing unpopularity of dreary Irish themes, Trollope provides the novel with a London dimension which has to do with an emancipated Irish-American opera singer, Rachel O'Mahony, whose father is a Republican zealot who has come over from America to further the cause of Irish freedom. Rachel, surely one of Trollope's least attractive women, is outspoken to the point of being an arrant bore. She is also more than a little anti-Semitic in her sentiments. Her link with the Irish section of the novel's action is through her lover, Frank Jones. He is the son of a Mr. Philip Jones who has been for some thirty years an extensive landowner and benevolent landlord in Co. Galway. It is against Jones that the assault of the Land-League agitators is directed. They wreck his dykes and flood some of his most valuable lands, thereby causing him ruinous financial loss. Later, they institute a severe boycott of his family and property so that he and his children are totally isolated in their home and unable to sell their farm produce or employ local labour. This is all bad enough but what troubles Jones most of all is his fear that his young son, Florian, is in league with his enemies. At this point Trollope sinks into simplicities of a distressing kind. Florian, who is a mere ten years old, is won over to Catholicism by a fanatical local priest, one Fr. Brosnan. Why Trollope should have chosen to make master Florian, surely one of the most improbable converts in the whole history of either religion or the novel, a mere ten years old it is difficult to imagine. Having begun thus unconvincingly, Trollope spares us little in the way of melodramatic contrivance. Florian is won back to his Protestant loyalties by Captain Clayton, a gallant, true-blue police officer who makes Myles Ussher of *The Macdermots* seem a triumph of convincing characterisation. Florian agrees to testify against his wicked Irish Catholic Land-League associates but, on the way to the courthouse, he is shot dead by assassins and expires in his father's arms. It would obviously be quite unfair to ascribe any real significance to this unconvincing and unfinished work by an elderly and ailing man long out of touch with the disastrously complicated events of a country which he had once known very well indeed. In his handling of Ribbonism in *The Macdermots of Ballycloran* nearly forty years earlier, and particularly in his powerfully discerning account of the character and dilemma of Thady Macdermot in that novel, Trollope had amply demonstrated his ability to probe beyond the trite official explanations of the Irish situation and search out the fundamental causes of Irish misery, both as it concerned the community and as it afflicted the individual. A few years after the publication of *The Land-Leaguers*, an Irish landlord of genius who had little cause to love agitators of any kind, published an important novel which illuminates the whole period much more thoroughly than Trollope's last sad offering. George Moore's *A Drama in Muslin* (1886) offers a blend of irony and passion which goes a long way towards matching fictionally the contradictions and agonies of the Ireland of the period and a comparison between Moore's first Irish novel and Trollope's last adequately places the regrettable deficiencies of the latter.

In any summary of the achievement of Trollope's Irish novels, *The Land-Leaguers* must be charitably ignored as an aberration. His earlier and better Irish novels fulfil a dual purpose in relation to his mature achievement. On the one hand, they abound in characters and strategies of a familiar Trollopian kind. On the other, they establish his emotional range as extending all the way from Austenian social satire to the profoundest reaches of personal loneliness and despair.

NOTES

1 Hugh Sykes Davies, *Trollope*, London, 1960, 7–8.
2 Quoted by Marilyn Butler, *Maria Edgeworth: A Literary Biography*, Oxford, 1972, 452–53.
3 Michael Sadleir, *Trollope: A Commentary*, London, 1927, 143–44.
4 Bradford A. Booth, *Anthony Trollope: Aspects of His Life and Art*, London, 1958, 106.
5 E. W. Wittig, 'Trollope's Irish Fiction', *Eire–Ireland*, IX, 3 (Autumn 1974), 98–9.
6 Bradford A. Booth (Ed.), *The Letters of Anthony Trollope*, Oxford, 1951, 317.
7 *The Macdermots of Ballycloran*, i, 282–83.
8 Anthony Trollope, *An Autobiography*, ed. Sadleir, O.U.P., 1953, 55.
9 *The Macdermots of Ballycloran*, iii, 21–2.
10 ibid., iii, 344–45.
11 ibid., iii, 266.
12 James Pope Hennessy, *Anthony Trollope*, London, 1971, 107–8.
13 *Autobiography*, *op. cit.*, 64.
14 See Lance O'Tingay, 'The Reception of Trollope's First Novel', *Nineteenth-Century Fiction*, 6, 3 (1951), 195–200.
15 R. C. Terry, 'Three Lost Chapters of Trollope's First Novel', *Nineteenth-Century Fiction*, 27, 1 (1972), 74.
16 Quoted by Lance O'Tingay, *op. cit*, 199.
17 Sadleir, *op. cit.*, 142–43.

18   ibid., 150.
19   ibid., 387.
20   *The Kellys and the O'Kellys*, i, 223–24.
21   ibid., iii, 7.
22   ibid., i, 31–2.
23   Robert A. Donovan, 'Trollope's Prentice Work', *Modern Philology*, 53, 3 (1956), 179–86.
24   ibid., 179.
25   Sadleir, *op. cit.*, 387.
26   *Saturday Review*, 19 May 1860, ix, 643–44 (Quoted in *Anthony Trollope: The Critical Heritage*, ed. Donald Smalley, London, 1969, 113–14).
27   James Pope Hennessy, *op. cit.*, 386.
28   *Letters, op. cit.*, 475.
29   ibid., 478.
30   ibid., 481.
31   ibid.

2

Dialectics in *Barchester Towers*

by JOSEPH WEISENFARTH

Barchester Towers is a novel about ambition. It offers four prizes so representative of position and money that they are all but irresistible: the bishopric of Barchester, the wardenship of Hiram's Hospital, the cathedral deanery, and the hand of Eleanor Bold. Obidiah Slope contends vigorously for all four; Francis Arabin more moderately for two. Trollope saliently contrasts Arabin and Slope in relation to how they seek what they want. Their opposite approaches and the outcome of them conveniently organise the novel into three volumes.

Volume One (chs. 1–19) sets Slope in action. He vies with Mrs. Proudie for the bishopric while trying to retain the good will of the bishop; he uses the vacant wardenship as stick and carrot to manoeuvre Mr. Harding and Quiverful; and he plays suitor to Eleanor at the same time that he is Madeline's lover. The weakness of Slope's position is exquisitely revealed in chapter 19 when he visits the Stanhopes: he is uneasy that everyone expects Mr. Harding to be named warden and he is embarrassed that Madeline greets him as a lover while Eleanor looks on. Even when Slope gazes at the night-sky and hears Venus, Diana, and Jupiter discussed he is reminded once again of his Venus, the signora; his Diana, the widow; and his Jupiter, the London newspaper that, contrary to Mrs. Proudie's wishes, endorses Mr. Harding's return to the hospital. 'Barchester by Moonlight' is nicely arranged to remind the reader that Mr. Slope is always a man between alternatives: between Dr. and Mrs. Proudie, between Mr. Harding and Quiverful, and between Eleanor Bold and Madeline Neroni. Slope's constant dilemma is that he always wants everything and cannot decide who is most likely to satisfy him. Unlike Paris before him, he finds that no one bribe is complete enough to supersede other tempting alternative possibilities.

Volume Two (chs. 20–34) sets Arabin in action and develops his character in opposition to Slope's. Madeline puts their contrasting traits so neatly in a nutshell in chapter 38 that she reminds the reader how artfully Trollope has constructed his novel; she says to Arabin:

> He is gregarious; you are given to solitude. He is active; you are passive. He works; you think. He likes women; you despise them. He is fond of position and power; and so are you, but for directly different reasons. He loves to be praised; you very foolishly abhor it. He will gain his rewards, which will be an insipid, useful wife, a comfortable income, and a reputation for sanctimony; you will also gain yours. (p. 384)[1]

These and related qualities of character are developed in comparable chapters of each volume. 'A Morning Visit' (ch. 5), for example, shows Slope abusing the archdeacon with his discontent at the physical amenities of the palace; 'St. Ewold's Parsonage' (ch. 21) shows Arabin restraining the archdeacon from repairing the parsonage, which suits him well enough as it is. 'War' (ch. 6) finds Mr. Slope preaching his 'doctrine, and not St. Paul's' for thirty minutes in the cathedral and leaving 'all Barchester . . . in a tumult' (p. 62). 'Mr. Arabin Reads Himself in at St. Ewold's' (ch. 23) finds Arabin preaching 'the great Christian doctrine of faith and works combined' for twenty minutes and sending his congregation home 'to their baked mutton and pudding well pleased with their new minister' (p. 221).

Volume Three (chs. 35–53) disposes of the goals of ambition sought by Arabin and Slope. In Act II of Ullathorne Sports Slope loses Eleanor and leaves Arabin to win her hand. The chaplain's defeat finds its analogue in Harry Greenacre's wild charge at the quintain—a device that when awkwardly touched unhorses a clumsy sportsman with a merciless swat. Slope's grab at Eleanor's waist earns him an immediate slap in the face that ends his untimely pursuit forever. Slope also fails to dispose of the wardenship as he would like to. Quiverful gets the nod from Mrs. Proudie, who has become bishop, another goal that Slope has fruitlessly pursued. Finally Mr. Harding and then Arabin are offered the deanery and the bishop's chaplain is offered nothing. Arabin, the truthful man of moderate ambition, gets the better of Slope, the deceitful man of unbridled ambition. And Madeline, who helps Arabin with Eleanor, exposes Slope to the laughter of his political and clerical rivals, Thorne and Arabin, by revealing his double-dealing in preferment and romance. Unable to choose a mistress among his Juno, Diana, and Venus, he is expelled from the palace, slapped in the face, and laughed to scorn. Slope is made to eat the apple of discord that he brazenly set rolling through the Barchester diocese.

Trollope develops this classically spare outline of his comedy in the context of age-old wisdom. Reading *Barchester Towers* is at times like dipping into the *Oxford Dictionary of Quotations*. The novel is laced with aphoristic wisdom coming from proverbs, maxims, songs, and poetry. 'There is a proverb with reference to the killing of cats' (p. 11), says the narrator in chapter 1—'More ways of killing a cat than choking her with cream'—when he wants the reader to know that the outgoing prime minister has promised Archdeacon Grantly the bishopric of Barchester indirectly, not directly. Although John Bold has died an untimely death, Johnny Bold is born to Eleanor to show how 'God tempers the wind to the shorn lamb' (p. 24). Trollope re-enforces this divine wisdom with hard human prudence: 'Let me ever remember my living friends, but forget them as soon as dead' (p. 25). Mr. Harding hesitates to take the wardenship on Slope's terms because 'It's bad teaching an old dog tricks' (p. 122). Bishop Proudie rebels against his wife just as 'Dogs have turned against their masters, and even Neopolitans against their rulers, when oppression has been too severe' (p. 31). He casts his lot with Mr. Slope against Mrs. Proudie convinced that '*Ce n'est que le premier pas qui coute*' (p. 314); nevertheless, he is fairly warned not to: 'Better the d—— you know than the d—— you don't know' (p. 248). Mr. Slope is content to make slower progress with Eleanor because he knows that 'Rome was not built in a day' (p. 153). When Arabin tells Eleanor that 'Charity should begin at home' (p. 298), she replies, 'You should practise as well as preach' (p. 298). Looking for a candidate to charge the quintain, Miss Thorne becomes philosophical: 'One man can take a horse to water, but a thousand can't make him drink' (p. 353). Having drunk deeply at the *fête champêtre*, Mr. Slope resolves to go ahead with a proposal of marriage, saying to himself, 'That which has made them drunk has made me bold' (p. 401). But, as Mrs. Quiverful knows, 'There's many a slip 'twixt the cup and the lip' (p. 435).

This proverb appears a second time, slightly embellished, to characterize this indomitable wife's pursuit of preferment for her hapless husband. 'There might be some slip between the cup of her happiness and the lip of fruition,' but Mrs. Quiverful persists and wins the wardenship she sought. The use of the same aphoristic wisdom twice in the Quiverful story is characteristic of Trollope's using some simple sayings as leitmotifs to link segments of a strand of action. When in chapter 17, 'Who Shall be Cock of the Walk,' for instance, Mr. Slope challenges Mrs. Proudie for the bishop's apron, Trollope asks, 'Does not every cock fight best on his own dunghill?' (p. 158)—a question that is answered in chapter 26, 'Mrs. Proudie Wrestles and Gets a Fall'; here Slope comes to the aid of the henpecked bishop and helps him 'take a proud place upon a dunghill' (p. 247). Mr. Slope has already decided that 'either he or Mrs. Proudie must go to the wall' over Hiram's Hospital—'The weakest goes to the wall'—and he feels confident of victory because he has recently overcome Mr. Harding, who has had to 'go to the wall in the manner so kindly prophesied to him by the chaplain' (p. 281).

This one-line literature of worldly wisdom also shapes the matrix of Mr. Slope's most humiliating defeat. In matching wits with Madeline Neroni he more than meets his mistress: 'He was the finest fly that Barchester had hitherto afforded to her web' (p. 259). Indeed, she 'sat there . . . looking at him with her great eyes, just as a great spider would look at a great fly that was quite securely caught' (p. 266). And Mr. Slope is caught like Dido, who mingled 'love and business' and consequently 'fell between two stools' (p. 261).

> There's an old song [says Trollope] which gives us some very good advice about courting:
>
> It's gude to be off with the auld luve
> Before ye be on wi' the new.
>
> Of the wisdom of this maxim Mr. Slope was ignorant. . . . A man should remember that between two stools he may fall to the ground. (p. 258)

When Madeline brings Slope to the ground, she sings to him as he tumbles:

> It's gude to be merry and wise, Mr. Slope;
> It's gude to be honest and true;

It's gude to be off with the old love, Mr. Slope,
Before you are on with the new. (p. 471)

Slope is, in the end, the cock who is kicked off his dunghill and
the fly who is eaten by the spider. As one who is not off with the
old love before he is on with the new, who mixes business and
love, and who falls between two stools, he is presented as an
offender against the accumulated wisdom of the ages. This is one
reason why his foolishly pursued ambition makes him such a
threat to Barchester society. Should Slope succeed in his ecclesiastical designs, the Church would suffer from his lust for power;
should he succeed as a suitor, marriage would be nothing but an
economic adventure. Slope is consequently a threat to the family,
society's smallest unit, and to the Church, society's largest bul-
wark of right-conduct. Eleanor's situation is quite appropriately a
personal reflection of the Church's public position; one is an
image of the other. Both are misunderstood by clergymen who
are called 'men of the world'; both are worth £1,200 in yearly
income; both are pursued by Arabin and Slope; both are adhered
to unswervingly by Mr. Harding; and both, finally, get the same
dean. It is manifestly Trollope's opinion that Slope, whom he describes as a devil—and as befits the devil, a liar—is undeserving
of the good things that should belong to gentlemen only: a
powerful position, a handsome income, a beautiful wife, and a
comfortable house. These things, the action of the novel asserts,
belong by right to men like Arabin.

Such men, however, are not easily characterized. Trollope feels
his powers inadequate to present a faithful picture of Arabin. He
feels that 'words forsake, elude, disappoint, and play the deuce
with him, till at the end of a dozen pages the man described has
no more resemblance to the man conceived than the sign-board
at the corner of the street has to the Duke of Cambridge' (p.
181). Perhaps this is because Arabin at forty is somewhat like
Trollope at forty-two and the difficulty of disengaging one personality from the other is trickier than expected. Both Arabin and
Trollope were younger sons. Both attended Winchester and were
meant to be fellows of New College, where neither arrived.[2] Both
had a respect for the Oxford Movement but neither became
Roman Catholics.[3] Both were inarticulate with women. Both
relished the good life but neither lied or cheated to achieve it.

Arabin is a blend of the same kind of 'worldliness and idealism' that characterizes Trollope's public image—but a kind of worldliness and idealism, *Barchester Towers* finally suggests, that is not sufficiently inspiring to satisfy an artist's imagination. That Trollope's difficulty in presenting Arabin adequately is not just the novelist's toying with the reader is confirmed by one critic's seeing Arabin as rescuing the novel from triviality, satire, and pessimism[4] while another critic finds chapter 20, entitled 'Mr. Arabin,' so uncharacteristic of the rest of the novel that it becomes impossible for us to 'know how to take Arabin afterwards.'[5]

Following on Slope's chapter, 'Barchester by Moonlight', chapter 20 links Arabin to the bishop's chaplain by way of a proverb: 'Truly he had fallen between two stools' (p. 192). But Arabin fell because he underwent a series of changes connected with a growing understanding of himself and his place in life, not because he was an opportunist. He is not a trimmer who cannot decide between equally attractive alternatives; he is a late-starter who is slow to see his authentic goals in life. Arabin is shown as a man who was once a Tractarian, once an apostle, once a lonely bachelor, and once a poorly paid professor of poetry. He is now no longer content with these things because 'the daydream of his youth was over' (p. 190). That daydream was founded on a stoicism that Trollope exposes as a pernicious doctrine which 'can find no believing pupils and no true teachers' (p. 191). Indeed, the idea of renouncing 'wealth and worldly comfort and happiness on earth' is pronounced 'an outrage on human nature' (p. 191). When Arabin belatedly comes fully to understand his own human nature, he regrets not having the good things in life: 'no wife, no bairns, no soft sward of lawn duly mown for him to lie on, no herd of attendant curates, no bowings from banker's clerks, no rich rectory' (p. 192). Arabin's ambition, in short, is the natural complement of his maturity.

By way of the radical changes that Arabin undergoes Trollope maintains that to interfere with the comforts of an English gentleman—established religion, family, money, and position—is unnatural. Arabin at age forty is a convert to the doctrine that Trollope as narrator preaches at the age of forty-two. And, one should carefully note, Slope is a true believer too.

Slope wants only a little more than Arabin as far as the good life is concerned. Although Arabin never wants to be bishop, both he and Slope want to be Eleanor's husband and Barchester's dean. But Slope is an English gentleman neither by birth nor conduct, as even Mr. Harding reluctantly admits: 'He is not gentlemanlike in his manners, of that I am sure' (p. 122). Slope is Trollope's more elegantly named scion of Sterne's Slop family who tries to subvert High Church practice, who makes love to a married woman, and who lies repeatedly in seeking a wife and deanery. Slope's ends tally with natural ambition—'the *nolo epis-copari* . . . is . . . directly at variance with the tendency of all human wishes' (p. 14)—but Slope's means make him an over-reacher. Trollope makes him a red man—hair of 'pale reddish hue,' face 'a little redder,' and nose like 'red-coloured cork' (p. 37)—a liar, and 'the d—— you don't know' (p. 248). The low-bred, mean-minded, callously manipulative Slope is a comic form of devil. Arabin, on the other hand, has so forthright a character that he is seen as 'a little child' (p. 390). Therefore, whereas Slope is struggled against, Arabin is helped. Dr. Grantly gives him St. Ewold's, Madeline delivers Eleanor into his hands, Mr. Harding renounces the deanery in his favour, and a Whig government appoints him to clerical office. Arabin represents for every faction in the novel the best of what one reviewer of *Barchester Towers* called, in a happy phrase, 'the second-class of good people':

> [Trollope] has the merit of avoiding the excess of exaggeration. He possesses an especial talent for drawing what may be called the second-class of good people—characters not noble, superior or perfect, after the standard of human perfection, but still good and honest, yet with a considerable proneness to temptation, and a strong consciousness that they live, and like to live, in a struggling, party-giving, comfort-seeking world.[6]

With Arabin the second-class of good people finds its hero and *Barchester Towers* touches ground and stands four-square. His reasonable ambitions are completely satisfied and the novel's conventional wisdom is thoroughly justified. But if *Barchester Towers* were nothing more than this would it still be a masterpiece? I hardly think so. It is every bit as much about lack of ambition and contemporary events as it is about ambition and aphoristic wisdom. This dialectic has kept the novel alive and interesting six score years and more.

Barchester Towers is larded with references contemporary to and nearly contemporary with its writing. There is even a reference to *Little Dorrit* which Dickens was writing and serialising while Trollope was writing his novel.[7] And as an alternative to the kind of death-scenes that Mr. Popular Sentiment made famous, Trollope gives us one of another kind:

> 'God bless you, my dear,' said the bishop with feeble voice as he woke. 'God bless you—may God bless you both, my children.' And so he died.
>
> There was no loud rattle in the throat, no dreadful struggle, no palpable sign of death. . . . Neither Mr. Harding nor Dr. Grantly knew that life was gone, though both suspected it. . . .
>
> 'My lord's no more,' said Mrs. Phillips, turning round and curtseying low with solemn face; 'his lordship's gone more like a babby than any that I ever saw.' (p. 14)

Trollope prefers Donne to Dickens here and allows the old bishop to die as do 'virtuous men' who

> pass mildly away,
> And whisper to their souls to go,
> Whilst some of their sad friends do say,
> The breath goes now, and some say, No.

Trollope not only capitalises on Dickens and death as his novel opens but he also comments on the frequent demise of ministries in the 1850s.

There were two new governments in 1852: the Earl of Derby's in February and the Earl of Aberdeen's in December; and Palmerston formed his first cabinet in February 1855.[8] Trollope gives his novel a contemporary, candid, and worldly-wise cachet by giving a behind-the-scenes report of what happens—so different from what we think happens—when governments change. How the 'Earl of —— in his inner library'

> stamped his foot as he thought of his heavy associates—how he all but swore as he remembered how much too clever one of them had been—my creative readers may imagine. But was he so engaged? No: history and truth compel me to deny it. He was sitting easily in a lounging chair, conning over a Newmarket list, and by his elbow on the table was lying open an uncut French novel on which he was engaged. (p. 17)

Trollope's outgoing Tory prime minister is suspiciously like Lord

Stanley, Earl of Derby, who had a passion for books and race-horses. He preferred translating Homer to talking politics, and Disraeli complained that he could never find Derby because he was 'always at Newmarket or Doncaster.'[9] Derby, for his part, thought Disraeli a 'scoundrel'[10] even before his minister of the exchequer presented a free-trade budget too cleverly replete with unworkable compromises—a budget that Gladstone so mercilessly destroyed that his attack brought down Derby's government.[11] The ministry in *Barchester Towers* is a shadow of this reality, and gives one the sense of reading a *roman à clef*. This method of grounding today's lively fiction on yesterday's lively facts is also used in part to characterize the Proudie and Grantly parties in the novel.

Both Sabbatarianism and university reform were popular topics in the 1850s. When the archdeacon and Mr. Harding pay a courtesy call to the palace, they learn that the bishop is a patron of the 'Manufacturing Towns Morning and Evening Sunday School Society'. Mrs. Proudie and Mr. Slope then demand to know their visitors' views on 'Sabbath-day schools', 'Sabbath-travelling', and 'Sabbatical amusements'. 'Mr. Harding had never been so pressed in his life' (p. 48), and Archdeacon Grantly is forced to open 'the safety-valve of his anger' and emit 'visible steam' to prevent 'positive explosion and probable apoplexy' (p. 50). When Slope offers Mr. Harding the wardenship, he orders him to preside over 'a Sabbath-day school' and to conduct 'morning and evening service' for the pensioners' on the premises every Sabbath': 'for people of that class the cathedral service does not appear to me the most useful' (p. 114). Slope's class-consciousness reminds one that 'when the railways began to spread, an attempt was made to stop Sunday travel, or at least to prevent third-class carriages from running.'[12] Indeed, at the time that Trollope was writing *Barchester Towers*, the old problem of Sunday observance—it began with the Puritans—was once again to the fore. In 1856 a bill proposing the opening of the National Gallery and the British Museum on Sundays was defeated, and Palmerston was 'obliged to accede to the Archbishop of Canterbury's request, that in deference to public opinion, the military bands in Kensington Gardens and elsewhere should be silenced.'[13] Palmerston's friend, C. C. F. Greville, wrote in disgust that 'Cant and Puritanism are in the ascendant, and it will be well if we escape more stringent measures against Sunday occupations and amusements. It is stated that the Sabbatarians are so united and numerous that they could carry any election!'[14] Indeed, since *Barchester Towers* begins with a change of ministries, we know that the Sabbatarians have done just that.

If the palace is identified with Sabbath-day reforms, the arch-deaconry is identified with opposition to university reform at Oxford. University reform was a controversial political issue from 1850 to 1856—from Lord John Russell's letter to the Duke of Wellington announcing a Commission of Inquiry through the establishment of the Royal Commission in 1852 to the parliamentary acts of 1854 and 1856 implementing the reforms.[15] Bishop Proudie is a member of the 'University Improvement Committee', which is about to finish its 'final report' (p. 44) when Grantly and Harding pay 'A Morning Visit' (ch. 5) to the palace. That report is finished by the time of 'Mrs. Proudie's Reception' (ch. 11) where it is discussed by the bishop and the archdeacon and his friends:

> 'Well, Mr. Archdeacon, after all, we have not been so hard upon you at Oxford.'
> 'No,' said the archdeacon, 'you've only drawn our teeth and cut out our tongues; you've allowed us still to breathe and swallow.'
> 'Ha, ha, ha!' laughed the bishop;. . . . 'Why, in the way we've left the matter, it's very odd if the heads of colleges don't have their own way quite as fully as when the hebdomadal board was in all its glory; what do you say, Mr. Dean?'
> 'An old man, my lord, never likes changes,' said the dean. (p. 104)

And some young men are like the old man too. Tom Staple, Arabin's and Dr. Gwynne's advisor in chapter 34, is one of them: 'Tom Staple would have willingly been impaled before a Committee of the House, could he by such self-sacrifice have infused his own spirit into the component members of the hebdomadal board' (p. 344). And Arabin is another: he 'opposed tooth and nail all projects of university reform, and talked jovially over his glass of port of the ruin to be anticipated by the Church and of the sacrilege daily committed by the Whigs' (p. 186). Having been seasoned at the battle of Oxford, Arabin is imported, almost as a mercenary, to fight in the battle of Barchester. But his standing with old men like Dean Trefoil on the issue of university reform is rather a weakness than a strength of character in the 'new champion'.

Most historians agree with Woodward's assertion that 'the condition of Oxford and Cambridge invited criticism'.[16] Like the old dean, soon to die of apoplexy, the hebdomadal board, the governing body at Oxford, 'was composed mainly of heads of houses, elderly and safe men who did not wish for change';[17] it was described as 'an organised torpor'.[18] The 'sacrilege' that Arabin opposes is the decision to award degrees to those who do not subscribe to the Thirty-nine Articles.[19] Fittingly, the free-thinking Stanhope, a Cambridge drop-out, feels free to interrupt the bishop and the archdeacon's conversation to suggest further the need for university reform: 'In Germany the professors do teach; at Oxford, I believe, they only profess to do so, and sometimes not even that' (p. 104). These extravagant remarks are true: the verdict of the Royal Commission was that at Oxford 'teaching was nearly extinct, and that professorial lectures had suffered something more than what the friends of the existing system called "a temporary interruption".'[20] The Oxford partisans at Mrs. Proudie's reception nevertheless refuse to discuss the matter 'with a young man with such clothes and such a beard' as Bertie Stanhope's.

Many critics of *Barchester Towers* argue that Trollope sides with conservative clergymen against their liberal counterparts in the novel. But clearly, in chapter 11, both Bishop Proudie and Bertie have the better of the argument, as the history of university reforms that Trollope alludes to demonstrates. A univocal reading of the novel, therefore, will not do. 'It is a poor reader of Trollope,' says Ruth apRoberts, 'who finds only custom and the ordinary in the novels.'[21] The contemporary events just canvassed suggest that a dialectical reading is necessary and that to achieve it we need to identify the heroes of Trollope's imagination—those who in his 'loving detailed anatomies of custom and its interplay with the endless variations, depths, inventions and ingenuities of the human psyche' foster 'the sense of wonder in existence'.[22]

'La Signora Madeline Vesey Neroni—Nata Stanhope' causes wonder with her gilt-edged visiting cards alone; she is presented, from the point of view of 'the second-class of good people', as decidedly dangerous and immoral. She makes only two excursions into society: at one, 'Mrs. Proudie's Reception', she defrocks an ultra-Whig female bishop; at the other, 'Miss Thorne's *Fête Champêtre*', she brings an ultra-Tory country squire to his knees. Madeline awakens all the suppressed sexual life in Barchester; men love her and women hate her:

> 'She is the most insolent creature I ever put my eyes on,' [said Mrs Proudie].
>
> 'Indeed she is,' said Lady de Courcy. 'And her conduct with men is so abominable that she is not fit to be admitted into any lady's drawing-room.'
>
> 'Dear me!' said the countess, becoming again excited, happy and merciless.' (pp. 374–75)

And Trollope, like Thorne, Arabin, and Slope, is half in love with his 'insolent creature' himself: 'She was a basilisk from whom an ardent lover of beauty could make no escape' (p. 81).

If Arabin represents one side of Trollope's character in his gentlemanliness and decency, Madeline represents another side in her ruthless love of truth. Her function in the novel is to reveal hidden motives and expose hypocrisy; she works hand-in-glove with Trollope to get out the truth. Not only does she hold hypocrisy up to ridicule in the persons of Mrs. Proudie and Mr. Slope but she also promotes actions based on truth. Madeline's function in chapter 38 is therefore similar to Trollope's in chapter 20. Trollope reveals the unfolding character of Arabin to the reader; we know what he once wanted and what he now wants. Madeline forces Arabin to admit to himself what he wants.

> 'The greatest mistake any man ever made is to suppose that the good things of the world are not worth the winning. . . . You try to despise these good things, but you only try—you don't succeed.'
>
> 'Don't I?' said Arabin, still musing, not knowing what he said.
> 'I ask you the question: do you succeed?'
>
> Mr. Arabin looked at her piteously. It seemed to him as though he were being interrogated by some inner spirit of his own, to whom he could not refuse an answer and to whom he did not dare to give a false reply.
>
> 'Come, Mr. Arabin, confess; do you succeed? Is money so contemptible? Is worldly power so worthless? Is feminine beauty a trifle to be so slightly regarded by a wise man?' (p.386)

Madeline draws out of Arabin that rejection of stoicism that Trollope earlier endorsed. She is an intensification of the narrative voice that refuses to live with lies. She ranges from low to high, from Mr. Slope to Mr. Thorne, revealing what should be revealed about each. But since her weapon is sex, the Victorians objected to her and called her 'desperately wicked'.[23] Trollope even crippled her to keep her from circulating too much; nevertheless, he refused to give her up when Longman's reader called her 'a great blot on the work'.[24] After all, she was part of himself; she was his truth within the action of the novel; she was Arabin's 'inner spirit'; she even delivered Arabin into Eleanor's hands. In Madeline's case, actions speak louder than words. And this is a principle to be kept in mind when judging Bertie Stanhope and Mr. Harding, the heroes of Trollope's imagination in *Barchester Towers*.

Some pretty harsh things are said about Bertie Stanhope in the course of the novel, the harshest being that 'he had no principle, no regard for others, no self-respect, no desire to be other than a drone in the hive, if only he could, as a drone, get what honey was sufficient for him' (p. 86). Yet he refuses to propose marriage to Eleanor in any way that could tempt her to accept him. The idea of a prudent marriage and domestic tranquillity that attracts Arabin and Slope gives Stanhope's stomach a turn: 'the most desirable lady becomes nauseous when she has to be taken as a pill' (pp. 422–23). Rather than being a man without self-respect, principle, and a concern for others Bertie is a free spirit, a Bohemian oddity perhaps,[25] who does not share the financial or marital goals of other more ambitious men. What has Bertie to look forward to as Eleanor's husband?

> Having satisfied his creditors with half of the widow's fortune, he would be allowed to sit down quietly at Barchester, keeping economical house with the remainder. His duty would be to rock the cradle of the late Mr. Bold's child, and his highest excitement a demure party at Plumstead Rectory. . . . (p. 422)

Bertie cannot bear the idea of living by the code of 'the second-class of good people'. Is he, therefore, to be condemned? If the narrator says *yes* in his harsh words, the novel says *no* in its most brilliant episodes. The artistic truth about Bertie is that he has the very best scenes in the novel.

Bertie's first great scene is a delightful social disaster. At Mrs.

Proudie's reception he deflates the obsessive preoccupation of High and Low Church clergymen with their intense partisan versions of ritual and doctrine by announcing himself as having been, first, an Anglican who aspired to a bishopric; next, a Roman Catholic who was an acolyte of the Jesuits; then, a Jew who admired Sidonia; and now, obviously, a genially persistent tormenter of clergymen. Bertie also deflates the timely preoccupation of these contentious churchmen with the English university system by suggesting in no uncertain terms, as we have already seen, that the German universities are far superior. And in the justly famous unveiling scene, Bertie defrocks the pretentious, usurping lady bishop and calls forth Trollope's finest burlesque style: 'As Juno may have looked at Paris on Mount Ida, so did Mrs. Proudie look on Ethelbert Stanhope when he pushed the leg of the sofa into her lace train' (p. 99). In chapters 10 and 11, Bertie deflates everything that is overblown in Barchester's clerical politics and serves the office of novelist-surrogate even more delightfully than his alluring sister.

Bertie's other great scene is a domestic triumph. He is equally adept at destroying pretension at home as he is abroad. Dr. Stanhope turns his illogical, sanctimonious parental wrath on his son when he learns that Eleanor is not to marry Bertie. As the son draws caricatures from his recollection of Miss Thorn's *fête*, his father rages against him while his sister tries to mediate between the wrath of the one and the wit of the other.

'Give over drawing,' said Charlotte, going up to him and taking the paper from under his hand. The caricatures, however, she preserved and showed them afterwards to the friends of the Thornes, the Proudies, and De Courcys. Bertie, deprived of his occupation, threw himself back in his chair and waited further orders.

'I think it will certainly be for the best that Bertie should leave this at once; perhaps tomorrow,' said Charlotte; 'but pray, Papa, let us arrange some scheme together.'

'If he will leave this to-morrow, I will give him £10, and he shall be paid £5 a month by the banker at Carrara as long as he stays permanently in that place.'

'Well, sir, it won't be long,' said Bertie, 'for I shall be starved to death in about three months.'

'He must have marble work with,' said Charlotte.

'I have plenty there in the studio to last me three months,'

said Bertie. 'It will be no use attempting anything large in so
limited a time—unless I do my own tombstone.' (p. 459)

Bertie manages this confrontation by the simple device of taking
his father's pretensions of generosity to their logical conclusion,
and he finds the task so easy that he can leave a record in pencil
—not unlike the one Trollope has left in ink—of the social-
climbing he witnessed at Ullathorne. I know of no scene in English fiction equal to this one in its use of logic to expose what is
ridiculous since Elizabeth Bennet, point for point, destroyed Lady
Catherine de Bourgh's ludicrous demand that she refuse to marry
Darcy.[26] Bertie Stanhope unimpeachably shares the honours of
comic success with the heroine of *Pride and Prejudice*—a book
that Trollope regarded as among the three best novels in the English language.[27]

'Mr. Harding was by no means a perfect character,' says the
narrator. 'In his indecision, his weakness, his proneness to be led
by others, his want of self-confidence, he was very far from being
perfect' (p. 166). Harding is dismissed as not in the least suited
to the warfare that gives the conflict its metaphorical texture in
the novel. He subscribes to peace and not to Arabin's doctrine
that 'Peace on earth and goodwill among men, are, like heaven,
promises for the future' (p. 200). He believes in 'that beautiful
love which can be true to a false friend' (p. 275). He is by temperament and principle unsuited to Barchester's peculiarly frac-
tious interpretation of the church militant; he is 'a man devoid of
all the combative qualifications' (p. 273) of a soldier in Archdeacon Grantly's army. He would rather direct the cathedral choir
and play the violoncello than fight tooth and nail. Yet in spite of
all these things Mr. Harding is given the last word in the novel:
'The author leaves him in the hands of his readers: not as a hero,
not as a man to be admired and talked of, not as a man who
should be toasted at public dinners and spoken of with conventional absurdity as a perfect divine, but as a good man, without
guile, believing humbly in the religion which he has striven to
teach, and guided by the precepts which he has striven to learn'
(p. 524). What this sentence says, in effect, is that Mr. Harding
cannot be judged by the conventions of Barchester society. It
affirms the very things that make him seem weak: 'Ah, thou weak
man; most charitable, most Christian, but weakest of men!' (p.

274). No word of condemnation, one suspects, could be sweeter to a clergyman's ear.

Mr. Arabin is the novel's successful priest and Mr. Harding its failure, we are told. But it is well to remember that what Arabin gets, Harding gives away—his daughter and his deanery. Also, what Arabin represents is less satisfactory to Trollope's mind than what Harding represents. In his *Clergymen of the Church of England* Trollope praises the parson of a parish above the dean of a chapter. 'A dean,' he says, 'has little to do and a good deal to get.'[28] Indeed, if one adopts a hard line toward Arabin, one could say that he is made a dean because he is not suited to be a parson. Trollope objects to a man who 'is ordained in order that he may hold his fellowship'[29] accepting in middle age the functions of a parish parson: 'Can anyone, we say, believe that such a one at the age of forty can be fit to go into a parish and undertake the cure of the parochial souls?'[30]

Yet Arabin at age forty does precisely this; but the former professor of poetry is rapidly promoted to the deanery, to which he is more nearly suited: 'It is required that a clergyman shall have shown a taste for literature in some one of its branches before he can be regarded among the candidates proper for a deanery.'[31] Mr. Harding, however, does not get to be warden and refuses to be dean; he remains vicar of St. Cuthbert's—he remains parson of a parish. His essential charity, which makes him fail as a combatant, allows him to succeed as a parson; and by the word *parson* 'the parish clergyman is designated as the palpable and visible personage of the church of his parish, making that by his presence an intelligible reality which, without him, would be an invisible idea.'[32] Mr. Harding finds at St. Cuthbert's the truth of his calling: 'the parson in his parish must know that he has got himself into a place for which he has been expressly fitted by the orders he has taken.'[33]

Bertie Stanhope and Septimus Harding are heroes in *Barchester Towers* because they are essentially unambitious men. It is good to be Arabin and get Eleanor and the deanery; but it is just as good, if not better, to be Bertie and Mr. Harding and refuse Eleanor and the deanery. Arabin is more typical and satisfies a conventional demand; they are unconventional and satisfy an imaginative demand. Arabin's path leads to domestic contentment; theirs to wit and wonder. Bertie scales the height of Trol-

lope's comic genius and Mr. Harding sounds the depth of his
moral sensibility. In *Barchester Towers* Trollope gives Victorian
society one hero and himself and posterity two heroes,[34] for in
the working-out of his novel he is finally unable to resist his
fellow artists. *Barchester Towers* itself proves that the novelist has
cast his lot most imaginatively with a sculptor and a musician.

NOTES

1 Anthony Trollope, *Barchester Towers*, New York, 1963.
2 C. P. Snow, *Trollope: His Life and Art*, New York, 1975, pp. 19–20, 28–9.
3 Ruth apRoberts, 'Carlyle and Trollope' in John Clubbe, ed., *Carlyle and His Contemporaries*, Durham, North Carolina, 1976, p. 219.
4 Robert M. Polhemus, *The Changing World of Anthony Trollope*, Berkeley and Los Angeles, 1968, p. 47.
5 William Cadbury, 'Character and the Mock Heroic in *Barchester Towers*', *Texas Studies in Literature and Language*, 5 (1964), p. 513.
6 *Saturday Review*, 30 May 1857, quoted in Donald Smalley, ed., *Anthony Trollope: The Critical Heritage*, 1969, p. 48.
7 Dr. Proudie 'read the last number of the *Little Dorrit* of the day with great inward satisfaction' (p. 432). On Trollope's own reading of *Little Dorrit*, see John Halperin, *Trollope and Politics*, 1977, p. 74.
8 Llewellyn Woodward, *The Age of Reform*, 2nd ed., 1962, pp. 664–65.
9 ibid., p. 166.
10 ibid., p. 115.
11 ibid., pp. 164–66. P. D. Edwards argues that 1852–53 is 'the period covered by the novel' in Appendix 1, 'The Barset Novels and History', *Anthony Trollope his Art and Scope*, St. Lucia, Queensland, 1977, p. 224. Since Sir David Brewster's *More Worlds than One*, 1854, is alluded to indirectly in ch. 19, Edwards cannot be correct. That Derby's ministry served Trollope in creating the one that fell in *Barchester Towers* does not require the novelist to limit himself to the date of the original in his novel.
12 H. D. Traill and J. S. Mann, *Social England*, 1904, VI,325.
13 ibid., p. 325.
14 ibid.
15 On university reform see G. M. Young and D. W. Hancock, eds., *English Historical Documents*, XII (1), *1833–1874*, ed. David C. Douglas, 1956, pp. 869–91.
16 Woodward, p. 489.
17 ibid.
18 Traill and Mann, VI, 848.
19 Woodward, p. 491.
20 Traill and Mann, VI, 848.

21 *Carlyle and His Contemporaries*, p. 212.
22 ibid.
23 *Spectator*, 16 May 1857, quoted in *Critical Heritage*, p. ¯42. For alternative views of Madeline Stanhope, see Robert W. Daniel, Afterward, *Barchester Towers*, New York, 1963, p. 533; U. C. Knoepflmacher, *Laughter and Despair*, Berkeley and Los Angeles, 1971, pp. 37–9; Murray Krieger, *The Classic Vision*, Baltimore, 1971, p. 251; Polhemus p. 48.
24 Michael Sadleir, *Trollope: A Commentary*, New York, 1947, p. 170.
25 See Polhemus, p. 45; also Daniel, p. 533; Edwards, p. 26; James R. Kincaid, *The Novels of Anthony Trollope*, Oxford, 1977, pp. 107–8.
26 *Pride and Prejudice*, vol. III, ch. 14.
27 Anthony Trollope, *An Autobiography,* ed. Bradford A. Booth, Berkeley and Los Angeles, 1947, p. 35.
28 Anthony Trollope, *Clergymen of the Church of England*, Leicester, 1974, p. 42.
29 iibid., p. 84.
30 ibid., p. 86.
31 ibid., p. 36.
32 ibid., p. 54.
33 ibid., p. 57.
34 Trollope allows himself one hero and his reader another in Ch. 1 of *Dr. Thorne*: 'Those who don't approve of a middle-aged bachelor country doctor as a hero, may take the heir to Greshamsbury in his stead, and call the book, if it so pleases them, "The Loves and Adventures of Francis Newbold Gresham the Younger." '

3

Patterns of Excellence: Theme and Structure in *The Three Clerks*

by TONY BAREHAM

> 'You must not compare me with them. . . . They are patterns of excellence, I am all the other way.' (Charley Tudor, *The Three Clerks*[1], p. 321).

1

Though Trollope had thought 'it was a good novel'[2] Sadleir set the tone for most modern assessment of the book when he called *The Three Clerks* 'shrill and facetious; its background is mere "painting in" and not a fertile soil from which spring character and happening'.[3] The book has received little attention since this dismissive fiat yet, coming as it does after Trollope had begun to find his style and matter in the Barsetshire series, though before he had settled to the writing of consistent novels, *The Three Clerks* has a special interest. It presents a method and a subject slightly outside those which he later made so successful, so that it should engage the attention even of those critics who might disagree with the present writer's claim for the specific quality of the book in itself.

The Three Clerks was begun in the spring of 1857 and published on 30 November of the same year.[4] Some of the writing overlaps with *The Struggles of Brown, Jones and Robinson*—Trollope's most resounding failure—yet it also overlaps with *Doctor Thorne*, 'which . . . has a larger sale than any other book of mine'.[5] Tucked away between some of his best and some of his worst work, *The Three Clerks* shows Trollope using his own youthful experiences in London to give impetus to his story, whilst his methods are somewhat different from those he usually employed.

A summary of the plot may be helpful, since the novel is unfamiliar to many readers. It concerns the lives of three young men in the Civil Service. Two are in the prestigious Weights and Measures Office, the third and youngest is employed by the inefficient and slovenly Department of Internal Navigation. Trollope emphasises the contrast in the characters of Henry Norman and Alaric Tudor, the senior pair. Norman is introspective, dominated by a reserved almost brusque temper. His character is marked by an unshakeable if not always superficially attractive honesty. This makes him at first sight seem ultra-conservative, almost priggish, though it hides an innate romanticism and chivalry. Alaric Tudor is more flamboyant, more ambitious and, as events prove, more morally pliable. Charley Tudor, Alaric's younger cousin, is a scapegrace; disorderly and lonely, he seems to be going to the dogs whilst his seniors flourish in their different ways.

Through Norman's kinship with Mrs. Woodward, who lives at Surbiton Cottage close by Hampton Court, the three young men have a weekend retreat from the cares and pressures of their lives in the City. Mrs. Woodward is a widow with three daughters. Gertrude, the eldest, is assumed to be tacitly engaged to Norman; her character is marked by control over her emotions, and a steadfastly realistic view of life. Linda, the middle daughter, is less intractable than Gertrude, more able to compromise and to take life as she finds it. In the early stages of the novel there seems to be an attraction between Linda and Alaric. Though Katie is still a teenage girl when Charley first meets her, an attachment develops between them; Mrs. Woodward disapproves because of Charley's wild life in London, though she has a touching maternal affection for him. She is constrained to forbid any communication between Charley and Katie, despite the fact that Charley saves her youngest daughter's life in a boating accident. The combination of accident and emotional deprivation seems to be driving Katie towards a serious illness.

Alaric is sent to report on the Government's interest in a Devonshire tin mine. His energetic work brings him to the notice of his superiors and enhances his chance of promotion. Yet while on official business at the mine he is persuaded to accept a present of some shares in the company he is investigating. His probity and his ambition are brought into conflict. Through his financial speculations he comes increasingly under the influence of Undy Scott, a ruthless stock-jobber with seedy Scottish aristocratic connections.

A new system of public examination is instituted at the Weights and Measures Office, and Alaric gains promotion through this over the head of Norman, who is his senior. Norman, whilst feeling the blow to his pride attempts to be altruistic towards his rival. Yet, after Henry has unsuccessfully asked Gertrude to marry him, Alaric steals this prize from him too. Abandoning his suit of Linda, he marries Gertrude, part of whose superior attraction lies in a small inheritance she receives from her uncle, Captain Cuttwater. There is now open schism between Norman and Tudor.

Alaric is persuaded to become trustee of the fortune of a society heiress related to Undy Scott, who subsequently manipulates Tudor into using her money to speculate on the stock-market. The speculation is then deliberately uncovered by Scott when Alaric refuses to yield to his blackmail, and his fall from grace is the greater because of the outward success of the career which has taken him towards a Civil Service Commissionership and a seat in Parliament. His disgrace culminates in a set-piece trial scene which introduces the lawyer Chaffanbrass (who reappears in *Orley Farm* and in *Phineas Redux*), and Alaric is sent to prison where he is forced to re-assess all the premises of his life and conduct. During this period he is supported by the heroic forgiveness of Gertrude, whose strength in adversity provides one of the book's most touching sketches. The counter-themes of Charley's gradual self-discovery and redemption, and of the developing love between Linda and Norman, move the book towards its conclusion.

This bare outline necessarily ignores the deftness of manipulation, and the enriching detail with which Trollope brings his story to life. Though it depends upon many of the trappings of the conventional Victorian love story it attracted the appreciation of several eminent contemporaries; Thackeray and the Brownings admired as well as respected it:

> When *The Three Clerks* appeared, a copy found its way into the Browning household, and they, like Thackeray, read it entranced.

'We both agree with you,' Elizabeth Browning wrote to Tom Trollope's wife, 'in considering it the best of his three clever novels. My husband, who can seldom get a novel to hold him, has been held by all three and by this the strongest. It has qualities of which the others gave no sign.'[6]

This does not sound like Sadleir's 'shrill and facetious' book at all. Perhaps both problem and solution are implicit in another of the same critic's comments. Sadleir found *The Three Clerks* 'derivative from Dickens'.[7] By this he presumably meant that the scenes of low life in the streets, the taverns, and the offices of the City—and also the kind of humour in parts of *The Three Clerks*—are outside Trollope's normal range. With the exception of the passages in *The Small House at Allington* which describe Johnny Eames's sojourn at Mrs. Roper's lodging house, it is acceptable to regard the 'City' material in *The Three Clerks* in this way. It is a mistake, however, simply to assume that this material is necessarily inferior merely because it is different, or even because Trollope chose not to write often in this vein. Both Eames and Charley Tudor are very close to Trollope's own experiences as a junior clerk at the Post Office. Perhaps because our view of Victorian City life is inevitably coloured by *Copperfield*, by Mr. Wilfer, and the other denizens of Dickens's London, something of this is bound to rub off on *The Three Clerks*. Trollope's use of the City environment is judicious and original however. Whilst Charley's entry exam (again a close approximation to Trollope's own experience) and the bating of Mr. Snape are excellent comic material, and whilst the atmosphere of the back parlour at the 'Cat and Whistle' is caught to perfection, we are aware that such detail is part of a plan. It is a moral sleaziness to which we are being subjected.

The Three Clerks is 'Dickensian' in a more interesting way than in this use of local colour, however. Trollope considered that there were two rival schools of fiction during his formative years, of which Dickens and Thackeray respectively were the masters. Trollope's avowed discipleship was to the latter. Broadly, the school of Thackeray stood for depth of characterisation, for 'knowledge of human nature', and 'purity of style'. The school of Dickens was less realistic, was marked by strong idiosyncrasy of manner, and by a palpable desire to 'teach'. Both the concept and the terms are those which Trollope himself expresses in *An Autobi-*

ography.[8] Thackeray was the naturalist, Dickens the symbolist: of course there are reservations and exceptions to any generalisation as sweeping as this, though modern criticism seems to concur with the broad gist of the proposition as well as with Trollope's uncompromising affirmation of his adherence to the school of Thackeray. His gifts are principally within the naturalistic ambit. Hawthorne summed it up in a passage Trollope was fond of quoting:

> Have you ever read the novels of Anthony Trollope? They precisely suit my taste,—solid and substantial, written on the strength of beef and through the inspiration of ale, and just as real as if some giant had hewn a great lump out of the earth and put it under a glass case, with all its inhabitants going about their daily business, and not suspecting that they were being made a show of. . . .

Trollope adds:

> If I could do this, then I thought I might succeed in impregnating the mind of the novel-reader with a feeling that honesty is the best policy; that truth prevails while falsehood fails . . . such are the lessons I have striven to teach; and I have thought that it might best be done by representing to my readers characters like themselves,—or to which they might liken themselves.[9]

The Three Clerks stands out as Trollope's most 'Dickensian' book because it seeks to inculcate these qualities by techniques which are in part outside the 'normality' of the world with which he customarily asks us to identify in his fiction.

By the late 1850s Dickens had produced a number of novels which deployed symbols and motifs to give depth of meaning to the narrative flow. Though nowadays almost an essential part of the serious novelist's craft, the technique was far from commonplace in English fiction at this period. The Marshalsea prison (*Little Dorrit*), and the Court of Chancery (*Bleak House*), for all their grim actuality, are clearly also symbols of social evil and personal corruption. In *The Three Clerks* Trollope seems to have made an attempt to shape a novel in this manner. The book contains a number of recurrent themes and images, and it uses places and incidents so that they assume a poetic resonance beyond their factual entity. They range from the mine which Alaric is sent to inspect to the purse which Katie makes for Charley after he saves her from drowning. The river is a central linking emblem, carrying the clerks from urban work-a-day London to the Hampton world of love and peace. The fact that Henry Norman is an accomplished oarsman, and that Charley learns to row, whilst Alaric refuses to acquire the skill becomes significant in the novel's pattern of meaning. So of course does the boating accident in which Charley rescues Katie. Even a narrative necessity like the Civil Service exam assumes an extra-realistic aspect; the book forces us to see it as a metaphoric examination of human nature at large, conducted by arbitrary and de-humanised means; it represents the judgements of the arid head as opposed to those of the full heart. The modern reader may well feel that the symbolism is perverse at this point. Public examination was introduced into the Post Office during Trollope's tenure of office there, and he detested it, as *An Autobiography* makes clear. Whether or not we accept the implications of his pattern, the fact remains that the pattern is there, a principal element in the structure and the meaning of the book. This and other motifs will be examined later in the essay. They are, however under the control of a larger design—a design which is constant in nearly all Trollope's novels, though never more rigorously applied than in *The Three Clerks*.

2

Trollope believed that human actions spring from either the benevolent impulses of the heart, or from the careful calculations of the head, and that men can be categorised and should be assessed according to the control which either impulse may have in dictating final actions. Though either may be dangerous if not balanced by a leavening of the other, he seems to have felt that the heart is the true seat of human benevolence and love whilst the head is mercenary, calculating and cold. It should bring experience to judgements which the heart makes, but in the last resort the heart must decide. Benevolence of intention is of prime importance to him rather than success of execution. *Doctor Wortle's School* offers a clear example; though Wortle, a rather dry and domineering scholar, knows that he is making a wilful and socially dangerous decision, and one which runs quite counter to his own professional interests, yet he refuses to dismiss his assistant master who is living 'in sin'. There are meliorating factors which appeal so strongly to his heart that the offended intellect is made to bow to the aroused emotion. Trollope is full of admiration for a man who can behave in this way. Though he might have been shy of so high-flown a phrase as 'the holiness of the heart's affections,' there can be no doubt he approved of the underlying concept.

Charley Tudor is a case of the undisciplined heart leading a man astray. In his loneliness and moral torpor he gets drunk, falls into debt and indulges a morally ambiguous relationship with a barmaid. Yet he does promise marriage to Nora—his heart enters the relationship, sleazy as his head may tell him it is, and he acts quite without calculation of gain or self interest. Hence, though Trollope is firm in his disapproval of the effects of Charley's behaviour, he is deeply sympathetic about the causes, and he never loses his basic affection for his scapegrace character. Mrs. Woodward is given the role of expressing the author's own sentiments.

Trollope's cads and his crooks—men like Undy Scott—are invariably men who seem to have no heart, or who suppress residual instincts of love for the sake of selfish gain. There are two distinct categories. Scott, and George Hotspur (*Sir Harry Hotspur of Humblethwaite*) are irredeemable because they show no signs of benevolent impulse. Characters like Adolphus Crosbie (*The Small House at Allington*) belong to the second class of Trollope villain. Crosbie is a sad and accurate study of a young man whose first and proper instinct is to love the socially insignificant Lily Dale through the impulses of the natural heart. The artificial pressure of social ambition prompts him to jilt her in favour of Lady Alexandrina de Courcy, however. Trollope's punishment for this defection gives us some of his finest writing in the chilling descriptions of the collapse of Crosbie's marriage, and the cerebral stoicism with which he faces the knowledge of his apostacy and self-inflicted emotional atrophy.

Phineas Finn vacillates through the course of two long novels between the instincts of his romantic Irish heart (often singularly ill disciplined), and the dictates of his political head. Only after something like two thousand pages of fiction is he deemed to have learned enough to be 'rewarded' with the hand and fortune of Madame Max, who represents the proper fusion of love, experience and affluence. Trollope was far from despising money or the good things it brings with it, but he felt there were inexorable rules governing the ways by which a man should acquire those good things. The theme applies to the women in his novels as well as to the men. Lady Laura Kennedy in the two Finn novels is a moving study of a woman who ignores the impulses of her heart, and who is driven into a lonely miserable exile as punishment for her head-motivated choice of the wealthy but loveless Kennedy as her husband. Perhaps nothing Trollope wrote is so moving as her confession to Finn that she loved him, and always had done, yet, knowing her love, still persevered with the apparently preferable match with Kennedy (*Phineas Redux*, ch. 12). Kennedy himself is the tragic antithesis of Lady Laura, a man led to dominate himself and others by dictates of the head alone. It is significant that when his attempt to buy love fails, he declines into imbecility—his head fails him both literally and metaphorically.

Trollope's women, once their heart is given to a man, seldom can or will redeem or re-bestow it. Hence despite the pressure following a violent quarrel with her fiancé, Violet Effingham tells Phineas, 'I told Lord Chiltern in the autumn of last year that I loved him. And I did love him. I shall never have the same confession to make to another man. . . . A woman cannot transfer her heart. . . . I was perhaps mistaken in saying I would be,—his wife. But I said so, and cannot now give myself to another.'[10] *Sir Harry Hotspur*, that spare and moving story of love inappropriately bestowed, suggests not only the constancy of a woman's heart, but the fatal effects such constancy may have. Overwhelming evidence of her suitor's vileness is put to Emily Hotspur, and it is argued that surely she cannot love him in the face of this: 'Every reader will know how easily answerable was the argument. Most readers will also know how hard it is to win by attacking the reason when the heart is the fortress in question.'[11] Maintaining her love against such cruel and logical pressures literally kills Emily. Lily Dale is more resilient in that she recovers from the loss of Crosbie's heart, but she subjects herself to the deliberate spiritual exile of old-maidism.

The Eustace Diamonds gives us a rarer kind of Trollopian woman—one who simply has no heart. Witty, personable, shrewd, Lizzie Eustace is entirely motivated by calculations of the head.

She plays at having feelings, and is sometimes almost self-persuaded by her charade. Her ventures into poetry reading are meant to illustrate the point:

> . . . Lizzie was lying listlessly on a sofa with a volume of poetry in her hand. She had in truth been reading the book, and in her way enjoying it. It told her the story of certain knights of old, who had gone forth in quest of a sign from heaven, which sign, if verily seen by them, might be taken to signify that they themselves were esteemed holy and fit for heavenly joy. One would have thought that no theme could have been less palatable to such a one as Lizzie Eustace; but the melody of the lines pleased her ear, and she was always able to arouse for herself a false enthusiasm on things which were utterly outside herself in life. She thought she too could have travelled in search of that holy sign, and have borne all things, and abandoned all things, and have persevered,—and of a certainty have been rewarded. But as for giving up a string of diamonds, in common honesty,—that was beyond her.[12]

Lizzie's moral and aesthetic obtuseness stems from her complete ignorance of the better impulses of the heart.

It is, of course, those not directly touched who can best discern the difference between actions of the head and those of the heart. Bell Dale, for instance, receives from her cousin Bernard a letter proposing marriage. (The very fact that the proposal is written rather than spoken tells with Trollope.) Bernard is an affable, easy-going man, genuinely fond of Bell as far as his tepid nature allows, and he is eager to please his uncle who controls the family purse-strings; 'Bernard Dale was a man capable of doing anything well in the doing of which a little time for consideration might be given to him; but he had not in him that power of passion which will force a man to eloquence in asking for that which he desires to obtain.'

Bell understands clearly; ' "It is, at any rate, a good letter, and, as I believe, tells the truth" ', Mrs. Dale affirms. Bell's reply is singularly sharp for so gentle a girl; ' "I think it tells a little more than the truth, mamma. As you say, it is a well-written letter. . . . But yet——" "Yet what, my dear?" "There is more head than heart in it." ' The narrator emphasises the point:

> Had the letter been writen with the view of obtaining from a third person a favourable verdict as to his suit, it would have

been a very good letter indeed; but there was not a word in it that could stir the heart of such a girl as Bell Dale.[13]

The notion behind Trollope's head/heart schism is common enough. Indeed any novelist who describes relationships between intelligent and articulate people is inevitably dealing with it, but none of Trollope's contemporaries emphasises it so clearly and consistently. If it is a variation on Jane Austen's 'sense' and 'sensibility' this should not surprise the reader who knows how deeply Trollope admired her work. Nor should it obscure the freshness of emphasis which Trollope brings to the familiar theme. Social conventions in his novels assume a benevolent, Austenish role and enforce a moderation between extremes. Thus cash and passion do not have to be incongruous bedfellows, for in Trollope's best work each is subjected to the control of a happy partnership between educated head and enlightened heart.

One final example takes us back towards *The Three Clerks*, where the stock theme of head and heart is strongly present, and is sharpened by the special emphasis and nature of the corroborative detail. In *The Claverings*, Harry nurses a passion for his cousin Julia Brabazon. Lacking both private means or a lucrative profession he is rejected by the brittle, ambitious and careful Julia. His way is natural, though fraught with all life's natural hazards; hers is artful, though apparently safe, for she has chosen to wed the wealthy but decadent Lord Ongar. Throughout the book the natural surroundings which the characters choose or in which they find themselves reinforce the head/heart schism. Thus Harry confronts Julia with the sterile worldliness of her choice in the ugly arid gardens of Clavering Park:

> It was now the end of August, and the parterres, beds, and bits of lawn were dry, disfigured, and almost ugly . . . everything was yellow, adust, harsh . . . and to Harry it seemed that the question of profession was, after all, but dead leaves to him who had a canker at his heart, a perpetual thorn in his bosom.[14]

Here there is a heightening of environment into metaphor. It is this, sustained and emphasised in far greater consistent detail, which makes *The Three Clerks* unusual among all these novels which have the heart/head theme in common, and which makes it a 'Dickensian' novel.

3

The Three Clerks has all those tendencies towards circumstantial actuality which conventionally mark Trollope's view of the world, but it organises these into a sustained and coherent pattern which emphasises, gives point to, and illuminates the meaning of the story. Character studies, situations and narrative details are all subjected to the essentially Dickensian method of presentation.

Each character is built up through careful contrasts of temperament which make their impact through reference to the schism between head and heart. Thus Henry Norman was

> . . . somewhat shy and reserved in his manners. . . . He showed it, however, rather among men than with women, and, indeed in spite of his love of exercise, he preferred the society of ladies to any . . . bachelor gaieties. . . . He was, nevertheless, frank and confident in those he trusted, and true in his friendships, though, considering his age, too slow in making a friend. . . . (pp. 5–6)

This is a man who undoubtedly has a heart, but who keeps its impulses banked down, suppressing the innate passions. It is not a flexible nature, nor will it prove pliant under stress. When Alaric wins Gertrude away from him, Norman will be unable to forgive from the heart, though his head will persuade him to offer financial help when his rival is in prison. The man's stiffness and emotional reticence attract the reader only slowly. One of the surprises in reading *The Three Clerks* lies in finding how Norman does grow upon one. Trollope seems to have had plenty of admiration for the character he created, but never to be quite easy in his company.

The situation soon offers an insight into this quiet man's heart. When Charley Tudor first arrives in London he is in need of lodgings where he can be under supervision. His mother appeals to cousin Alaric, who is typically hesitant to undertake the family responsibility of accepting Charley into the flat he shares with Norman. Mrs. Tudor then turns to Norman, though he is virtually a stranger to her:

> . . . with the eloquence of maternal sorrow, she made her request. Mr. Norman heard her out . . . begged to have a day to

consider, and then acceded to the request.

'I think we ought to do it,' he said to Alaric. The mother's tears had touched his heart, and his sense of duty had prevailed. (p. 20)

Heart and duty: in Norman all actions are governed by a balance between the two. Thus when he and Alaric discuss the propriety of introducing the scapegrace Charley into the Woodward household, it is Norman who makes the charitable judgement:

'I am afraid you will find him very rough,' said his cousin Alaric. 'At any rate you will not find him a fool,' said Norman, who was always the more charitable of the two. (p. 29)

One of Trollope's problems is to make the reserved and diffident Norman credible as a suitor, whilst retaining those un-romantic qualities which make him the soul of probity and discretion. Hence, the author emphasises the fact that behind the façade of dispassion, there lurks a purer kind of romanticism than anything Alaric can understand. In possessing this Norman is closer to Charley than to Alaric. Early in the novel a conversation is arranged to illustrate the point, heightened by illuminating detail:

Norman had told his friend scores of times that it was the first wish of his heart to marry Gertrude Woodward; and had told him, moreover, what were his grounds for hope, and what his reasons for despair.

'She is as proud as a queen,' he had once said as he was rowing from Hampton to Searle's Wharf, and lay on his oars as the falling tide carried his boat softly past the green banks of Richmond—'she is as proud as a queen, and yet as timid as a fawn. She lets me tell her that I love her, but she will not say a word in reply; as for touching her in the way of a caress, I should as soon think of putting my arm round a goddess.'

'And why not put your arms round a goddess?' said Alaric, who was perhaps a little bolder than his friend, and a little less romantic. (p. 28)

There is in Gertrude a worldly wisdom which is totally un-responsive to this element in Henry Norman's nature. She has mistaken his covert romanticism for coldness. Norman lacks the sparkle she craves. Trollope emphasises the point at the moment when Norman asks for her hand:

65

. . . his own heart beat so fast, his own confusion was so great, that he could hardly see the girl whom he now hoped to gain as his wife. Had Alaric been coming to his wooing, he would have had every faculty at his call. But then Alaric could not have loved as Norman loved. (p. 144)

When Norman is rejected he sits 'with a dreadful look of agony on his brow', and excuses himself from company on the grounds of a headache. The physiology and the iconography of love coincide, and the incidence of heart and head is sustained through the novel. When rejected by Gertrude Harry Norman intellectualises his emotional malady; 'he had rejected from his mind all idea of hope', as Trollope puts it. He thus survives his disappointment. It also subtly prepares the way for us to accept him later as the suitor of Linda. Norman's love for Gertrude is described as stiff, idealised, inadequately balanced between emotion and intellect. That which subsequently grows between himself and Linda is founded upon a far stronger and broader basis. Yet, Norman 'was not a man to seek for sympathy in the sorrow of his heart' (p. 187), and the wound left by the betrayal (as he sees it) of Gertrude and Alaric will rankle for the rest of his life, because Alaric 'had stolen his very heart's blood'.

Later events offer him a chance of revenge. Trollope continues to describe psychological states in terms of his division between the heart and the head, presenting us with an inner portrait of an interesting and unusual man:

> Norman talked of forgiveness, and accused himself of no want of charity in this respect. He had no idea that his own heart was still as hard as the nether millstone against Alaric Tudor. But yet such was the truth. . . . He thought . . . he was forgiving; but there was no forgiveness in (his) assistance. There was generosity in it, for he was ready to part with his money; there was kindness of heart, for he was anxious to do good to his fellow creature; but there were with these both pride and revenge. . . . Alaric had injured him, and what revenge is so perfect as to repay gross injuries with great benefits? Is it not thus that we heap coals of fire on our enemies' heads? . . . He was unconscious of his own sin, but he was not the less a sinner. (p. 459)

It is by such careful and well charted analysis that the novel avoids mawkishness or 'shrillness'. Norman is once nearly swayed into a sentimental response. The worn and harassed Gertrude, on the eve of her departure for Australia with her disgraced husband, makes to Norman a final plea for his reconciliation with Alaric. Norman's 'heart palpitated' at this plea (p. 528), but he cannot bend his mind simply to the dictates of the heart. His integrity and his emotional intransigence are hopelessly inter-locked. The author is closely engaged in Norman's feelings, which he calls, perhaps surprisingly, a 'manly hatred'. (p. 366)

Norman is, of course, one corner of a triangular structure. With Alaric and Charley as the others, Trollope has given us here a book more obviously planned in structure than is his norm. The author's ideal man might occupy the ground somewhere between all three. If Charley embodies much of the recklessness and loneliness—together with the amazing resilience—of Trollope's own youth, and Norman represents the restrained gentleman he could never quite become, then Alaric is ambitious and emotionally fallible as his creator was afraid of being.

Trollope is careful not to make Alaric utterly self-involved. As a study in unmitigated selfishness he would interest us less, and would never attract and hold the affections of Gertrude Woodward. His ambition and his folly in business must be carefully contrasted, and the way he is drawn into Undy Scott's net is completely convincing, because it is so well related to the understanding of Alaric's character which we have been given. There is real depth to the contrast between himself and Norman; if the one is apparently reticent, reserved and stiff, whilst the other shows to the world as debonair gifted and charismatic, the reader can see behand this façade by means of the heart/head character structure, and by means of the coherent organisation of illuminating detail.

Very early in his study of Alaric Trollope shows us that he has suffered emotional deprivation. Like his author he lacked a complete family background. The broken domestic circle, the experiences as an assistant in a continental academy, and the false start in life in Europe are common to Alaric Tudor and Anthony Trollope. Goodness knows whether the identical initials are conscious or not. In any case Alaric has been brought up by a widowed father who dies when he is sixteen; the orphan boy is shuffled from place to place, and thrust into the world of banking at an early stage:

. . . but here he soon gave signs of disliking the drudgery which
was exacted from him. Not that he disliked banking. He would
gladly have been a partner with ever so small a share, and would
have trusted to himself to increase his stake. . . . Alaric was aware
that no such good luck as this could befall him, at any rate
until he had gone through many years of servile labour. . . . (pp.
8–9)

By a calculated irony, after he is disgraced and forced to emi-
grate to Australia, Alaric again finds himself occupying a lowly
position in the banking world. (p. 559)

He first comes to the Civil Service, however, with all the apparent attributes of the conventional Victorian hero. He is diligent,
energetic and talented. Yet Trollope's initial sketch sounds a
warning note. Alaric's ambitious drive includes a willingness to
cut corners, and lacks the moral integrity which can only come
from emotional assurance coupled with intellectual talent. Hence
the absence of description of qualities of the heart in this intro-
ductory portrait should sound a warning for us. Trollope quietly
but firmly emphasises the point:

He was ambitious; and lived with the steady aim of making the
most of such advantages as fame and fortune had put in his
way. Tudor was not perhaps superior to Norman in point of
intellect; but he was infinitely his superior in having early
acquired a knowledge of how best to use such intellect as he had.
(p. 8)

Early in his intimacy at Surbiton Cottage we are shown Alaric's
heart in contrast with Henry Norman's. After the description of
Norman's lovemaking Trollope comments:

Alaric Tudor had no defined intention of making love; but he
had a sort of suspicion that he might, if he pleased, do so
successfully; and he had no defined intention of leaving it alone.
He was a far-seeing, prudent man; for his age perhaps too prudent . . . and though he knew that marriage with a girl without
a dowry would for him be a death-blow to all his high hopes,
he could hardly resist the temptation of conjugating the verb to
love. (p. 52)

This describes a man impelled by his head, not at all by his
heart, even to the concept of 'conjugating' an emotion. And Alaric
continues true to this type. Just prior to the Civil Service exam

Norman declares altruistically that he will strive to accept defeat by Alaric:

> 'By God's help I will get over it; and if you succeed it shall go hard with me, but I will teach myself to rejoice at it. Look at that fawn there,' said he, turning away to hide the tear in his eye, 'did you ever see more perfect motion?'
>
> Alaric was touched; but there was more of triumph than sympathy in his heart. . . . As the acknowledgement was made to him by the man whom . . . he certainly ranked second to himself, he could not but feel that his heart's blood ran warm within him.
> (p. 68)

Norman's appeal away from commerce and the head to nature and the heart, and Alaric's self-involved preoccupation with the exam and its consequences show how apparently incidental detail is organised to assist the understanding of character and function in *The Three Clerks*. The suppression and subversion of his heart eventually becomes a moral disease in Alaric under the tutelage of Undy Scott. Both business and private life are corrupted. Thus when Norman confesses that Gertrude has refused his proposal of marriage, Alaric is genuinely sorry, 'for his heart was not yet so hardened . . . as to render him callous to the sight of grief' (p. 149), yet within a lamentably short space of time Alaric has made his own proposal to her. Now he must face Linda, with whom he has flirted and prevaricated. He puts a bold face upon his defection—'his assurance told more for his head than for his heart' (p. 165). Mrs. Woodward's occasional inclination to distrust Alaric is now confirmed as she is repelled by his 'cold-hearted propriety of demeanour' in facing Linda.

Yet outwardly he prospers. His chief, Sir Gregory Hardlines, praises Alaric because 'his heart is at The Weights and Measures'. And Sir Gregory boasts of the benefits he has heaped on Alaric's head at precisely the moment when worldly success is corrupting his heart. In Alaric's disgrace the motif receives its strongest emphasis:

> And so he went on thinking, thinking, thinking, but ever as though he had a clock-weight fixed to his heart and pulling at its strings.
> (p.465)

Then, when forced to confess to Gertrude that he has disgraced and ruined them both, the images of mechanical head yield to those of spontaneous heart:

69

> . . . she answered by opening her arms to him with more warmth
> than ever, and bidding him rest his weary head upon her breast.
> (p. 461)

Husband and wife are tellingly contrasted, and we realise that
through Gertrude's maternal love which, for the first time offers
Alaric a true life of the heart, there is hope for him even in his
exile and his long slog to begin again:

> 'Poor little wretch!' said Alaric [as he stoops to kiss the child
> born during his imprisonment].
> 'Wretch!' said Gertrude, looking up at him with a smile on
> her face,—'he is no wretch. He is a sturdy little man, that shall
> yet live to make your heart dance with joy.' (p. 520)

There are not many children in Trollope's novels. Alaric's children
are deployed several times in the last chapters of *The Three Clerks*,
however, to demonstrate the strength of the redemptive heart-
bond.

Charley Tudor is the converse of Alaric—too much heart and
insufficient discipline by way of restraint and self-knowledge; 'A
lad of kindly heart, of a free, honest, open disposition, deficient in
no proportion of mind necessary to make an estimable man. But
he was easily malleable.' (p. 18) This malleable nature inspires
the best as well as the worst of his conduct; it leads to his emotional entanglement with Nora Geraghty at the 'Cat and Whistle',
but even at his most self-involved moment of distress, the accus-
ation of a street beggar that he has a hard heart makes Charley
attend to her plea for alms. He sounds very like the young Trollope of chapter 3 of *An Autobiography*, striving, against worldly
odds, to be 'kind of heart, and open of hand, and noble in
thought'. At the very time she is steeling herself to forbid his
future visits to Katie, Mrs. Woodward recognises Charley's innate
quality; 'his heart is good, and I will speak to him openly.' (p.
371) His final redemption is achieved by Katie who, in her serious
illness appeals to both his intellect and his passion that he should
reform. The success of her plea is signalled by Charley 'bowing
his head before her and before his God'. The heart has always
been right in essence; now the head is in accord with it.

The same methods characterize and individualise the Woodward family. Gertrude is withdrawn and composed. She is incapable of responding to Norman who is ostensibly like her, since

he has failed to touch her heart. She is drawn by a romanticism which she reads into Alaric's extrovertly successful career. She simply cannot love Norman:

> Prudent, sensible, high-minded, well-disciplined Gertrude! But had her heart really felt a spark of love for the man . . . how much would prudent, sensible, high-minded considerations have weighed with her? Alas, not a feather! (p. 59)

She is caught between the emotional pre-suppositions of her mother, whose heart can discern the superior merit of Norman, and the instincts of her own nature which cannot respond to so reticent a brand of romance. Hence she makes an interesting psychological study. The more so because when Alaric is disgraced she finds unexpected depths in herself. She genuinely grows as the story develops, and many of the structural emblems around which the novel is constructed come to centre upon Gertrude.

Linda is more lightly sketched. Her heart is 'full of dreams of love'—how unlike her sister—yet Linda's softness hides a special kind of strength:

> We talk about the weakness of women—and Linda Woodward was in many ways, weak enough—but what man, what giant, has strength to equal this? It was not that her love was feeble. Her heart was capable of truest love, and she had loved Alaric truly. But she had that within her which enabled her to overcome herself, and put her own heart, and hopes, and happiness—all but her maiden pride—into the background, when the hopes and happiness of another required it. (p. 165)

The idea is discussed again at the time of Gertrude's wedding, when Linda might be expected to break under the disappointment:

> We are not all of us susceptible of being torn to tatters by an unhappy passion; not even those who may be susceptible of a true and honest love. And it is well that it should be so. It is one of God's mercies. . . .
> Linda was, perhaps, one of those. She was good, affectionate, tender and true. But she was made of that stuff which can bend to the north wind. The world was not all over with her because a man had been untrue to her. . . . (pp. 179–80)

One suspects this is Trollope's own temperament, making him

particularly sensitive to the unheroic and undemonstrative nature of this unusual girl among Victorian heroines.

Katie Woodward does nearly die of a broken heart. In her yet another variation upon the theme of the heart's endurance is sounded. Katie grows from girlhood during the course of the story so that we can trace the full curve of her inner development. Her love for the scapegrace Charley is an involuntary and gradual thing, finally sustained despite physical and intellectual pressure. Not even her mother's open opposition can change the course of the heart's affections in Katie, though her head is ready to obey parental orders even to the death. It is a strength different from Gertrude's, and a pliancy nicely distinguished from Linda's.

The threat of Katie's death also gives Trollope the chance to open his own and the reader's heart as neither of her sisters can. Elizabeth Browning was 'wrung to tears' by it,[15] and the author himself declared that 'the passage in which Katie Woodward, thinking she will die, tries to take leave of the lad she loves, still brings tears to my eyes.'[16] It is a recognition of the clear purpose served by this passage within the novel's overall investigation of the head and the heart which saves it from the sentimentality of many Victorian death-bed scenes.

Katie is changed from girlhood to womanhood by the boating accident. Natural gratitude to her preserver changes to something deeper. With a nice assimilation of setting and symbol the river becomes the agent of her near death and her re-birth into womanhood; 'she was sinking deep deep, in waters which were to go near to drown her warm heart . . .' (p. 304). The realisation of adult love involves, for the first time, a recognition by Katie of the dual potency of heart and head; 'an instant light flashed across Katie's heart—across her heart and brain and senses' (p. 365).

Mrs. Woodward, whom Trollope describes as 'my chief favourite character in the tale' (p. 28) has her own warm individuality:

> She was a quick little body, full of good humour, slightly given to repartee, and perhaps rather too impatient of a fool. But though averse to a fool, she could sympathise with folly . . . there was something of the rake at heart about Mrs. Woodward. She never could be got to express adequate horror at fast young men, and was apt to have her own sly little joke at women who prided themselves on being punctilious. (p. 24)

She is a degree too indulgent to her daughters, but if there is a fault in this it is forgiven since it springs from her warmth of heart. Scarcely an action of hers is not described by Trollope as affecting her heart; 'her heart melted' for Norman when Gertrude chose Alaric (p. 170); 'her heart was wrung to its very core' for Charley's anguish (p. 337), though it is her head which has insisted on his banishment; and Katie, in her distress 'would creep as it were into her mother's heart of hearts'. (p. 369) It is the telling accretion of such conventional-looking descriptions which gives Mrs. Woodward a central position in the book's structural pattern.

The most striking of the minor characters is Undy Scott. 'Heart' is mentioned only once in all the episodes concerning Undy. Alaric makes an impassioned plea for Scott to sell the shares which would make possible a concealment of Tudor's peculation:

> Undy for a while seemed staggered. . . . Whether it was Alaric's extreme simplicity . . . or whether by chance some all but dormant remnant of feeling within his heart was touched, we will not pretend to say. But for a while he walked on silent, as though wavering. . . . (p. 419)

The narrator's tone of hesitation implies clearly enough that there *is* no heart in him, and, ironically, as he stiffens his resolve to refuse the plea, Undy jibes that Alaric's stomach must be out of order! When further pressed he retorts:

> . . . you will make me think your head is wrong as well as your stomach if you go on like this. (p. 420)

Driven at last to open confrontation with Alaric's new-found scruples Undy boasts, 'I am free to hold my head before the world' (p. 441), and Trollope dismisses him as a man 'blessed with a total absence of sensibility, and an utter disregard to the pain of others . . . [having] . . . no other use for a heart than that of a machine for the maintaining of the circulation of the blood'. (p. 529)

In an extraordinary authorial intrusion into the course of his story Trollope sums up Undy Scott as far worse than Bill Sykes because he is capable of awareness of his crimes, and lacks Sykes's justification in social deprivation. Trollope declares that his fingers itch to be at the rope which might string Undy Scott up at the broad end of Lombard Street—a most violent separation of head and heart!

4

If the characters are sketched in with the help of this unifying theme of heart and head, common to much of Trollope's work, but never elsewhere emphasised quite as it is in *The Three Clerks*, there are other structural devices which are equally pervasive here, and almost entirely without parallel in the other novels. Ordinary objects, places and phenomena assume a fetishistic significance. The characters' names have a less arch significance than in many of Trollope's stories. Tudor and Norman are appropriate surnames for the clerks: the solid, almost gloomy Norman contrasts with the more flamboyant Tudors, and the novel's geography, varying between Hampton, Westminster and the fashionable West End becomes a related part of the meaning of the story.

The settings are linked by the river Thames. Trollope's use of the river with its life-giving upper reaches and its more forbidding City aspect, with its potential for both death and re-baptism, with its suggestion of flux and of highway between life's choices seems almost to foreshadow Dickens's later use of the Thames in *Our Mutual Friend*. For Katie in her girlhood the river is the innocent path to a dream-land. She makes both Norman and Charley row her out to an eyot close by Surbiton Cottage, where she builds childish palaces of pleasure. It betokens their innate altruism and a shared sympathy that neither man resents these damp and muddy forays; Alaric is never asked to take Katie to her island—he can't row, cannot negotiate this path to the heart's innocent release. When she thinks she is dying 'Katie could look out upon the water and see the reedy island, on which in happy former days she had so delighted to let her imagination revel'. (p. 511) Trollope's geography constructs two bridges over the river. One is at Hampton, the other downstream in central London. Whilst the former of these arches over the stream of life is the agent of Katie's awakening to adult love, the other is Charley's projected means of suicide when he is forbidden to visit Katie. The boundary between geography and iconography is sometimes difficult to place in *The Three Clerks*; whilst the cumulative effect impinges properly upon the reader's sub-conscious, the material is handled with a discretion which is not intrusive. There are areas in which authorial intention and critical ingenuity become debatable, perhaps. Captain Cuttwater is a sturdy, forthright character, whose blunt pragmatism ploughs across the more subtle emotions of the other characters. The Captain understands comparatively little of what is going on around him; it is his championship of Alaric, and his offer of a dowry for Gertrude if she weds his favourite clerk, which precipitates the split between Norman and Tudor. Hence it is clear that Trollope intends his name to have a bluff, nautical tang. Since a cutwater is the sharp angle of a ship's prow the name is good enough, having a slightly Dickensian alliterative roll to it as well. But since the angular edge of a bridge pier also has the same technical name, it may be that we are intended to see the Captain as occupying a place in the book's bridge and river patterning as a sturdy, unshakeable but essentially unmoved entity.

Charley's Internal Navigation Office is concerned with the locks of waterways having no natural flow. Naturally he stagnates in such a place, and needs the revitalising experience of his trips up the Thames to Hampton to offer hope of redemption. Toilers in the dim basements of this office are known among the rest of the Civil Service as 'the Infernal Navvies'. Though Charley's life is pulled downward by the Internal Navigation, it may be argued that he is undergoing a voyage of self-discovery. But the book's patterning contrasts this with another 'infernal' motif, where self-loss not self discovery is the result. This is the material concerned with Alaric's investigation of Wheal Mary Jane, the Tavistock tin mine. This occupies a place in *The Three Clerks* akin to that of the dustheaps in *Our Mutual Friend*.

Money and commerce pre-occupy Trollope as they do most of his contemporaries. They are frequently a source of moral corruption, of course. But Trollope had a sturdy respect in money honestly earned—*An Autobiography* actually records to the penny all his profits from literature. Money from speculation, money not earned directly by a man's labour is another matter. This is no matter for surprise amidst the scandals of mid-Victorian stock-jobbing and financial chicanery. Trollope's view of the subject is usually sought in *The Way We Live Now*. Arguably, that given in *The Three Clerks* is every bit as forceful and well written.

That part of the book in which Alaric investigates the tin mine

is full of splendid tactile detail, and of ominous suggestions
behind its vigorous factuality. It also contains some of the novel's
finest comic writing; the rivalry between Alaric and his fellow
commissioner, Fidus Neverbend is some of the best comedy Trollope ever wrote.

He goes to 'investigate the provocations of evils not yet dug
out from their durable confinement' (p. 110):

> 'And what on earth is it that you are to do down in the
> mines?' asked Mrs. Woodward. . . .
> 'Nothing on the earth, Mrs. Woodward—it is all to be below
> the surface, forty fathom deep,' said Alaric.
> 'Take care that you ever come up again,' said she.
> 'They say the mine is exceedingly rich—perhaps I may be
> tempted to stay down there.'. . .
> 'Isn't it very dangerous, going down into those places?' asked
> Linda.
> 'Men go down and come up every day of their lives, and what
> other men do I can, I suppose.'
> 'That doesn't follow at all,' said Captain Cuttwater. (p. 75)

This kind of conversation which crackles with suggestions of
hidden metaphor is certainly not the Trollopian norm. The
comedy of the mine inspection is nicely judged to help us accept
the episode as both realistic and symbolic of Alaric's danger.
Before his departure Katie predicts 'that Alaric would certainly
marry Mary Jane Wheal, and bring her to Surbiton Cottage' (p.
73). Since it is during his stay in Tavistock that he is first corrupted by Scott with a bribe of shares in the mine, her remark
has an ironic undertow which reacts on the entire episode.

Nursing a hangover—a malady of the head acquired during his
evening's devious business with Undy Scott, Alaric has to rouse
himself and gallop to the mine lest he be outdone by Fidus in his
visit to the nether regions:

> It was an ugly uninviting place to look at, with but few visible
> signs of wealth. The earth, which had been burrowed out by
> these human rabbits in their search after tin, lay around in
> huge ungainly heaps; . . . dirt and slush, and pools of water con-
> fined by muddy dams, abounded on every side; muddy men with
> muddy carts and muddy horses slowly crawled hither and
> thither. . . . The inferior men seemed to show no respect to those
> above them, and the superiors to exercise no authority over those

below them. . . . On the ground around was no vegetation;
nothing green met the eye, some few stunted bushes appeared
here and there, nearly smothered by heaped-up mud, but they
had about them none of the attractiveness of foliage. The whole
scene, though consisting of earth alone, was unearthly, and
looked as though the devil had walked over the place with hot
hoofs, and then raked it with a huge rake. (p. 111)

This is redolent of Chancery fog, and of the landscapes of *Hard
Times*, with Old Hell shaft waiting to swallow Stephen Blackpool.
Yet the rhythmic energy it generates is not merely derivative from
Dickens.

There is an irony in Alaric's eagerness to descend; 'I've caught
you at the first stage,' he boasts to Fidus Neverbend, 'it shall go
hard but I'll distance you before we are done.' (p. 114) 'Down to
hell itself' the shaft seems to go. Neverbend baulks at it and is
carried back up to the surface. Alaric cheerfully makes his way to
the bottom, down the slimy perpendicular ladders. (Later, after
his success in the Civil Service exam Trollope remarks that Alaric
'never for a moment rested content with the round of the ladder
on which he had placed himself'.) And later still we find this:

Excelsior! Yes. How great, how grand, how all-absorbing is the
idea! But what if a man may be going down, down to Tophet
and yet think the while that he is scaling the walls of heaven?
(p. 287)

The ladder and the mine are two of the motifs of ascent and
descent which run through *The Three Clerks*, echoed by the jour-
nies up and down the river. Trollope uses the latin tag 'facilis
descensus Averni' in the chapter on the mine, and chapter XXIX
is entitled 'Easy is the slope of Hell'. 'Excelsior!' becomes a veri-
table leitmotif through the book. The echo from Longfellow's
famous poem on heroic but self-destructive aspiration was familiar to English ears by the late 1850s, ensuring the full play of
ironic resonance which Trollope clearly intends for it. It first
crops up when Alaric is contending for promotion—'his motto
might well have been "Excelsior!" if only he could have taught
himself to look to heights that were really high.' (p. 133). Alaric
then uses the cry as a magic charm to ward off incipient attacks
of conscience, as in chapter XXIV. Charley uses it with a rueful
sense of his *downward* path; ' "Excelsior!" such was the thought

77

of his mind; but he did not dare to bring the thought to utter-
ance' (p. 335). The same chapter puts the cry into the mouth of
Clementina Golightly, the brainless social butterfly whom Undy
Scott intends Charley to marry, and Nora Geraghty the Irish barmaid whom Charley nearly condemns himself to wed.

By chapter XXXIII Alaric's use of the totem-phrase has become
desperate:

> But still that watchword of his goaded him on—'Excelsior!' he
> still said to himself . . . if he halted now . . . he might never have
> another chance. (p. 409)

And Mrs. Val, Undy's socialising sister-in-law 'had her ideas of
"Excelsior!", her ambition to rule . . .' (p. 410) Alaric comes to
rely on the sound of the word to bolster his desperate financial
juggling in face of his growing moral awareness. The cry becomes
more desperate, culminating in the Westminster Hall scene, when
he realises Undy Scott is deliberately set upon his ruin:

> Where now were his high hopes, where now his seat in Parlia-
> ment, his authority at the board, his proud name, his soaring
> ambition, his constant watchword? 'Excelsior!'—ah me—no! no
> longer 'Excelsior!'; but he thought of the cells of Newgate, of
> convict prisons, and then of his young wife and baby. (p. 425)

It returns to his mind as he sits in the Old Bailey, (chapter
XXXVIII), and is then, marvellously, taken up by Gertrude as she
prepares herself for the bitter struggle to begin a new life in Australia. It is as though the music shifts from a long sad passage in
the minor key, and out of the grey mists comes a clarion call in
the major:

> She would go to a new land, new hopes, new ideas, new freedom,
> new work, new life, and new ambition. 'Excelsior!' there was
> no longer an excelsior left for talent and perseverance in this
> effete country. She and hers would soon find room for their
> energies in a younger land. (p. 526)

The last iteration of the cry comes in the final chapter, as the narrator muses on Gertrude's letter from her new home in the An-
tipodes;

> And had he utterly forgotten the stirring motto of his early days?
> Did he ever mutter 'Excelsior!' to himself as, with weary steps,
> he dragged himself from home to that hated counting-house? Ah!

he had fatally mistaken the meaning of the word he had used so often. There had been the error of his life. 'Excelsior!' When he took such a watchword for his use, he should surely have taught himself the meaning of it.

He had learned that lesson in a school somewhat of the sternest; but as time wore kindly over him, he did teach himself to accept the lesson of humility. His spirit had been wellnigh broken as he was carried from . . . the Old Bailey to his prison on the riverside; and a broken spirit, like a broken goblet, can never again become whole. But Nature was a kind mother to him, and did not permit him to be wholly crushed. She still left within the plant the germ of life . . . He still repeated to himself the old watchword, though now in humbler tone . . . and it may be presumed he now had a clearer meaning of its import. (p. 559)

The passage serves as summation of several of the principal strands of imagery in the novel. River, motion, natural and artificial growth are among these. Numerous incidental tokens help to enrich the warp and weft. The most striking is the purse which Katie makes for Charley, after he rescues her from drowning. It is intended as a girlish gesture of innocent thanks, but even as she weaves it Katie begins to realise that her heart is touched, that she is changing from girl to woman. The purse symbolises a healthy union of money with passion—the thing Alaric fails to achieve—and this balance, granted to Charley and Katie, is at the root of the message of *The Three Clerks*. As 'Excelsior!' clings to Alaric, so this purse is passed several times between the younger couple. When he is banished from Surbiton Cottage. Charley slips it back into Katie's workbox, and returns to his tainted London life:

> When he got back to town he felt that he had lost his amulet; his charm had gone from him, and he had nothing left now whereby to save himself. (p. 382)

The purse is given back to him when Katie thinks she is dying:

> 'There, Charley, you must never part with it again as long as there are two threads of it together; but I know you never will. . . .'
>
> He took the purse, and put it to his lips, and then pressed it to his heart. . . . (p. 514)

The 'two threads' are money and love, Charley and Katie, 'Excelsior!' and humility. The ritual of carrying 'the charm' to the heart via the head confirms the final message of assimilation through experience.

A schematic summary of this kind allows too little space for discussion of the book's incidental excellences and weaknesses. Charley's entry exam, the cavortings of the terpsichorean Miss Golightly and her French suitor M. Jaquêtanàpe, and gruff old Captain Cuttwater who stinks of grog, evinces a dreadful line in social snobbery, gets everything wrong and still emerges triumphantly likeable; all these add much to the enjoyment of *The Three Clerks*. At the other extreme 'Crinoline and Macassar', the novelette Charley is writing for the *Daily Delight* is aweful quite beyond Trollope's intention. The book is, on the whole, a richly interesting attempt by Trollope to assay the Dickensian mode of novelwriting. Employing the head/heart dichotomy familiar enough in his other novels, *The Three Clerks* extends the use of that motif and surrounds it with an encrustation of images until the book operates on a level quite beyond Hawthorne's 'lump of earth hewn by a giant'. *The Three Clerks* is a work finely cut, not 'hewn' at all.

NOTES

1 All references to *The Three Clerks* are to 'The World's Classics' edition, London, 1907.

3 Michael Sadleir, *Trollope, A Commentary*, London, 1933, p. 373. Hereafter referred to throughout this essay as *Sadleir*.

2 Anthony Trollope. *An Autobiography*, London, 1950, p. 112. Hereafter referred to as *An Autobiography*.

4 *Sadleir*, p. 406.

5 *An Autobiography*, p. 116.

6 *Sadleir*, pp. 187–88.

7 ibid, p. 374.

8 *An Autobigraphy*, pp. 243, 244, passim.

9 ibid, pp. 144, 145, 146 passim.

10 *Phineas Finn*, edited by John Sutherland, Penguin Books, Harmondsworth, 1972, p. 616. Phineas offers an interesting male rationalisation of this on the next page.

11 *Sir Harry Hotspur of Humblethwaite*, London, 1871, p. 301.

12 *The Eustace Diamonds*, London, 1953, pp. 170–71.

13 *The Small House at Allington*, London, 1915, p. 495.

14 *The Claverings*, London, 1867, p. 1.

15 *Sadleir*, p. 188.

16 *An Autobiography*, p. 111

4

The Last Chronicle of Barset

by WALTER ALLEN

'The best novel I ever wrote was *The Last Chronicle of Barset*.' So wrote Trollope to an admirer in 1874. Though posterity has not invariably agreed with him, there are few critics today who would not put *The Last Chronicle* among the first half dozen of his novels. To claim more for it than this is scarcely possible in view of the diversity and range of scenes and characters Trollope's forty-eight novels display.

That it is the best of the novels in the Barsetshire series seems to me unquestionable. The others are *The Warden*, *Barchester Towers*, *Doctor Thorne*, *Framley Parsonage*, and *The Small House at Allington*. All deal with life and society in the imaginary county of Barsetshire, in the south-west of England, and its capital, the cathedral city of Barchester. In a famous passage in his autobiography Trollope writes:

> In the course of the job I visited Salisbury, and whilst wandering there one mid-summer evening round the purlieus of the cathedral I conceived the story of *The Warden*—from whence came that series of novels of which Barchester, with its bishops, deans and archdeacons, was the central site. I may as well declare at once that no one at their commencement could have had less reason than myself to presume himself to be able to write about clergymen.

At first, Trollope had one novel only in mind, *The Warden*, the germ of which he found in a current ecclesiastical scandal that had been widely discussed in the newspapers. But the place and characters he created in that novel so seized his imagination that he went on developing them, discovering new facets, exploring

their relations one with another, until, as he says in his autobiography, discussing *Framley Parsonage*:

> as I wrote it I became more closely than ever acquainted with
> the new shire which I had added to the English counties. I had it
> all in my mind—its road and railroads, its towns and parishes,
> its members of Parliament, and the different hunts which rode
> over it. I knew all the great lords and their castles, the squires
> and their parks, the rectors and the churches. . . . Throughout
> these stories there has been no name given to a fictitious site
> which does not represent to me a spot of which I know all the
> accessories, as though I had lived and wandered there.

The result is an imaginary region that, in the solidity of its
creation, the range and depth of its reference, the sense it carries
of complete authenticity and actuality, can be compared, for all
the almost grotesque differences between them in setting, history
and characters, only with the Yoknapatawpha County of the
twentieth-century American novelist, William Faulkner.

After *The Warden* Trollope went on to become one of the most
successful writers who ever lived. In *An Autobiography* he tells us
that, to date, he had earned £68,939 17s. 5d. from his books, and
when he wrote down the figure he still had thirteen more to write.
Yet the frankness of *An Autobigraphy* when it was published in
1883, a year after his death, was disastrous to his reputation. With
its apparent emphasis on the commercial side of authorship, its
details of his methods of literary composition, its account of how
he rose at 5.30 every morning and wrote for three hours, with
his watch in front of him, requiring of himself two hundred and
fifty words every quarter of an hour, it seemed to reveal him as,
at best, 'a magnificent example of plain persistence', in Henry
James's phrase, and more often as a manufacturer of merchandise
who made money by spinning yarns.

His very prolificness was against him; how could a novelist
who wrote so much be any good? And this general reaction to his
attitude in *An Autobiography* more or less coincided with a change
in the conception, particularly on the part of novelists themselves,
of what a novel should be. He had no notion, it seemed plain, of
the novel as an art-form or of the novelist as artist; and a writer
who could say, as he did, that 'a novel should give a picture of
common life enlivened by humour and sweetened by pathos',
appeared to have little to offer readers accustoming themselves to

the work of Hardy and Zola and the Russians. He appeared indeed, quintessentially Victorian, and so long as the Victorians were out of favour and the adjective itself a term of abuse, Trollope was out. When he was praised, as he was for example by Henry James, the praise was tinged with patronage, as though his good qualities were no more than happy accidents.

The praise Trollope himself most valued came from Nathaniel Hawthorne, 'a brother novelist very much greater than myself'.

> Have you ever read the novels of Anthony Trollope? [wrote Hawthorne] They precisely suit my taste,—solid and substantial, written on the strength of beef and through the inspiration of ale, and just as real as if some giant had hewn up a great lump out of the earth and put it under a glass case, with all its inhabitants going about their daily business, and not suspecting that they were being made a show of. And these books are just as English as beef-steak.

This is a fine and just appreciation. It expresses perfectly the impression of immediate reality Trollope seems effortlessly to evoke in his fiction. Yet it does so by over-stressing the side of Trollope that can be summed up in beef and ale and ignores qualities in him that one doesn't normally associate with such robust fare. Admittedly, Hawthorne was writing of him at a comparatively early stage in his career, before he had written *The Last Chronicle of Barset*. It is true also that it was what might be called the John Bull aspects of him that struck his contemporaries as they met him in society.

The American poet James Russell Lowell reported an encounter he had with Trollope, in the company of two other American writers, Emerson and Oliver Wendell Holmes, in these terms:

> I dined the other day with Anthony Trollope, a big, red-faced rather underbred Engishman of the bald-with-spectacles type. A good roaring positive fellow who deafened me.

The effect of Holmes' famous paradoxes on Trollope, Lowell said, was like 'pelting a rhinoceros with seed-pearls'. Trollope's heartiness, exuberance and assertiveness seem often to have disconcerted Americans; it was what they had in mind when they called him underbred—and we have to remember that Lowell, Holmes and Emerson were all Boston Brahmins. He was a great arguer too; when he argued he argued for victory, and to win he was prepared to shout down his opponents. And he had his own sense of humour; it is clear from Lowell's report of the dinner-table exchanges between Trollope and Holmes that Holmes never realized his leg was being pulled.

Still, the general impression made by Trollope in society was that of a blustering, cheerfully bellicose extrovert, almost of a professional 'good fellow' or of a fox-hunting clubman—as indeed he was—who has the same no-nonsense attitude towards his writing as towards his duties as a civil servant. He appears a Victorian philistine.

A very different man emerges when we turn to Trollope as we find him in his novels, both in his authorial comments and, more important, in his analysis of character and in his sense of what is significant in human behaviour and the situations in which men and women get themselves. The massive common sense is always there, but with it there is an extraordinary delicate moral sensibility that results in a wonderful charity, a magnificent fairness. This charity, which is quite unsentimental, is the offspring of an unillusioned knowledge of men and women as they are and of his own moral code. It comes from his acute recognition of, his sensitivity to, the gap between ideal human behaviour and actual human behaviour.

This makes him the best delineator among Victorian novelists of young men. There is a type that recurs in his novels: the young man, generally ambitious and with his way to make in the world, whose susceptibility to women leads him to be at any rate half unfaithful to the girl who loves him and with whom he has an understanding. Johnny Eames, in *The Last Chronicle*, is a variant on the type. His strong suit is fidelity to a love that he cannot quite persuade himself is hopeless. His passion for Lily Dale, though unrequited, is as it were the cardinal principle by which he lives. It does not, however, prevent him from attaching himself to young women he recognizes as inferior and indeed worthless. Trollope does not approve of Johnny's behaviour; but neither does he upbraid him, scold or hold him up for our censure. One might say that his attitude towards Johnny is the opposite of what George Eliot's would have been and similar to Fielding's towards Tom Jones. Like Tom Jones, Johnny is a young man whose 'life was a constant struggle between honour and inclination, which alternately triumphed over each other'. The difference between

Fielding and Trollope is, of course, one of explicitness. Tom Jones seduces or is seduced: the Victorian moral code means that Johnny can do no more than flirt.

This charity of Trollope's, with its roots in his sympathetic understanding of temptation and human weakness, is related to something else. For all he wrote so much and so well about clergymen, we do not normally think of Trollope as a religious novelist. He is concerned with clergymen not as priests or as men of God, but as men whose mode of life is conditioned by the requirements of their profession, as, for example, in the case of professional soldiers. There was never, on the face of it, a more 'professional' or a more worldly clergyman than Archdeacon Grantly. He is one of Trollope's triumphs, and he is a triumph in part precisely because every so often Trollope jerks us once again into the realization that neither the professional aspect of him nor the worldiness is the whole truth about him. He is also a sincere Christian, and his sense of Christian obligation is the constantly, if intermittently, humbling factor in his worldliness. We find it in such a passage as this one, in *The Last Chronicle of Barset* after he has decided to disinherit his son for declaring his intention of marrying Grace Crawley:

> 'You will find that I shall be of the same mind tomorrow—exactly,' he said to his wife. 'I have resolved about it long since; and it is not likely that I shall change in a day.' Then he went out, about his parish, intending to continue to think of his son's iniquity, so that he might keep his anger hot—red hot. Then he remembered that the evening would come, and that he would say his prayers; and he shook his head in regret—in a regret of which he was only half conscious, though it was very keen, and which he did not attempt to analyse—as he reflected that his rage would hardly be able to survive that ordeal. How common with us it is to repine that the devil is not stronger over us than he is.

That last sentence speaks volumes for Trollope's view of Christianity. It was perhaps a very Anglican view. It was certainly optimistic rather than not: if it is not easy to be good, it is also not easy to be wicked. But the present point is that the Archdeacon's sense of a religious obligation gives him a complexity that is permanently interesting. It is also what gives him reality as a character.

Trollope, it is tempting to think, had learnt both his compassion for human weakness and his optimism from his own experience of life. *An Autobiography* relates a remarkable success story, the more remarkable because of its very unpromising beginnings. He summed up the first twenty-six years of his life as 'years of suffering, disgrace and inward remorse', during which he felt that he 'had been looked upon always as an evil, an encumbrance, a useless thing,—as a creature of whom those connected with him had to be ashamed'.

He was born in Bloomsbury, London, on 24 April 1815, the son of a barrister who was also a farmer and was unsuccessful as both. 'The touch of his hand', Trollope wrote, 'seemed to create failure. . . . His life as I knew it was one long tragedy.' For years the family was supported by the earnings of his wife, Frances Trollope. When Trollope was twelve she sailed to the United States, to open, in an effort to restore the family fortunes, a 'bazaar for the sale of fancy goods' in Cincinnati, Ohio, and the rest of the family, except Anthony, followed her. The bazaar was not a success, but when Mrs. Trollope returned to England four years later she brought back with her the manuscript of her book, *Domestic Manners of the Americans*, which was an immediate success and set her on the path she was to follow for the rest of her life as a prolific writer of fiction and non-fiction alike.

Trollope's boyhood was passed in humiliation and loneliness. At the age of seven he went to Harrow School as a dayboy, for the Trollopes had moved to the family farm at Harrow. He was at Harrow School for three years and was flogged 'constantly'. At a private school at Sunbury, in Middlesex, he was 'always in disgrace'. At twelve, he was sent to Winchester College, where his condition was, if anything, worse. His school fees unpaid, without pocket money, he became a 'pariah'.

> I suffered horribly [he wrote]. I had no friend to whom I could pour out my sorrows. I was big, and awkward, and ugly, and I have no doubt, skulked about in a most unattractive manner. Of course I was ill-dressed and dirty. But, ah! how well I remember all the agonies of my young heart; but I considered whether I should always be alone; whether I could not find my way up to the top of that college tower, and from thence put an end to everything.

After he had been three years at Winchester his father returned from America and sent him to Harrow again. He had twelve miles to walk to school and back each day.

> I had not only no friends but was despised by all my companions. . . . As I look back it seems to me that all hands were turned against me,—those of masters as well as boys. I was allowed to join in no plays. Nor did I learn anything,—for I was taught nothing.

He was acutely and miserably conscious all the time that he was at Harrow on charity.

The success of *Domestic Manners of the Americans* meant a temporary improvement in the Trollope's condition, but the 'absolute isolation' of Trollope's life at school continued.

> Of the cricket field or racket-court I was allowed to know nothing. And yet I longed for these things with an exceeding longing. I coveted popularity with a longing that was almost mean. It seemed to me that there would be an Elysium in the intimacy of those very boys whom I was bound to hate because they hated me.

Looking back on his school-days when he was over sixty, he could write:

> I feel convinced in my mind that I have been flogged oftener than any human being alive. It was just possible to obtain five scourgings in one day at Winchester, and I have often boasted that I obtained them all . . . if I did not, nobody ever did.

When Trollope left school at about nineteen it was at a time when it seemed that the family fortunes had touched bottom. He was summoned very early one morning to drive his father, who was ill, to London. When they got there, his father told him to put him on the boat for Ostend. He did not explain why, but the reason was plain when Anthony returned home. His father had fled abroad to escape arrest for debt, and the bailiffs were in possession of the house. Soon after, the family was reunited in Bruges, the father, a son and daughter all ill and indeed dying from tuberculosis, the mother nursing them and also keeping the family by her writing. 'The doctor's vials and the ink-bottle held equal places in my mother's rooms.' As for Trollope himself, he was, he tells us, 'An idle, desolate hanger-on, that most hopeless of human beings, a hobbledehoy of nineteen, without any idea of a career, or a profession, or a trade.' For a time there was a scheme for him to become an officer in an Austrian cavalry regiment, and he went to Brussels in order to learn German and French. But at the end of six weeks there he was offered, by influence, a clerkship in the General Post Office, which he accepted. Within a matter of months both his father and his brother were dead.

Trollope's entry in the Post Office was the turning-point in his life. Even so, its very beginnings were anything but auspicious. 'The first seven years of my official life', he wrote, 'were neither creditable to myself nor useful to the public service.' He was crippled by debt and he hated his office, the work he did there, and above all his own idleness. But in 1841 he volunteered for a position in western Ireland. It was regarded as an inferior position socially derogatory to its occupant. but it was in Ireland that he found himself. He discovered the joys of fox-hunting.

> I have [he wrote] ever since been constant to the sport, having learned to love it with an affection which I cannot myself fathom or understand . . . I am very heavy, very blind, have been—in reference to hunting—a poor man, and am now an old man . . . Nor have I ever been in truth a good horseman . . . But it has been for more than thirty years a duty to me to ride to hounds; and I have performed that duty with a persistent energy. Nothing has ever been allowed to stand in the way of hunting,—neither the writing of books, nor the work of the post-office, nor other pleasures.

It was in Ireland that he met his wife, Rose Heseltine; of his wedding day he said, 'perhaps I ought to name that day as the commencement of my better life.' It was in Ireland, too, soon after meeting Miss Heseltine, that he began to write, initally novels about Irish life, the first of which, *The Macdermots of Ballycloran*, appeared in 1847. His first success he achieved eight years later with *The Warden*, the first of the Barsetshire novels.

By that time he was back in England. When he retired from the Post Office twenty years later he had risen high in the service. It was he who originated the scarlet pillar box for the collection of letters; he also travelled far and wide on Post Office business, to the United States, Egypt and the West Indies. When he retired it was to become editor of the *St. Paul's Magazine*, and by then he was one of the three or four most famous living English novelists.

The Last Chronicle of Barset appeared in 1866 and 1867 in

sixpenny monthly numbers, the publisher having paid £3,000 for the novel. In the *Autobiography* he tells us:

> I was sitting one morning at work upon the novel at the end of the long drawing-room of the Athenaeum Club,—as was then my wont when I slept the previous night in London. As I was there, two clergymen, each with a magazine in his hand, seated themselves, one on one side of the fire and one on the other, close to me. They soon began to abuse what they were reading, and each was reading some part of some novel of mine. The gravamen of their complaint lay in the fact that I had reintroduced the same characters so often! 'Here,' said one, 'is that archdeacon whom we have had in every novel he has ever written.' 'And here,' said the other, 'is the old duke whom he has talked about till everybody is tired of him. If I could not invent new characters I would not write novels at all.' Then one of them fell foul of Mrs. Proudie. It was impossible for me not to hear their words, and almost impossible to hear them and be quiet. I got up, and standing between them, I acknowledged myself to be the culprit. 'As to Mrs. Proudie,' I said, 'I will go home and kill her before the week is over.' And so I did.

So, though the Barsetshire novels are not sequels of one another *The Last Chronicle* is in a real sense a winding up of the sequence. Not only does Trollope kill Mrs. Proudie, the bishop of Barchester's wife, he also allows Mr. Harding, the hero of the first of the Barsetshire novels, *The Warden*, to die. With these gone, it is impossible for the reader not to think an epoch of Barchester is at an end. Trollope also brings to a resolution situations previously developed in earlier novels in the series. The heart of the novel tells the later history of Mr. Crawley, the poor curate of Hogglestock, whom we first met in the flesh, as it were, in *Framley Parsonage*; and the chapters dealing with Lily Dale and Johnny Eames continue a story begun in *The Small House at Allington*.

Trollope's account of why he 'killed' Mrs. Proudie is valuable, among other things, for the light it throws on the way he wrote his novels. It shows how much Trollope's art was that of the improvisator, at least in the sense that he was not a schematic planner of his work. As he said himself:

> I have never troubled myself much about the construction of plots . . . But the novelist has other aims than the elucidation of his plot. He desires to make his readers so intimately

acquainted with his characters that the creatures of his brain should be to them speaking, moving, living human beings. This he can never do unless he knows these fictitious personages himself, and he can never know them unless he can live with them in the full reality of established intimacy.

It is because he did so live with them—the reality of the characters proves that—that one feels that he would have killed Mrs. Proudie even without benefit of advice from the clergymen at the Athenaeum. She was doomed as soon as Mr. Crawley refused to recognise her authority.

But the improvisatory nature of Trollope's art was also, of course, encouraged by the kind of novel he was writing, which was essentially discursive; and he did not always know where to stop, where to draw his boundaries. *The Last Chronicle* has often been criticised precisely on this score. The eminent American authority on Trollope, Professor Bradford A. Booth, has declared: 'Few of his stories have more irrelevant plot material.' This seems to me to be going much too far. But there is, certainly, one sub-plot that is artistically irrelevant, distracts from the main centres of interest of the novel and therefore mars the whole. This is what may be called the 'Jael' plot, the episode in Londen dealing with the relations between Conway Dalrymple, Mrs. Dobbs Broughton and Clara Van Siever. It is, as it were, an illegitimate extension of the Lily Dale–Johnny Eames sub-plot, and the most glaring cause for complaint is that it is much too far removed from the Barchester scene and the unity it gives the novel.

But it offends no less seriously against another kind of unity, what may be called the thematic unity. 'The central issue', Professor Booth writes in *Anthony Trollope: Aspects of His Life and Art*, 'is, I believe, merit v. special privilege'. But this is to see the novel as essentially Mr. Crawley's story. If Trollope had intended this he would have given the novel some such title as *The Curate of Hogglestock*. He called it *The Last Chronicle of Barset*, and though Mr. Crawley's is the central story, the sub-plots, the 'Jael' sub-plot apart, are organically linked to it because all explore a common theme. The theme is pride, pride in the sense of self-respect, the consciousness of what is due or befitting a man's conception of himself.

It is pride in this sense that determines the behaviour of Mr. Crawley in his long agony under suspicion of stealing the cheque for £20, as it is pride that leads Archdeacon Grantly to disinherit his son, the Major, for declaring his intention of marrying Grace Crawley. Pride dictates the refusal of Major Grantly, the figure of the Trollopean gentleman in the novel, to be deflected from his chosen course by his father's financial power over him, just as it prompts Grace Crawley's refusal to receive him as a suitor while her father's innocence is still in doubt. Pride, again in the sense of her consciousness of what is befitting her conception of herself, compels Lily Dale steadfastly to reject Johnny Eames, as, in the last analysis, pride makes Johnny flirt with Madalina Demolines. One could even say that it is pride that allows Mr. Harding, though he is not a man one associates with the quality, to slip so quietly out of life, and it is the shattering blow to her pride that kills Mrs. Proudie.

These examples of pride vary greatly in kind and in complexity. The Archdeacon's approximates, much more than any one else's, to the sin of pride in the theological sense, an over-weening opinion of his own importance as a bureaucrat of the Church, the son of a bishop and the father-in-law of a peer. As we have seen, his pride is constantly at odds with his Christianity and constantly humbled by it. Major Grantly's is much simpler; it is the sense of honour, held almost unconsciously, of a gentleman. Grace's is its feminine equivalent. Lily Dale's is more complex again and for us perhaps more interesting. Trollope was certainly no feminist, but in Lily he creates a young woman for whom independence, the right to control her own life, is more important than marriage for its own sake. In her intransigence, honesty, humour, as well as in the idealism that enables her to withstand the pressures of the society about her to persuade her into marriage with Johnny Eames, she is one of Trollope's finest and most sympathetic women characters.

But Mr. Crawley's pride is much the most complex, and because of this Crawley is not only one of Trollope's finest character-creations but also one of the finest in fiction. It is the greatness of Mr. Crawley that enables us to say that *The Last Chronicle* is the best of the Barchester novels. In him, Trollope is seeing and creating with profundity for which there is no parallel in the other novels in the series.

'It is significant', says Booth, 'that Trollope makes the lowliest cleric in the Barsetshire hierarchy the most spiritually dedicated of its members.' It is equally significant that Mr. Crawley is even more deeply entrenched in his self-regard than Mr. Grantley himself. Indeed, the Archdeacon's pride in his status is naïve compared with the curate's in his lowliness and humility. Mr. Crawley's pride is positively ferocious; and it is fed all the time by his sense of merit despised. His unworldliness, in other words, is anything but unflawed; as Trollope says:

> He pitied himself with a commiseration that was sickly in spite of its truth. It was the fault of the man that he was imbued too strongly with selfconsciousness. He could do a great thing or two. He could keep up his courage in positions which would wash all the courage out of most men. He could tell the truth though truth should ruin him. He could sacrifice all that he had to duty. He could do justice though the heaven should fall. But he could not forget to pay tribute to himself for the greatness of his own actions; nor, when accepting with an effort of meekness the small payment made by the world to him, in return for his great works, could he forget the great payments made to others for small work. It was not sufficient for him to remember that he knew Hebrew, but he must remember also that the dean did not.

His humility is genuine and intensely moving, never more so than when he is unable to decide whether he is sane or not. It is the fruit of years of struggle with himself and it bestows on him something like sanctity; but, as Frank O'Connor says in his fine appreciation of Trollope in *The Mirror in the Roadway*, 'Crawley's sanctity has had to take a terrible beating from his vanity'. The worldly view of him—it is in part Trollope's—we see through the eyes of his fellow-clergyman, Mr Robarts:

> . . . even in his own house, Mr. Crawley affected a mock humility, as though, either through his own debasement, or because of the superior station of the other clergyman, he were not entitled to put himself on an equal footing with his visitor: He would not have shaken hands with Mr. Robarts—intending to indicate that he would not presume to do so while the present accusation was hanging over him—had not the action been forced upon him. And then there was something of a protest in his manner, as though remonstrating against a thing that was unbecoming to him. Mr. Robarts, without analyzing it, understood it all, and knew that behind the humility there was a crushing pride—a pride which, in all probability, would rise up and crush him before he could get himself out of the room again. It was, perhaps, after

all, a question whether the man was not served rightly by the
extremities to which he was reduced. There was something radically wrong within him, which had put him into antagonism with
all the world, and which produced these never-dying grievances.

He is a man of a kind that, met in the ordinary traffic of life, is
called impossible. He is as impervious to help as a rock-face. And
he reminds us of something in Trollope for which even now he has
not had sufficient recognition, his ability to create obsessional
characters, characters who exist on the boundaries of abnormal
psychology. In this respect, Mr. Crawley was to be followed by
Louis Trevelyan in *He Knew He Was Right* and Mr. Kennedy in
Phineas Finn and *Phineas Redux*. Mr. Crawley was the first of them
and the greatest. Such characters have an added importance in
novels such as Trollope wrote, novels that aim at a plane surface
realism, because they hint at the instability that underlies the
social scenes depicted.

Mr. Crawley is the greatest of Trollope's obsessed characters
because he is the one who most truly approaches the tragic. *The
Last Chronicle* lacks a tragic *denouement*; Mr. Crawley is not only
freed from the suspicions of theft that pursue him throughout the
book but, at the end of the novel, is incomparably better off
materially and in prestige than he is at the beginning. Yet, without any question, he dominates the novel. He is a giant. When,
reading the Polyphemus passage in the *Odyssey* with his daughter
and making the parallel with *Samson Agonistes*, he says:

> These are old thoughts with me. Polyphemus and Belisarius, and
> Samson and Milton, have always been pets of mine. The mind of
> the strong blind creature must be sensible of the injury that has
> been done to him! The impotency, combined with his strength, or
> rather the impotency with the memory of former strength and
> former aspirations, is so essentially tragic!

We smile partly because of the pedantic mode of expression— the
Johnsonian orotundity which is his normal manner of speech is
not merely a comic device on Trollope's part; it is also an expression of the carapace he has evolved to protect him against
the world, a sign of his inability to converse with the world in the
world's language—partly because we recognise his unconscious
identification with the blind heroes. But though we smile, we do
not find the identification ludicrous. His stature, as Trollope has

revealed him to us in the course of the novel, is such that we acknowledge it as apposite. We feel that he is a figure capable of tragedy in the full sense. In his suspicions of his sanity and his humble acceptance of them—and here he attains a humility untainted by pride—he reminds us of King Lear. That is the index of Trollope's achievement with him.

The excellences of *The Last Chronicle of Barset* do not end with Mr. Crawley. The novel is full of splendid things. There are notable death scenes of Mrs. Proudie and Mr. Harding, all the scenes in which the Archdeacon, Mrs. Proudie and Lily Dale appear, and passages of exquisite humour, in many of which, incidentally, Mr. Crawley figures. And Trollope's sweetness of mind, his sanity and charity, irradiate all. The impression is precisely as Hawthorne said, as if a giant had hewn a huge lump out of the earth and put it under a glass case, with all its inhabitants going about their daily business and not suspecting they were on show. But this, though much, is what we take for granted in Trollope, and any consideration of *The Last Chronicle* must begin and end with Mr. Crawley, for it is through him that Trollope transcends himself. Mr. Crawley we cannot take for granted.

5

Jealousy, Mastery, Love and Madness: A brief reading of He Knew He Was Right

by SIMON GATRELL

Louis Trevelyan, the central character of *He Knew He Was Right*, is impelled towards death by three forces that dominate his personality: jealousy; a desire for mastery in his marriage; and a reluctance, eventually an inability, to admit he could be wrong. It is possible to consider each of these elements in his nature separately and then to look at the consequence of their combination; such an examination will offer an insight into Trollope's achievement in the novel as a whole.

> That his wife was innocent he was quite sure. But nevertheless, he was himself so much affected by some feeling which pervaded him in reference to this man, that all his energy was destroyed, and his powers of mind and body were paralysed. (17)[1]

It may be that any writer in English dealing with jealousy so violent as this felt by Trevelyan for Colonel Osborne cannot avoid association with *Othello*, but Trollope goes further than association or allusion: in the main strand of the novel he attempts to examine the relevance of Shakespeare's play to mid-Victorian society. Much is changed: for instance Trevelyan's jealousy of the rather obscene middle-aged Cassio Colonel Osborne needs no stimulating—indeed, in the apparently instinctive quality of his emotion the stimulation at first more resembles that at the opening of *The Winter's Tale*. But at the same time there are distinct and evidently deliberate echoes of *Othello* even in the novel's beginning: for example the colour difference between the main characters is maintained, though the sexes are reversed. It would be inconceivible that such a one as Louis Trevelyan should marry a Moorish girl, but he comes as close to it as Victorian probability would allow: he journeys to the tropical Mandarin Islands for a bride who had

> dark eyes—eyes that looked to be dark because her eye-brows and eye-lashes were nearly black. . . . Her brown hair was very dark and very soft; and the tint of her complexion was brown also . . . and she was very strong, as are some girls who come from the tropics. (6–7)

and Trevelyan a little later remembers to have heard that

> women educated amidst the langours of those sunny climes rarely came to possess those high ideas of conjugal duty and feminine truth which a man should regard as the first requisites of a good wife. (41–42)

But it is in the relationship between Trevelyan and the private detective Bozzle that the most clear connections between the play and the novel are drawn. Half way through the novel the narrator comments

> We remember Othello's demand of Iago. That was the demand which Bozzle understood that Trevelyan had made him, and he was minded to obey that order. (419)

Initially Trevelyan only considers the possibility of his wife's sexual infidelity to reject it at once, but his employment of Bozzle co-incides with an intensification of his suspicion. Bozzle fosters this suspicion until Othello's 'Villain be sure you prove my love a whore' might reasonably be accepted as Trevelyan's instruction to him. Later in the same chapter, in response to a letter from Bozzle, Trevelyan muses over the course of events:

> He had sent his wife first into a remote village on Dartmoor, and there she had been visited by her—lover! How was he to use any other word? Iago;—oh, Iago! The pity of it, Iago! (422)

It can hardly be a coincidence that he is in Venice when he reflects this.

What Trollope does with this *Othello* parallel is to show that his society was unheroic, that the tragic intensity, the immense nobility of delusion that Shakespeare was able to create were not possible in Victorian England; and moreover, that though the evil created by jealousy, here in combination with other factors, is no less evil for being unheroic, society itself must take a proportion of the blame for the evil that is produced. This he does chiefly through the relationship between Bozzle and Trevelyan.

The narrator does not much care for Bozzle; his activities and character are presented in a mixture of sarcasm, comedy and disgust:

> Mr. Bozzle was, of course, convinced that the lady whom he was employed to watch was—no better than she ought to be. That is the usual Bozzlian language for broken vows, secrecy, intrigue, dirt, and adultery. It was his business to obtain evidence of her guilt. There was no question to be solved as to her innocency. The Bozzlian mind would have regarded any such suggestion as the product of a green softness, the possession of which would have made him quite unfit for his profession. He was aware that ladies who are no better than they should be are often very clever, —so clever, as to make it necessary that the Bozzles who shall at last confound them should be first-rate Bozzles, Bozzles quite at the top of their profession. . . . (318)

But Bozzle's view has been formed by experience, as the narrator also allows, and this experience has been gained, firstly as a policeman in the employment of society, and then as a private detective in the pay of individual representatives of society. Trevelyan would gladly have tracked Colonel Osborne into Devonshire himself, but how could a gentleman do such a thing? So Bozzle takes his place; becomes. in effect, part of Trevelyan's consciousness. When Trevelyan experiences at the thought of Bozzle 'a crushing feeling of ignominy, shame, moral dirt, and utter degredation' (253), it is for himself that he feels it; if 'He was paying a rogue to watch the steps of a man whom he hated' (253), the rogue is himself. Bozzle's certainty of Emily's guilt is only a reflection of what Trevelyan wants to hear:

> 'If there's billy-dous going between 'em we shall nobble 'em,' said Bozzle. Trevelyan tore his hair in despair, but believed that there would be billy-dous. (364)

When Bozzle's name appears on the page, it appears in clusters, in droves of repetitions, almost as if it were a talisman:

> He was filled with disgust by Bozzle's words, and was made miserable by Bozzle's presence. Yet he came gradually to believe

in Bozzle. Bozzle alone believed in him. There were none but Bozzle who did not bid him submit himself to his disobedient wife. (363)

It is as if Trevelyan is invoking a minor fiend, and finds that fiend in himself.

If there were not a market for Bozzle's services, then he would not survive. Because, as he writes in his *Autobiography*, Trollope wished to create sympathy for Trevelyan he attempts through the narrator to excuse him from responsibility by connecting the first mention of Bozzle with insanity, in a portentous, almost Biblical phrase: 'In these days of his madness, therefore, he took Mr. Bozzle into his pay' (177). Society however cannot escape responsibility for the misery caused by the activities of Bozzle and his ilk —unless indeed you wish to consider that society itself has gone mad, a conclusion not altogether inapplicable to much of *The Way We Live Now*.

Like Iago, Bozzle feeds his master's jealousy at almost every opportunity by telling him what he wants to hear, but there is a crucial difference between them. Iago is quite conscious of what he is doing, his malice is vivid, uncontrollable, personal, utterly evil; Bozzle on the other hand has no personal feelings at all, and his 'malice' consists simply of a mean opinion of human nature. The same petty meanness of emotional and moral stature is reflected in the comparison between Trevelyan and Othello; Trevelyan's jealousy, leading from self-deception to self-neglect and destruction is ignoble, almost sordid; his self-pity is almost as far from

> Blow me about in winds, roast me in sulphur,
> Wash me in steep-down gulfs of liquid fire!
>
> *Othello* V ii (280–1)

as possible. This unheroic quality is emphasised by Trevelyan's invocation of Lear; on his isolated hill-top near Siena he says to Hugh Stanbury 'with an affected air of ease':

> Ha, my friend, all your leading articles won't lead you out of that. What's the news? Who's alive? Who dead? Who in? Who out? (868)

The vision of the deranged Trevelyan in Casalunga echoing Lear's words to Cordelia is almost grotesque. Trollope deliberately asks us to consider Shakespeare's tragic intensity, and shows us the absurdity of the comparison he has made. On the one hand we have made present to us the universal scale of a heroic world—on the other a world epitomised by the observation that 'the real disgrace of England is the railway sandwich'. (351)

Emily Trevelyan considers her husband's jealousy of Colonel Osborne completely unjustified, and an implicit criticism of herself; she is not slow to tell him so, pitting her will against his. He feels himself threatened, and more specifically the mastery of husband over wife that is at the centre of his view of marriage; and so he demands of her obedience, submission to his will, and an acknowledgement of her error. Her resentment of unjust suspicion, as she feels it, is so strong that in Louis' eyes it amounts to a refusal to submit to him, and thereupon jealousy and the need for mastery fuel each other until they begin to corrupt his judgement quite seriously. The idea of mastery is the one that links all the strands of the novel, and in this instance the Trevelyans are not at the centre of the analysis Trollope initiates. Instead we must turn to an apparently minor character.

Towards the end of the novel the narrator says of Priscilla Stanbury that she 'from the first has been intended to be the real heroine of these pages' (826). The tone of the paragraph in which this assertion occurs is jocular, and the reader may be encouraged to doubt its sincerity. She appears in the novel relatively infrequently, and her misanthropic view of life as 'mere vanity and vexation of spirit' (238) might be thought directly opposite to that which Trollope would wish to preach through his novels. But she has qualities of moral and intellectual insight which make her one of the characters in the novel whom we most trust. Above all she has that immense gift—self-understanding—which is given to few in fiction or in life. She has measured her eccentricities, her desires, her limitations:

> I stand alone, and can take care of myself . . . I defy the evil tongues of all the world to hurt me . . . I am not fit to marry. I am often cross, and I like my own way, and I have a distaste for men. (151)

She is the nearest to an unsatirised intellectual woman in Trollope's major fiction; he was not fond of intellectual qualities in women, and it is with the air of a great concession that he says of Priscilla that she was 'a young woman who had read a great deal, and even had some gifts of understanding what she read' (135). This combination of power of thought and self-knowledge is brought to bear on the desire for mastery that we have already seen her confess ('I like my own way'); her response is to withdraw wherever possible from situations where it is likely to be aroused—from marriage, for instance. Indeed she determines to withdraw as far as possible from contact with all society, desiring almost to assume the role of anchorite. Paradoxically the only way she can achieve this is through a mastery-struggle with her brother Hugh; the efficiency of her victory is testimony to her power, but at the same time it is made clear that Hugh's motives for wishing his mother and sister to remain in the Clock-House are essentially selfish, and that Priscilla has exercised her strength of will in a right cause.

While recognising the problem of the desire for mastery in herself, Priscilla also recognises that it is a characteristic of all men, and expresses this understanding theoretically:

> What is it we all live upon but self-esteem? When we want praise it is only because praise enables us to think well of ourselves. Every one to himself is the centre and pivot of all the world. (152–53)

The implication of this insight suggested by the narrative is that the desires of each self-centered isolated individual will conflict with those of others, and unless there are checks then each will seek domination in order to achieve his desires. Trollope's fiction as a whole shows that social codes and structures exist to provide this check; but if there is a change in his writing as he grows older it rests in his growing uncertainty whether society is capable of coping with the drive to power of the individual. While in the Barsetshire series collective responsibility, the sense of functioning societal organisations underlies the individual idiosyncrasies of his characters, what the Palliser novels suggest about politics is not so much the activity of minds combined for the country's welfare, as the isolation of each individual within his wrap of intelligence, or ambition, or indolence, or ignorance; and what *He Knew He Was Right* shows above all is the utter isolation and increasing madness of Trevelyan, the man obsessed by the idea of mastery.

Indeed society has institutionalised this one form of mastery, that of husband over wife; and we have already seen in the comparison with *Othello* how Trollope assesses this society. But there are two alternatives which are subversive of the desire for mastery, withdrawal and love. Neither is often completely effective—Priscilla's rational desire for withdrawal is only accomplished through the exercise of mastery; but Priscilla herself is also thoroughly aware of the value of love. Both Nora Rowley and her sister Dorothy ask her for help, and her advice in either case establishes the primacy of love in personal relations; it is valued as the only way that the borders of the self can be broken, in the process of fusion with another.

Nora Rowley has just refused for the second time her aristocratic and wealthy suitor Mr. Glascock, and is in great distress. Her social conditioning has encouraged her to set the highest value on securing a husband of wealth and position who would provide for her and whose patronage would create similar marital opportunities for her six younger sisters, just as they were provided for her by Emily's husband; moreover though she does not love him as she does Hugh Stanbury, still she likes him and respects him, and is aware that she would be safe, and even moderately happy if married to him; we have seen how honourable and generous and kind Mr. Glascock is—in fact the narrator has done all he can to convince us that Nora's dilemma is a real one, almost the only one in the novel. Of course, since it is a Trollope novel, the dilemma is not resolved by reason, which Nora so painfully employed upon Dartmoor earlier in the same day (the conclusion of which was that should Mr. Glascock ask her again, she should accept him), but rather by instinct and emotion. Almost always for Trollope the appropriateness of any decision depends in the end not upon logic, but partly upon circumstances, and to a greater extent on the nature of the individual making the decision; here Nora makes the choice she does because she is loving, honest and true. Nevertheless we believe in the value for her of what she has rejected, and we sympathise with, or at least understand her misery at its rejection. However Priscilla's response to Nora's sorrow is utterly uncompromising:

> . . . you have already refused to be this man's wife because you
> could not bring yourself to commit the sin of marrying him when
> you did not love him. . . . There was a choice given you between
> the foulest mire of the clay of the world, and the sunlight of the
> very God. You have chosen the sunlight, and you are crying after

> the clay! I cannot pity you; but I can esteem you, and love you, and believe in you, And I do. (165–66)

This is the strength of belief in the primacy of love which is at the root of Jane Austen's fiction, as it is of Trollope's.

Priscilla's sister Dorothy writes to her about the respectable minor canon Mr Gibson, who is going to make her an offer of marriage, asking her advice. The position is somewhat different, because aid is asked before and not after the event, and because she knows her sister much better than she knows Nora. It is clear from the letter that Dorothy doesn't love Mr. Gibson, but as Priscilla considers the advice she should offer she says to herself that 'she knew her sister's heart so well as to be sure that Dorothy would learn to love the man who was her husband' (323). Priscilla here reflects one of Trollope's favourite ideas, that love grows slowly, and even as an act of will, is no less to be valued than the instantaneous love-at-first-sight sort. This contrast, for instance, is at the centre of *The Belton Estate*, where Will Belton falls utterly and forever in love with Clara Amedroz in just over twenty four hours, and Clara has to spend the whole novel learning that she does not love Captain Aylmer, but does love Will; even more lengthy is Plantagenet Palliser's process of learning to love Glencora his wife—it is only after her death, in *The Duke's Children* that he fully comes to realise what she meant to him. Glencora too has to learn to love him, and to forget Burgo Fitzgerald, for whom she was prepared to sacrifice everything in one of those over-mastering passions that are so often destructive in Trollope's novels. Nora Rowley too is a case in point—she says of Mr. Glascock that 'he was a man whom any girl might have learned to love' (124–25)—but of course she has already, presumably instantaneously, fallen in love with Hugh Stanbury.

Despite her conviction regarding Dorothy's heart, and the poverty of the Stanbury's, Priscilla's advice is finally

> I can find no escape from this,—that you should love him before you say that you will take him. But honest, loyal love need not, I take it, be of that romantic kind which people write about in novels and poetry. You need not think him to be perfect, or the best or grandest of men. (324–25)

This too is absolute for love, but in one way it is unusual; if evidence is taken from all his fiction it does appear that Trollope

on the whole believes that satisfactory marital love should be once
it is given, whether instantaneously, or learned more slowly, for
the woman at least 'of that romantic kind which people write
about in novels and poetry'. It is very easy to find examples of his
approval of girls who see their lovers or husbands as heroes:

> if to be his wife seems to me to be the greatest bliss that could
> happen to a woman; if I feel that I could die to serve him, that
> I could live to worship him, that his touch would be sweet to me,
> his voice music, his strength the only support in the world on
> which I would care to lean,—what then? . . . It is after that fashion
> that I love him. He is my hero. . . . (382)

this is what Isabel Boncassen says to Lady Mary Palliser of Silverbridge in *The Duke's Children*, vividly echoing what that most
perceptive and unfortunate girl Lady Mab Grex says after she has
just refrained 'out of sheer downright Christian charity' from
encouraging Silverbridge to ask her to marry him 'I know the sort
of girl he should marry. . . . She should be able not only to like
him and love him, but to worship him. . . . She should have a
feeling that her Silverbridge is an Apollo upon earth.' It is part of
Mab Grex's misfortune that to her 'he is a rather foolish, but very,
very sweet-tempered young man;—anything rather than a god'
(160–61). Mary Lowther in *The Vicar of Bullhampton* refuses to
engage herself to the pleasant eligible squire Harry Gilmore because
she does not feel for him what she observes her friend Janet feels
for her husband: 'Janet loved her husband's very footsteps. . . .
She was, as it were, absolutely a bone from her husband's rib.' The
same idea is expressed from another point of view in the lament of
Arabella Trefoil during her hunt of Lord Rufford in *The American
Senator*:

> What a shame it is that a man like that should have so much
> and that a girl like me should have nothing at all. I know twice
> as much as he does, and am twice as clever, and yet I've got to
> treat him as though he were a god. (171)

The examples could be multiplied; it is what the young men
expect; society conditions them to expect it, and their women-
folk to offer it. In this novel, both Dorothy—'[Brooke Burgess] had
already become her god, though she did not know it' (488)—and
Nora, in a significant passage, reflect this prevailing view:

> Whether it be right and wise to covet or to despise wealth and rank, there was no doubt that she coveted them. She had been instructed to believe in them, and she did believe in them. In some mysterious manner of which she herself knew nothing, taught by some preceptor, the nobility of whose lessons she had not recognised though she had accepted them, she had learned other things also,—to revere truth and love, and to be ambitious as regarded herself of conferring the gift of her whole heart upon someone whom she could worship as a hero. (161)

The implication here is that this worship of the woman for the man is somehow God-given, an idolatry fair in the sight of heaven.

Thus Priscilla's view seems opposed to that most frequently expressed by the narrators of her author's novels. Yet it is so sensible, so consonant with the reality we observe around us, and we have so learned to trust and admire her insight that we may well be justified in suggesting that she is indeed in one sense the heroine of the novel, and that she is closer in her perceptions about love to those deeply held by Trollope himself than are the narrators of his novels, bound as those characters must be by the conventions and pressures of mid-Victorian society and fictional practice. Robert Polhemus in his book *The Changing World of Anthony Trollope* (1968) has suggested that Trollope at times attempted to defend the ideal of love epitomised in Coventry Patmore's *The Angel in the House*, though personally aware that it was a decaying illusion: here there is further evidence of such a claim.

The love that combats the isolationist tendencies of the desire for mastery is not necessarily sexual. At the beginning of the novel Jemima Stanbury, the maiden aunt of Hugh, Priscilla and Dorothy, has abandoned her support of Hugh because he would not submit himself to the control she tried to exercise over him; (one may well sense a parallel here with the situation between the Trevelyans). She still feels that it is her duty to help the family in some way, and so invites Dorothy to Exeter to stay with her, determining to assert the same control over her. When Dorothy arrived Miss Stanbury

> went downstairs looking sternly, with a fully developed idea that she must initiate her new duties by assuming a mastery at once. (74)

and at their first meal together Trollope is careful to repeat the word in a different context:

> Miss Stanbury was standing up . . . as she always did on such
> occasions, liking to have a full mastery over the dish. (76)

She has the reputation of being a wilful domineering old lady,
which these quotations may seem to reinforce; but we see her growing love for Dorothy gradually overcome one apparently fixed
prejudice after another. She tries to arrange a marriage for her, is
at first angry that Dorothy will not comply with her arrangement,
but soon accepts that she was right. Then she tries to forbid the
marriage that Dorothy has found for herself, and even forces her
to decide to leave Exeter and return to her mother and sister; but
she relents again, moved by her feeling for Dorothy, which comes
to seem more important than any need to rule others' lives. In
assenting to this marriage between her niece and her heir Brooke
Burgess, she has resigned all her desire for mastery; the visit that
she makes to Dorothy's room in the middle of the night to tell her
is one of the most moving moments, in a simple way, in all of
Trollope's novels. And once she has agreed she abandons all her
other prejudices in order to further Dorothy's happiness: she
invites Hugh to the wedding, and her favourite enemy Priscilla;
she receives Barty Burgess, another most inveterate foe, in her
house in order to try to make arrangements that will allow Dorothy
and Brooke to remain in Exeter—and finally she gives up the keys
of her house and prepares to retire into senile decay, sensing how
futile were her desires and prejudices now they have been dissipated
by love. But that very love contains its own reward; because she has
sought with her whole self the good of others beyond herself, others
respond to her in the same way. Her keys are handed back to her.

Thus the love that can destroy mastery need not be erotic, and
through the musing of Hugh Stanbury over a pipe in Nuncome
Putney graveyard, Trollope gives us a definition of it:

> And then he began to speculate on love,—that love of which
> poets wrote, and of which he found that some sparkle was neces-
> sary to give light to his life. Was it not the one particle of divine
> breath given to man. . . .

Then Hugh suggests to himself that such love is as a distant land
which once reached will offer only a humdrum family life:

> Did the love of the poets lead to that, and that only? Then,
> through the cloud of smoke, there came upon him some dim
> idea of self-abnegation,—that the mysterious valley among the

mountains . . . was, in fact, the capacity for caring more for other human beings than for himself. The beauty of it all was not so much in the thing loved as in the loving. (236–37)

Priscilla Stanbury realises all this quite consciously, and tries to communicate it to others; her aunt reaches the same point through experience.

Trollope shows, in the strand of the plot that brings Nora Rowley, Hugh Stanbury, Charles Glascock and Caroline Spalding together, how the qualities of generosity, honesty and steadfastness in love, that have been advocated by Priscilla, and intuited by Hugh, create joy and contentment, breaking through the isolating tendencies of the individual. The only justification for the inclusion in the novel of the occasionally tedious entanglement of the minor canon Gibson with the two French sisters is that it offers a parallel situation demonstrating the effect of the reverse of these qualities, —covetousness, deceit and treachery in relationships that have only to do with the pretence of love, and that achieve nothing but an economic and social contract, each remaining essentially dominated by self-interest.

In the central relationship of the novel, that between Emily and Louis Trevelyan, there seems also to be little room for love between the jealousy, the claims of mastery and the resentment. Their courtship is narrated almost entirely on the first page of the novel, and the tone is strongly ironic; we are told simply that he fell in love with her, nothing more; and it is implied that she married him chiefly for his money and status in society. By the time the first chapter is over, we have had the cause of dissension between them vividly narrated; and from then on, if there is any mention of love, it is always in terms of 'I love you, but . . . .'.

We have already seen how the desire for mastery can be controlled by self-knowledge, and how it can be melted by love; in this relationship Trollope shows how mastery, if unchecked by love can destroy the self. The idea of the mastery of husband over wife was socially institutionalised, the most deeply entrenched form that Trollope could find; his case against it rests not on the right of women to equality in the relationship, though the narration shows in several places that he has sympathy with the role they were forced to assume (for example pp. 39–40), and some understanding of how things were changing in his time: Lady Milborough says to Hugh Stanbury of Nora

'She is very amiable, and if she will only submit to you as well as she does to me——'

'I don't mean to submit to him at all, Lady Milborough;—of course not. I am going to marry for liberty.'

His case is based rather on the perception illustrated in other relationships in the novel that mutual and equal love is essential to a living marriage, and on a more practical insight which is expressed most clearly in *The Belton Estate*. Clara Amedroz, in accepting Captain Aylmer says to herself that she would 'let him know that she recognised in him her lord and master as well as her husband.' On this resolve the narrator comments:

> The theory of man and wife—that special theory in accordance with which the wife is to bend herself in loving submission before her husband—is very beautiful; and would be good altogether if it could only be arranged that the husband should be the stronger and the greater of the two . . . In ordinary marriages the vessel rights itself . . . but there sometimes comes a terrible shipwreck. . . .

It will be seen from the unironical phrase 'and would be good altogether' that Trollope was no feminist; but this passage might almost be taken as a scenario for the central strand of *He Knew He Was Right*. Trevelyan is weaker than his wife, and thus needs the support of his 'right' to obedience from her; but in the first part of the novel we are asked to see that if it is the husband's jealousy and desire for domination that begins the quarrel, the wife is not guiltless. In fact the conduct of the relationship between Emily and Louis required a different kind of narration from that which Trollope most frequently used; there is still the variety of dialogue, internal monologue, narratorial commentary and letters used to expose states of mind and to stimulate action, but the pattern is altogether different. The characteristic shape of a Trollope plot is of a central character or characters facing a dilemma, usually of a moral variety, the resolution of which, in whatever manner, leads in turn to a further dilemma, until the process is ended by marriage, oblivion or occasionally death. In this element of *He Knew He Was Right* there are no dilemmas to be resolved; the progression is through an alternation of responsibility for the estrangement, in which Trollope attempts to hold a balance between the husband and wife. The balance begins with Lady Rowley's slight anxiety when she realises how much both Emily and Louis like to have their own way, and moves through a set of situations connected with Colonel Osborne (whose attentions to Emily are the immediate cause of dissension) in which both knew they were partially wrong, but were by their inflexible self-centred natures constrained to assert that they were altogether right. Two brief examples will suffice to show how this balance works, one in dialogue, the other in narrational commentary. On p. 53, though Louis does not at bottom suspect Emily of any unfaithfulness even in spirit, yet he is beginning the process of arguing himself into the position where he wishes she had been unfaithful and his actions certainly might be held to belie his statement to Emily; 'I have never had any suspicions.' We are thus initially sympathetic when she answers

> A husband without suspicions does not intercept his wife's letters. A husband without suspicions does not call in the aid of his servants to guard his wife. A husband without suspicions—

But by this time her tone of voice has turned distinctly aggressive, and we at once accept the truth of her sister's interjection: 'Emily, . . . how can you say such things,—on purpose to provoke him?' The provocation on either side is real; the reader hardly knows where to turn, for he is anxious to place the blame somewhere; Trollope never lets it rest. In summarising the position the narrator says

> In the matter of the quarrel, as it had hitherto progressed, the husband had perhaps been more in the wrong than his wife; but the wife . . . had proved herself to be a woman very hard to manage. (83)

The equivalents of 'perhaps' and 'but' are ever present in detail and generalisation while the estrangement is being developed. The husband's softer nature is bolstered by his belief in his right to mastery to equal the greater strength and hardness of his wife.

This balance continues until Trevelyan's need to be right begins to dominate both his jealousy and his desire for obedience. It was from the first shown to be a significant element in his nature:

> he was one to whose nature the giving of any apology was repulsive. He could not bear to have to own himself to have been wrong. (8)

But it comes to assume the dominant role, so that his increasing desire to discover that his wife had been unfaithful, and his continuing demands for her submission are motivated more by his refusal to admit he could have been wrong to act as he did, and to continue acting as he does. When his friends tell him that he is acting foolishly, even madly, he rejects them and their advice, one by one, until Bozzle, the extension of his own mind, is the only character he will trust, because only Bozzle believes in him.

It seems probable that Trollope did not at first expect his novel to take quite this course, because in the face of the growth of this imbalance in Trevelyan, he cannot hope to hold the balance of responsibility between husband and wife; and soon after the employment of Bozzle there are narratorial summaries that seem almost to absolve Emily from all blame:

> There be men . . . who seem absolutely unfitted by nature to have the custody or guardianship of others. A woman in the hands of such a man can hardly save herself or him from endless trouble. (257)

or again:

> he had subjected her to a severity of rebuke which no high-spirited woman could have borne. His wife had not tried to bear it,—in her indignation had not striven to cure the evil. . . . Though every friend he possessed was now against him . . . he was certain he was right. (362)

The balance has decisively shifted, because while Emily's response remains rational, if bitter and obstinate, Louis's has become obsessive; and the centre of interest has also moved from the development of the estrangement itself to the analysis of Trevelyan's mania. There are occasional attempts to show that Emily is still at least partially responsible for the trouble, particularly in her continuing attitude to Colonel Osborne; but from the moment the narrator links the employment of Bozzle with Trevelyan's madness it is on him that attention primarily focuses.

We have already seen how Bozzle's unthinking conviction of Emily's guilt feeds Trevelyan's jealousy: but it does more; it forces the substratum of doubt that exists beneath Trevelyan's certainty that he is right to be buried deeper and deeper, till it becomes inaccessible to his consciousness. Trevelyan considers the private detective a utilitarian agent, the only one capable of discovering the facts that will conclusively prove what he does not in the roots of his mind believe. In the end he out-Bozzles Bozzle by fantasising facts that even the detective cannot find out, and it is ironically in response to a 'fact' which has no basis in reality, but which is nevertheless discovered by Bozzle, that Trevelyan writes the unforgivable letter which begins the reader's alienation from him in earnest (255). As he abandons reasonable behaviour, he abandons his friends, his country, his civilisation, his health; and most destructively, is abandoned by his familiar. Eventually he abandons his life, all because it becomes more and more essential to him that everyone should acknowledge that he was right. It is an excellent analysis of the probability of human behaviour.

But there is a crucial question that the reader cannot help but ask, because in the end Trollope himself seems unsure of the answer: is Trevelyan mad—and if he is, when does he become so? The narrator, apparently in no doubt here as elsewhere in the novel, relates its inception to the employment of Bozzle. This is the moment when Trevelyan's jealousy and his obsession over the right to mastery become uncontrolled, so that he can no longer contain them within himself and he has to employ an agent to share the burden; once this happens he has lost the mental balance of the sane man. This is the narrational view, and it is soon reinforced by the opinions of others who are more closely involved in the action:

> *Nora:* 'To depend upon the caprice of a man who must be mad!' (240)
> *Hugh:* 'I cannot understand how you can be so mad as to say so.' (245)
> *Mr. Outhouse:* 'The only possible excuse is that he must be mad.' (310)

But these characters have an interest in suggesting that Trevelyan must be insane, and their judgements seem to be at least as much a conventional response to the apparently irrational as the result of considered thought about what madness is. And the narrator makes this point:

> There is perhaps no great social question so imperfectly understood among us at the present day as that which refers to the line which divides sanity from insanity. (361)

In the sentences which follow he does not attempt to suggest that

110

he understands it very clearly himself. They are illustrative rather than instructive, and when half way through the paragraph he asserts 'Now Trevelyan was, in truth, mad on the subject of his wife's alleged infidelity', the confidence of the claim comes as a surprise. In the face of such an authoritative statement it is hard for the reader to think otherwise; but it is probable that each of us, informed on the subject or uninformed, will have his own view of what constitutes madness. For my own part, the moment that I am convinced that Trevelyan's mind has so far lost balance and rational understanding as to justify the deliberate, as opposed to the casual use of the word mad is when, quite as a matter of course, he says to himself 'Mr. Bideawhile had probably been corrupted by Colonel Osborne' (427). Such corruption is utterly inconceivable— (a long acquaintance with the lawyer through a number of Trollope's novels gives strength to this impression).

The heavy-handed anger of Emily's father Sir Marmaduke adds a further dimension to the question of Trevelyan's madness. For the first time he is confronted with the possibility of action against him:

> Do you know what people are saying of you;—that you are mad, and that you must be locked up, and your child taken away from you, and your property? (648)

This has the effect of driving him further into isolation, which becomes complete when Bozzle takes the pay of his enemies, confessing that his client needed to be 'looked after'. Trevelyan in any case no longer requires a surrogate to share the developing burden of the certainty of Emily's guilt; it is now fixed deeply in himself. Sir Marmaduke tries to invoke the law, but finds that the process is involved, and success doubtful, the law partaking of society's uncertainty in the matter (as is not unreasonable). Trollope further emphasises the ignorance of society by counterpointing the narrative of Trevelyan's growing mental imbalance with numerous examples of the way in which people use the language of madness quite unthinkingly:

> I am driven nearly mad (228); I thought at first that C. G. must have been cracked (376); I shall be in Bedlam (494); you will drive that man mad before you have done (692); poor Lady Rowley should be nearly out of her mind (747).

When it is considered that we have been shown how slender yet strong is the root of mental disturbance, apparently growing with the inevitability of a natural growth, this polite dementia sounds especially hollow, almost dangerous in its lack of understanding of what the words really imply.

Trevelyan leaves England for the arid hilltop near Siena which so vividly reflects his state of mind just before he journeys to it: 'Everything for him now was hot and dry and poor and bitter' (634). Henry James rightly praised the scenes at Casalunga, where physical neglect and mental oscillations between confusion and clarity make Hugh Stanbury's assessment of him appear perfectly accurate:

> He is undoubtedly so mad as to be unfit to manage anything for himself, but he is not in such a condition that anyone would wish to see him put into confinement. If he were raving mad there would be less difficulty, though there might be more distress. (878)

It seems that though there may be different views about when Trevelyan could properly be considered mad, by the time that Stanbury arrives to help Emily bring him back to England, he is indeed insane.

But just as I have suggested that perhaps Trollope himself had a different attitude from his narrator to the kind of love a girl should feel for the man she wishes to marry—expressed in this novel through Priscilla Stanbury—so too he is to the end uncertain about Trevelyan's madness, though the narrator is quite sure. For instance, as the narrator considers Trevelyan in Casalunga, he says:

> At this time Trevelyan's mind was so far unhinged, his ordinary faculties were so greatly impaired, that they who declared him to be mad were justified in their declaration. His condition was such that the happiness and welfare of no human being,—not even his own,— could safely be entrusted to his keeping. (786)

But we have already seen (quotation on p. 109 above) that it was suggested earlier in the novel, by way of absolving Emily from much of the blame for the quarrel, that Trevelyan was at no time fit to have responsibility for others; this failing in him can then hardly be used with any justice as evidence of his madness.

The confusion is at its height in the penultimate chapter of the novel: Acquitted. The difficult question to resolve in this context is how we value the judgement of Dr. Nevill:

He would not admit, even when treating his patient like a child, that he had ever been mad. (919)

He convinces Emily that such was indeed the case; and the doctor's statement in response to Emily's question 'Can he then be in his sane mind?' seems final, in spite of all the assertions of madness that we have heard, and most probably accepted:

> In one sense all misconduct is proof of insanity. . . . In his [Trevelyan's] case the weakness of the mind has been consequent upon the weakness of the body. (923–24)

We think back to the evidence of Trevelyan's self neglect; his eventual similarity to Bozzle in seediness; the intervention of Mrs. Fuller, his landlady at Rivers Cottage, who describes 'them sweats at night as'd be enough to kill any man'; and the grotesquely-dressed emaciated figure at Casalunga; and we are influenced by the confident tone of the professional man, the specialist—so that we are convinced he is right, and adjust our retrospective impressions of the course of the novel accordingly. It comes then as a shock of a quite disorientating kind to read, a page and a half later the narrational comment:

> And he was mad;—mad though every doctor in England had called him sane. Had he not been mad he must have been a fiend,—or he could not have tortured, as he had done, the woman to whom he owed the closest protection which one human being can give to another. (925)

Who are we to believe? The narrator's view is more powerful emotionally, and it carries more weight because we have grown used to his voice in our ear as we read, conducting a dialogue with us as he presents the story, here as in all Trollope's novels. But on reflection such a view seems only to respond to the last part of the novel and certainly bears no resemblance to the progressive disintegration of the marriage as the narrator has earlier shown it to us. It echoes, perhaps unconsciously, Emily's sense of anguish at having confessed in order to try to save her husband's life to something she did not do:

> What is all that we have read about the Inquisition and the old tortures? I have had to learn that torturing has not gone out of the world;—that is all. (899)

I have already shown how the direction of the narration alters from a balance of responsibility for the quarrel to a gradual emphasis of blame on Trevelyan and absolution for his wife. Here, in this final narrational analysis, the process has gone as far as it well could. Or so one would think; but it is not until the beginning of the final chapter that we hear the last of Trevelyan—an epitaph it is, but such an epitaph:

> At last the maniac was dead, and in his last moment he had made such reparation as was in his power for the evil that he had done.

It seems astonishing that Trollope could write in his *Autobiography*

> It was my purpose to create sympathy for the unfortunate man who, while endeavouring to do his duty to all around him. . . . (293)

The desire to create sympathy may be active in the first quarter of the novel, but it becomes progressively less and less tenable until at the end the narrator would apparently have us despise him rather than sympathise with him. There is no way of reconciling the statement in the *Autobiography* with what appears on the page, but it is possible to come closer to understanding why Trollope said what he did if it is suggested, as I have, that there is a dislocation at times between Trollope and the narrator he has created to manage the progress of the story. In the end I do not think Trollope knows what conclusion to offer about the disintegration of Trevelyan that he, through his narrator, has so brilliantly charted. He would like to see the case dispassionately, but with sympathy, as Dr. Nevill does; but his emotional response is more powerful, and is allowed the final words. For Trollope, as for so many of his characters, the heart was stronger than the head.

In effect the reparation Trevelyan offers with his last act is to acknowledge that he was wrong. Only in the certainty of death does he have the will to wrench his mind from its encrustation of suspicion and certitude imposed by jealousy and the need for mastery. Whether Trevelyan is considered mad or not, the blame for the destruction of his life and the ruin of Emily's is neither his nor hers alone, nor Colonel Osborne's; the society which supports the concept of marital mastery, which condones Colonel Osborne, which maintains Mr. Bozzle, which plays with the idea of madness without understanding it, is awarded an equal share of the blame. Though love may cure the self-centredness of man, it can only do so at its most intense, whether instinctive or learned. Without this love, however, the outlook is bleak.

NOTE

1 Page references for all Trollope texts are to The World's Classics edition, with the exception of *The Duke's Children* which is referred to in the Oxford Trollope edition.

6

Trollope and *St. Paul's* 1866-70

by JOHN SUTHERLAND

1

In a life less crowded with literary and extra-literary incident than Trollope's, the conducting of a political journal for three years would loom large; more so as the three years cover the implementation of the second Reform Bill, the editor's own foray into parliamentary life and the opening of a major cycle of Trollopian political fiction. Yet the *St. Paul's* episode customarily rates little more than parenthetic reference, even in works as thoroughly specialist as John Halperin's *Trollope and Politics* (1978). The aim of this essay is to pull into focus what is known about Trollope's editorial adventure, to introduce the largely unpublished negotiation over the founding of *St. Paul's* and to throw some light on the contributions to the magazine, the majority of which are unattributed.

As elsewhere, his editorial career shows Trollope to have been 'the lesser Thackeray'. *St. Paul's* in name, content, form and tone aped the *Cornhill Magazine*. With Thackeray as its figurehead Smith's magazine had attained hitherto unheard-of sales for an English monthly periodical—as high as 120,000 for the early 1860 issues. Although his own self-aggrandizing account emphasises the outstanding originality of *Cornhill's* conception, Smith was, in fact, no innovator. *Cornhill's* low cost (1 sh.), its mix of high class fiction, illustration and general interest articles, all gathered under a relaxed, superintending editor, are evidently modelled on *Harper's New Monthly Magazine*, launched a full decade before *Cornhill*. (Thackeray was recently returned from America when Smith first approached him with vaguely formed proposals for a new monthly magazine. It is possible that the novelist may have given the publisher some formative ideas for *Cornhill*.) Nonethe-

116

less, Smith deserves substantial credit and certainly enjoyed the financial rewards of discovering an attractively new permutation of English quarterly gravity and miscellany levity.

Cornhill's spectacular success inspired a series of frankly imitative journals, many with a London-topographical title: Temple Bar, Belgravia, St. James's (Smith followed his own fashion in names with the weekly Pall Mall Gazette). As for St. Paul's, Trollope was candid enough to acknowledge a certain staleness in the name: 'If we were to make ourselves in any way peculiar, it was not by our name that we were desirous of doing so' (A. 286).[1] Trollope was inseparably associated in the public mind with Cornhill's triumph (he wrote the magazine's lead serial, Framley Parsonage, with its fine Millais illustrations); as Cornhill's primo violino (Thackeray's gracious compliment) Trollope was an obvious candidate for offers on the same comfortably honorific terms that Thackeray had enjoyed with Smith, Elder and Co. (Since Smith conducted all the magazine's business it was, in fact, a relatively thornless cushion Thackeray sat on, for whose occupancy he had up to £600 a month.) In 1861 Trollope had relayed to him the following proposal from the publisher of Temple Bar:

> Mr. Maxwell has asked me to offer you £1,000 a year for three or five years, with the ostensible editorship of Temple Bar, if you will undertake to supply a novel and fill the position that Mr. Sala now occupies. All the real work of editorship will be performed—as heretofore—by Mr. Edmund Yates, who would act with you as sub-editor.[2]

Trollope declined. He was too busy; he detested Yates and his career, as he then saw it, lay in the Post Office with a novel-writing stint every morning before breakfast.

By 1866–67 Trollope was more accessible to tempting overtures from the literary world. He was no longer happy in his profession and indignation at being passed over in favour of a younger man led him to resign his post in September 1867, a month before the first issue of St. Paul's. Moreover Trollope had evidently decided on an even more significant step in life, his entry into parliament and the achievement of what he held to be 'the highest object of ambition to every educated Englishman' (A. 290). When 'a little before the date of my resignation' (A. 284; in fact it was ten months before) James Virtue offered the editorship of a new magazine, Trollope was amenable.

To have a journal as his disposal (what Quintus Slide would call 'a horgan') as well as the guaranteed income which went with the editorship would be a clear career advantage for a new M.P. The stipend would secure him against the dilemma of a Phineas Finn—unable to sustain parliamentary independence without the servitude of office or the advantage of inherited wealth (judging by its prominence in the serial, written as he was tendering his resignation, this dilemma preyed on Trollope's mind in 1866). More importantly, *St. Paul's* would give Trollope a platform outside the house on which he could not only speak himself, but which he could hospitably make available to party friends. Trollope enunciated this intention to make the magazine a party organ, where powerful men might express their views incognito, in a letter to Grant Duff shortly after *St. Paul's* publication:

> Dear Sir, You may perhaps have seen the first number of the Saint Paul's Magazine, which is being edited by myself. If so you will have noticed that it is our object to make the magazine a vehicle for political articles on the Liberal side. I am not at liberty to mention the names of those who are already writing for us, but I believe you would find the matter such as you would approve in point of feeling and line of argument (L. 205).

The novelist-editor and future M.P. (as he fondly thought) must have foreseen a useful role for *St. Paul's*—a dream which evaporated with the Beverley debacle of Autumn 1868.

As it finally appeared, *St. Paul's* followed the physical layout of *Cornhill* exactly. Both cost 1 sh., appeared monthly, ran to 128 pages, carried two illustrated serial novels. The title page of *St. Paul's* first issues proudly proclaimed the services of two luminaries associated with the fabulously successful launch of the earlier magazine—Anthony Trollope and Millais, RA. Trollope originally intended to have another colleague of the old *Cornhill* days as his Assistant Editor. But Robert Bell, though he found Trollope's offer of £250 a year 'liberal and satisfactory'[3] had misgivings about the state of his health. Misgiving was in order: he died before being able to take up his position, and Trollope took as his lieutenant the younger and serviceable Edward Dicey.

In his first and only editorial Trollope again imitated the Thackerayan-Cornhill manner. This was to be a magazine for gentlemen, written and conducted by gentlemen. The only depar-

ture from the *Cornhill* was in *St. Paul's* party-political commitment. '*St. Paul's*, if it be anything, will be political' (I. 4).[4] One of
the few descriptions of content which Trollope vouchsafed Virtue
in the planning stages was that the journal would contain a
political article every month, alternating between 'foreign politics'
and 'home politics'. And judging by his own early contributions
('On Sovereignty' and 'Carlylism') it would appear that the editor
intended to keep the political ball rolling with a series of theoretical
pieces. In line with its 'gentlemanly' code *St. Paul's* disdained the
merely personal political commentary or 'Young Grubstreet' style
gossip, though in his indignation Trollope himself sometimes
violated this rule (notably in 'Mr. Disraeli and the Mint'; Disraeli
always brought out the worst in Trollope).

At this period politics was a man's business; hence *St. Paul's*
has a strong aroma of the club smoking-room about it. The magazine aims at professional and university men, with a series of
articles on outside manly pastimes: the turf, hunting (naturally),
Alpine climbing, rowing. In my view the journal's best contributions are in this sector with Trollope's vigorous pieces on field
sport and Leslie Stephen's dryly fanatic celebrations of rowing and
climbing. If nothing else, *St. Paul's* gives a reflection of the mid-
Victorian, Liberal gentleman's cultural and physical recreations.

In the largest sense *St. Paul's* represents a typically Trollopian
compromise of the three journals he had principally associated
with. Predominantly it was Cornhillian, and Trollope's editorship Thackerayan. Onto this stock Trollope intended to graft some
of the Liberal intellectualism current in the *Fortnightly* and the
close commentary on political affairs of the day featured in the
Pall Mall Gazette. It was just the kind of hybrid 'an advanced conservative Liberal' would devise, given his head.

2

Like Smith before him, Virtue was open-handed in his payments.
Trollope is generous to his publisher in the cheaper currency of
praise on this point:

> If the use of large capital, combined with wide liberality and
> absolute confidence and perpetual good humour on the part of
> the proprietor, would have produced success, our magazine
> certainly would have succeeded. A. 285)

But unlike Smith, Virtue's disbursements were unbalanced and came from a shorter purse; they also had the structural weakness that they tended from the first to risk all the publisher's eggs in the one Trollopian basket. It was never a healthy gamble nor, possibly, did Trollope think it so, even in his earliest dealings with Virtue.

The first intimation of *St. Paul's* is a letter from Strahan to Trollope in April 1866 in which the publisher mentioned, in passing, that he had recently taken over the *Argosy* magazine, intended to build it up 'and to stand or fall by its success'. He evidently fell. According to Sadleir the magazine 'was by December 1866 already so far gone in failure as to be cheaply purchasable'.[5] Strahan's relationship with the printer and blockmaker Virtue is obscure; from later correspondence it would seem that there was some degree of incorporation between the two. Whatever the relationship, Virtue was ambitious not merely to serve, but to join the ranks of the publishers. His first plan was to take over the unlucky *Argosy* and build his house around it. As Trollope observes in the *Autobiography*, magazines were customarily used by publishers to bring 'grist to the mill' (A. 284). Evidently Virtue opened this plan to Trollope and had some encouragement. The first letter we have from the publisher to his future editor on the matter clearly continues a previous correspondence. The letter is dated 13 November 1866:

> My Dear Sir, Upon further consideration I am inclined to think that instead of purchasing the 'Argosy' perhaps it would be better to start an entirely new Magazine. A new volume of the Argosy commences Decr. 1—you could not possibly venture any new arrangements before that time and we should then be committed to a new Volume, and you would be held responsible by the public for a tale or tales that you did not select and that you had little time to examine.
>
> What say you to a new Magazine to be started say Jany. 1 to be edited by you and so announced? Editor's salary to be £1,000 p. annum, this to include all editorial expenditure. All arrangements with contributors to be made by you entirely, upon such terms as we may agree upon together; but the management of the literary portion and illustrations must be entirely in your hands. Your own writings would be of course be paid for, same as if you wrote for any other magazine [this lapse in grammar, incidentally, and the general stylistic simplicity of the letter indicate one

reason why Virtue wished to leave literary matters entirely in Trollope's hands] I should propose to get up a magazine similar in appearance to the Argosy, but upon better paper and with more pages but if you feel inclined to entertain the idea we can discuss the details if we can first agree upon main principles, such as editor's salary and the like.

I am sure there is room for a good magazine, under your management. It will be hard if we cannot hold our own against such as 'Belgravia' and 'Temple Bar'.

According to Trollope in the *Autobiography*, 'a little before the date of my resignation [from the Post Office, in September 1867] Mr James Virtue . . . asked me to edit a new magazine for him, and . . . offered me a salary of £1,000 a year for the work, over and above what might be due to me for my own contributions' A. 284). The dates don't fit here; 'new magazine' must refer to the conception which Virtue announces for the first time in the 13 November letter—and this is hardly 'a little before' September 1867. We may also doubt the subsequent account of his dealings with Virtue that Trollope gives:

I very strongly advised him to abandon the project, pointing out to him that a large expenditure would be necessary to carry on the magazine in accordance with my views,—that I could not be concerned in it on any other understanding, and that the chances of an adequate return to him for his money were very small. (A. 284)

According to Trollope, Virtue came down to Waltham, listened to Trollope's arguments patiently 'and then told me that if I would not do the work he would find some other editor'. 'Upon this,' Trollope reports, 'I consented to undertake the duty.'

Trollope is, perhaps, conflating an earlier meeting with the precise negotiations for the 'new magazine' in November 1866. Possibly, too, a sense of guilt at having exploited the tyro publisher's ingenuousness leads him to fabricate a Cassandra-like scene. It is, surely, highly improbable that after correctly prophesying the dismal future of *St. Paul's* Trollope should have so enthusiastically involved himself in its debacle.

Trollope must have replied to Virtue's letter of 13 November by return of post, and judging by the publisher's equally prompt reply of 16 November, no misgivings were voiced by the editor-elect. Virtue begins with apologies for being unable to make a meeting on the 17th (one wonders, incidently, at the efficiency of the postal deliveries) and continues:

> My ideas are as yet very crude—I have no definite plan, as so much depends on our understanding together and what your ideas may be as well as mine.
>
> Briefly—I should say: Pay the contributors well to get good talent. If our magazine made 128 pages I should think an average of 20/- a page ought to do, but this must so much depend upon prices paid by other magazines, and the ability of the writers that it is difficult to name a definite sum.
>
> Certainly illustrators, with two full page illustrations, and perhaps a few others in the body of the magazine, but we should not commence with this probably.
>
> About the novel to commence with—I have nothing whatever in contemplation for this, my experience lies so little in that way that I fear I should have to look to you entirely for the literature—Is there no possibility of arranging even for a short one of your own? But perhaps when you have thought over the matter more fully—you would lay out roughly your plan for the whole Magazine and then we might determine which portion might be illustrated and such like.
>
> I should have no objection to guarantee the arrangement for two years but concerning this we had better talk when we meet, as I apprehend that if by any mischance the enterprise failed to get a sufficient circulation and that if, contrary to my expectations, it did not turn out a success, it might be advisable for both of us to consider the propriety of working a dead horse.

At the conclusion of his letter, Virtue adds: 'I calculate that a sale of 25,000 would pay—but I certainly expect a far higher circulation.'

Trollope's account in the *Autobiography* reflects this letter of Virtue's accurately enough, although he implies that such things as the rate of proposed payment (20 sh. a page was accepted as the standard payment for non-fiction) was his, Trollope's, 'stipulation' rather than Virtue's. Trollope's commitment to the project is witnessed by the fact that, denied a meeting in London with Virtue on 17 November, he actually began writing *Phineas Finn* on that day—thus supplying the want of a novel which Virtue expresses in the middle of his letter. And given that by Trollope's account the circulation actually achieved by *St. Paul's* was, on average, 'nearly 10,000' rather than the 25,000 which Virtue required to pay his way, it is clear that the novelist kept the proprietor strictly to the two year clause—in spite of *St. Paul's* proving a very dead horse indeed.

On 13 December, Virtue wrote Trollope a letter containing more precise business details of 'our publication'. He was inclined to publish later in the year than they first contemplated. April or May 1867 would clash with the Paris Exhibition and dull the new journal's impact. He was also concerned (as well he might be) that Trollope would be featured as author of *The Claverings*, running serially in *St. Paul's* main rival, *Cornhill*, until May 1867. He proposed January 1868, 'or perhaps a month or two earlier'.

Trollope replied to Virtue a day later, on 14 December. His preference for launching the magazine was October 1867. As to the vexed question of the periodical's name, Trollope found 'Trollope's Monthly' objectionable—it would mean nothing once he left the journal. (Trollope was also, as we shall see, very pre-occupied with the question of anonymity at this period.) He suggested 'The Monthly Westminster', 'The Monthly Liberal', and in a later letter, of 19 April, was to put forward 'The Whitehall Magazine'. What is significant here, is that Trollope clearly had a political mission in mind for the journal—something not touched on by Virtue. Trollope confirmed this by indicating that the magazine was to have a central political article every month—a design which may well have been news to Virtue. There should be little reviewing, Trollope proposed, 'or none'. In addition to his own novel—which was to receive £3,200—he proposed a second serial to run concurrently, 'of course written on cheaper terms'. The cheaper terms of 25 sh. a page (as opposed to 20 sh. for non-fiction) was in fact adopted for Mme Blaze de Bury, Frances Eleanor Trollope and Mrs. Oliphant—the lesser novelists who ran along-side Trollope.

There is some mystery in Trollope's other reason given in this letter for preferring the October 1867 publication date, namely that he could not start a novel until July. In fact, as we have seen, *Phineas Finn* was begun on 17 November 1866, and finished, according to schedule, on 15 May, 1867. It is unlikely that Trollope was deliberately duping Virtue in this, rather it would seem that he was keeping options open. Trollope was doing very good business with Smith, Elder and Co. over the period 1866–67. *The Claverings* ran in *Cornhill* from February 1866 to May 1867; 'for this', Trollope notes in the *Autobiography*, 'I received the highest rate of pay that was ever accorded to me' (A. 197). And on 6 February, 1866, Smith agreed to give £3,000 for *The Last Chronicle of Barset*, to be issued in 32 weekly instalments from December onwards. Both these novels were well out of the way when Trollope began to write *Phineas Finn* in November 1866. The manuscript of *Phineas Finn* suggests that Trollope was unsure of his mode of serialisation in the early stages of the novel's composition. One deduces that the novelist hoped for another sale to Smith of a novel in weekly numbers. But the newfangled serialisation adopted for the *Last Chronicle* was 'not altogether successful' (A. 274). Smith made a loss on the venture and this probably resulted in Virtue getting *Phineas Finn*, rather than the work which Trollope had planned to start in July 1867. Although he couldn't have realised it, Trollope had now burned his bridges with George Smith. For the rest of his writing career he published no further novel in the *Cornhill* and nothing substantial for Smith, Elder and Co., the house that had 'made' him and always been his most generous paymaster.

On 14 January 1867 Virtue wrote to Trollope, proposing to have 'regular formal agreements for our understanding together'. Trollope made a copy of his reply on the back of Virtue's letter.'I do not think we shall want any lawyers between us', he observed; a letter of proposal from Virtue would suffice. This was duly sent by Virtue on 21 January. It specified the £1,000 annual payment and its two years' guaranteed duration ('if we do not continue the magazine, we agree to still pay you £2,000 during two years, unless from any unforeseen occurrence you are unable to continue the editorship'). A further sum of £75 was to be advanced for editorial assistance in the three month period prior to publication; thereafter all editorial expenses to come from Trollope's own pocket. (Trollope gave Dicey a stipend of £250 a year, plus a generous allowance of article space in the journal.) Trollope's articles were to be paid for 'at [the] same rate as it is intended to pay other contributors, viz 20/- per page during the first twelve months'. Trollope evidently wrote two formal letters of reply to Virtue, one accepting the editorship, the other accepting Virtue's simultaneous bid of £3,200 for a new novel of 480 pages 'such pages as those of the Cornhill Magazine' to be 'published in your magazine in continuous monthly parts'.

In these contracts the failure of *St. Paul's* was prepared for.

Comparison shows that Trollope was—in spite of his later apology about 'fairly good' shares for all[6]—skimming all Virtue's cream for himself. He would receive £160 an issue for *Phineas Finn*, £83 an issue for editorial services, and £1 a page for any incidental material he cared to put in; and as editor with complete control over contributions this meant that he was free to top up his monthly income as it suited him. Thus for the first October 1867 issue Trollope had £160+£83+£23 (for his editorial and 'On Sovereignty'). Madame de Bury had a mere £24 for her instalment of *All for Greed*, and the other four main contributors £55 to share between them.

Trollope was in his full strength as a novelist in the mid-1860s. This is the peak of his earning achievement. But the canny Smith, while recognising Trollope's virtues, had never gauged him as a really top rate magazine writer. He was prepared to go to £5,000 for Wilkie Collins and as high as £10,000 for George Eliot. Trollope he rated at a little over Mrs. Gaskell's price, £3,000 a full length novel. Virtue was paying top price for Trollope and something more. Moreover he allowed himself to be rushed into committing himself far too exclusively to Trollope, something that Smith was very careful not to do. In January 1867 Virtue agreed to give Trollope £3,200 for an unseen novel, and to pay him £2,000 for editorial editorship, however well or badly he performed his duty and however well or badly the magazine sold. In November 1867, some three weeks after *St. Paul's* launch, Virtue made a further agreement to publish the as yet unwritten *He Knew He Was Right* in 32 weekly parts at a payment of £3,200. (Trollope clearly hadn't let on about the failure of the *Last Chronicle*'s publication in this form.) In one year Virtue made blind bargins with Trollope to the amount of £8,400.

The partners' motives were damagingly at cross-purposes. Virtue wanted to be a publisher, and immodestly patterned his dealings on 'the Prince of Publishers' George Smith. He set up a blatant copy of Smith's *Cornhill* with *St. Paul's*; imitated Smith's serial experiment with *He Knew He Was Right* and poached two Smith star performers in Trollope and Millais. He was, quite clearly, a rich would-be great publisher in a hurry.

Trollope, on the other hand, wanted money to cushion his departure from a salaried, pensioned profession and to bankroll his imminent entry into politics—an unpaid occupation for back-

benchers at this period and always an untenured one. He was prepared to take advantage of Virtue's inexperience. It was, after all,
extremely rare, if not unique, for a Victorian novelist to be in the
position to exploit a Victorian publisher. If an employer made bad
bargains that was his look-out.

There were other disagreements evident in the controversy over
the magazine's name. Virtue, already in for £5,200 to Trollope,
wanted 'Trollope's Monthly'. He judged that the novelist's name
and fame would sell the enterprise best to the fiction reading
public. Trollope demurred in January 1867 to this identification
of the magazine so prominently with him. In April he was still
suggesting alternative titles. Even as late as September 1867, a
month before publication, advertisements carried no title and
suggested vaguely that Trollope's fiction, not Liberal politics, was
to be the magazine's main fare:

> ANTHONY TROLLOPE'S New Magazine will have for its Contribu-
> tors THE BEST WRITERS OF THE DAY. . . . On the First of
> October will be published, price One Shilling, the first Number
> (to be continued Monthly) of a New Magazine, devoted to Fiction,
> and to subjects Artistic, Literary, Social, and Political, edited by
> ANTHONY TROLLOPE. (A. 287)

If Virtue wanted something Trollopian and prophetic of good
fiction, Trollope wanted a title which should be political sounding,
and suggestive of Liberal affiliation: 'The Monthly Westminster',
'The Monthly Liberal', 'The Whitehall Magazine'. It is also clear
that Trollope was strangely exercised at this period about keeping
his name out of the limelight. In the summer of 1867 he wrote
and published anonymously in *Blackwood's* the story *Linda Tressel*
(he also wrote in Autumn that year another story to be published
anonymously, *The Golden Lion of Granpere*, which Blackwood
declined). The experiment in invisible authorship was not profit-
able, and Trollope's reasons for suppressing his name, as expressed
in the *Autobiography*, are unconvincing. It seems likely that Trollope was testing the market, to see if he might continue surreptit-
iously to put out work to rival magazines while conducting *St.
Paul's*. And this, of course, would be easier if his attachment to
Virtue's magazine were not too ostentatious.

A related enigma is why Trollope should have enforced an anonymous contribution rule on *St. Paul's* (it was only relaxed for

poetry, where initials were given). In his work for the *Fortnightly*, just previous to the *St. Paul's* engagement, Trollope had come out strongly in favour of contributors always speaking 'with the responsibility of their names attached' (A. 189). In one of the early numbers for the other magazine Trollope wrote 'a paper advocating the signature of the authors to periodical writing' (A. 191–2; he did allow some exception for articles on political subjects). Trollope's reason for departing from this admirable forthrightness in *St. Paul's* can only be conjectured. In the first place, *Cornhill* was anonymous. In the second, the *Fortnightly* had not prospered with its 'responsible' philosophy, and Trollope chafed under its democratic conduct by board of management. Thirdly, Trollope may have felt that politicians, himself included, would be freer to speak their minds in an anonymous forum. Leslie Stephen puts this forward in an essay on 'Anonymous Journalism' which he contributed, anonymously, to the issue for May 1868. If editors abolished the anonymous principle, Stephen notes, 'we should throw a considerable obstacle in the way of the best class of contributors' (II. 229). A less high minded consideration is that in an anonymously conducted journal the public did not actually know what class of contributor they were getting for their shilling. This is important since although Trollope was doing very well, *St. Paul's* did not pay enough to recruit the great names of periodical writing. At 25 sh. a page, it could only purchase a very poor sort of novelist to pull with the editor—of Mme Blaze de Bury Trollope himself wrote, in January 1867, 'having many years ago made a reputation, she has not maintained it. . . . She must not . . . expect a long price' (L. 195); nor did she get one from *St. Paul's*. Frances Eleanor Trollope had only £333 for *The Sacristan's Household*, which ran from July 1868 to June 1869. Mrs. Oliphant was paid directly by Virtue, but one assumes that she too had the 25 sh. a page normal payment for fiction. Nor, for a pound a page, could Trollope entice, at least on a regular basis, distinguished non-fiction contributors. In the *Autobiography* he misrepresents somewhat the calibre of *St. Paul's* contents; implying that occasional contributors were the magazine's stalwarts:

> During the three years and half of my editorship I was assisted by Mr. Goshen, Captain Brakenbury, Edward Dicey, Percy Fitzgerald, H. A. Layard, Allingham, Leslie Stephen, Mrs. Lynn Lynton, my brother T. A. Trollope and his wife, Charles Lever, E. Arnold,

Austin Dobson, R. A. Proctor, Lady Pollock, G. H. Lewes, C. Mackay, Hardman (of the *Times*), George Macdonald, W. R. Greg,
Mrs, Oliphant, Sir Charles Trevelyan, Leoni Levi, Dutton Cook
—and others ... (A. 286)

Of these, between October 1867 and September 1869 (when Trollope's personal records stop), Layard and Stephen contributed three
articles each; Fitzgerald, Lady Pollock and Leoni Levi contributed
two articles each; Mrs Lynn Linton, G. H. Lewes, C. Mackay, Hardman, C. Trevelyan, and Dutton Cook each contributed only one
article; Allingham contributed two and Arnold one short piece of
poetry.

Of course Trollope is truthful enough in this roll call. But it
would seem evident that most of his notables could only be presumed on once or twice in the way of friendship. The bulk of the
24 months' 100 or so contributions came from pens which were
not only anonymous but obscure in themselves.

3

From the first *St Paul's* was a lame enterprise. The cool, judicious, 'manly' tone of the journal evidently missed its mark. In a
malicious notice of 5 October 1867 the *Spectator* hailed the new
arrival on the periodical scene as colourless, a 'blanc mange' of a
political paper. *St. Paul's* 'thoughtful liberalism' it found merely
dull. For all one's natural partisanship it is hard not to concur with
the *Spectator*'s opinion. Trollope's 'Introduction' is an extra-
ordinarily muffled fanfare, riddled with self doubts and anticipated
objections. The editor:

> begs to assure such of the public as will kindly interest them-
> selves in the matter, that the SAINT PAUL'S MAGAZINE is not
> established on and from this present 1st of October, 1867, on
> any rooted and mature conviction that such a periodical is the
> great and pressing want of the age (I. 1).

And again, on page 3:

> There is certainly no settled conviction in the minds of any of us,
> proprietors, contributors, or editors, that a SAINT PAUL'S
> MAGAZINE is the one great want of the age ...

To say it once is bad enough; repetition suggests a severe case of editorial cold feet. Indeed the only assertion which is made with any confidence is that there will be no reviewing: 'It is not intended that this magazine shall be a vehicle for literary criticism' (I. 7). What it *was* to be a vehicle for, other than 'gentlemanly' and 'independent' opinion is not clear. Trollope chooses his words so carefully as to the sides the magazine will take that one apprehends nothing except an overmastering caution: 'an editor need hardly declare that the cause to be supported here will be the free government of the country by that side in the House of Commons which in truth represents the majority of the constituencies' (I. 5).

Part of this equivocation must have arisen from the fact that Trollope, like the rest of the political community, had been wrong-footed by the events of 1866–67. In March 1866 Gladstone published his Reform Bill; but the Liberals fell to Dunkellen's motion in June. The Tories came in, Disraeli sacrificed the fancy clauses in the Spring of 1867 and passed a more radical act than the Liberals themselves had aimed at, in their bill of July 1867. While Trollope and Virtue laid their plans for *St. Paul's*, the familiar political world was thus turned upside down. How to strike a rational Liberal pose in the face of Conservative 'leaps in the dark' was clearly something of a poser.

Further upsets were to come. In Autumn 1868 Trollope made his attempt to enter parliament and failed miserably. The catastrophe at Beverley where he came bottom of the poll in an egregiously dirty contest was utterly demoralising. The disaster had long-reaching effects; he was never, for example, to write any fiction as optimistically and unequivocally 'Liberal' as *Phineas Finn* again. His later politics were increasingly Whiggish and emotionally reactionary. Moreover, he was £2,000 out of pocket; in a few unproductive days at Beverley he spent all that Virtue had guaranteed him for two years arduous editorial work.

Disaster of a more pressing kind was facing Virtue. As *St. Paul's* was launched the publisher was over-extended. And as Trollope records, the magazine never sold even half as many as Virtue needed to cover his expenses. It would seem that Trollope kept the publisher to their two year minimum agreement. But when it elapsed, Virtue was forced to make over the property to Strahan, who reasonably decided that the first economy should be the paid services of Trollope. On 25 January 1870, Virtue wrote what was effectively a letter of dismissal:

I hear from Messrs Straham today that they intend to write to you upon the subject of St. Paul's intending to try the Editorship themselves. But I could not let the intimation be made without saying that, personally, I so much regret that St. Paul's and you should part company—our relationship together has been so genial and pleasant that I much regret that any change should have become necessary—but when we parted with the Magazine from our charge here, we also parted from all control over it, as although I am largely interested in Strahan's business—I have always declined and intend to decline any active share in its management.

Virtue concludes his good natured letter ruefully: 'It is hard work to make a property of this description remunerative.'

The same day, Trollope received a letter from the more business-like Strahan declaring that 'we have been thinking that St. Paul's might be allowed to follow the example of Blackwood's, and "edit itself".' Somewhat tactlessly, in addressing its architect, Strahan goes on to explain: 'I would never think of making this proposal were the Magazine in a flourishing state.' Not that Trollope deluded himself. In the *Autobiography* he assesses *St. Paul's* as an outright 'failure' and concurs with Strahan's policy: 'I think, upon the whole, that publishers themselves have been the best editors of magazines' (A. 288).

Trollope 'gave up the seals' of *St. Paul's* in June 1870. It was, as Sadleir observes, the turning point in his fortunes as author. Hereafter his fame was 'slightly blown upon'.[7] He was never again to enjoy the payments Smith and Virtue had given him in the years 1865–69.

Even with hindsight it is not easy to apportion responsibility for the failure of *St. Paul's*. The following, however, are the main reasons which can be plausibly sustained from the evidence:

(1)   There wasn't room for two *Cornhill*'s in the market.

(2)   Virtue was over-eager and over-rated Trollope's value; Trollope took ruthless advantage of the publisher's miscalculation and inexperience.

(3)   The scale of payments to Trollope was too high, and to other than Trollopian contributors too low (more so as the anonymity rule did not even allow the consolation of name credit).

(4)   Proprietorial and Editorial motives were confused. Virtue wanted a literary magazine centred on the 'man of letters' Trollope.

Trollope, on his part, wanted a magazine centred on his brand of Liberalism.

(5) *St. Paul's* political bearings were confused by the political upheavals of 1866–67.

(6) Trollope's energy waned when his political future vanished, and Virtue's nerve failed as the magazine obstinately failed to prosper.

As the above schedule suggests, it is not entirely possible to exonerate Trollope from the charge of taking unfair advantage of Virtue. He could have allowed more play to be made with his name. He might have voluntarily surrendered his legal right to two years' editorial salary, when the magazine manifestly wasn't paying enough to justify it. He might have indicated to Virtue that the *Last Chronicle* was 'not altogether successful' in weekly numbers, before allowing the publisher to sink £3,200 in the same dubious experiment a few months later (with the same costly results). And in regard to *Phineas Finn* (which may have been dumped on Virtue), Trollope did not do his best for the magazine. *Phineas Finn* was written between November 1866 and May 1867; it assumes—as was quite logical in late 1866—that the Liberal party would pass the Reform Bill. When it came to be published in *St. Paul's* (October 1867–May 1869) this assumption as to Liberal reform was historically jarring. As a *roman à clef* many of *Phineas Finn*'s keys do not fit with his false prophecy as its centre-piece. Another kind of novelist might have rewritten, at least in part, a novel for which a publisher had obligingly given £3,200, sight unseen. But this would have meant putting off the writing of *He Knew He Was Right*, a diversion of earning capacity quite alien to Trollope's authorial instincts.

4

Trollope's Non-fiction Contributions to *St. Paul's*

Among Trollope's business papers, now in the Bodleian, are some ledger sheets with the amounts paid to various contributors over the period October 1867–September 1869. Since these are copies of what was forwarded to Virtue for monthly payment (one of Trollope's 'special stipulations' was that he should have charge of all dealings with contributors apart from signing the pay cheques), the editor's own monthly due is entered with all the others. Although he does not specify the articles, they can be worked out by correlating page-length and pound-payment. A list of Trollope's contributions is given in Sadleir's *Trollope: A Bibliography* (1928), but it is incomplete, slightly inaccurate and in places misleading. Short descriptions of the articles are given with the identification, and those missed by Sadleir are asterisked:

October 1867:   'Introduction' (7 pp.), *'On Sovereignty' (16 pp.). Trollope credits himself with £23 for the month. 'On Sovereignty' is a mechanical exercise in which following Aristotle's analysis of tyranny, Trollope draws an illustrative distinction between the rule of Emperors, Presidents and Constitutional Monarchs. The last, as exemplified in the throne of England, is the preferred *via media*. What is striking in this essay is how little Trollope's views have changed since 1856. *The New Zealander*[8] in its chapter 9 on 'The Crown' makes the same three part comparison, and draws the same extended analogy between the monarch's relationship to the state and the spire of Salisbury Cathedral's relationship to its supporting edifice.

November 1867:   'About Hunting' (14 pp.). Trollope credits himself with £14. This is the expected encomium on the sport from its most famous follower. Trollope celebrates hunting as a mature, civilised recreation and offers a practical breakdown of the annual cost of pursuing it.

December 1867:   'An Essay on Carlylism' (14 pp.). Trollope credits himself with £14. Trollope again uses *The New Zealander* as a quarry (the editor of Trollope's posthumously published work, N. John Hall, calls this article 'a small version of *The New Zealander*', p. xiv). Trollope repeats his main points in the *Autobiography*, pp. 353–

54. In all three places, he takes Carlylism as the profoundly pessimistic belief that 'the English speaking world is growing worse from day to day' and repudiates it.

January 1868:   'The Uncontrolled Ruffianism of London' (6 pp.). Trollope credits himself with £6. A whimsical piece about street crime: 'Our attention has been specially called to the subject above named by the fact that, after a somewhat prolonged and minute inquiry, we have been unable to meet anyone who has been garrotted.' Trollope introduced a garrotting episode centrally into *Phineas Finn*. It was scheduled to appear in the instalment for May 1868.

February 1868:   'Whom Shall we make Leader of the New House of Commons?' (15 pp.). Trollope credits himself with £15. Who, Trollope asks, should take over as Prime Minister when the Conservative Ministry has gone? Trollope short-lists the candidates for new leader: no Liberal would follow Disraeli. Lord Stanley, Lord Cranbourne, Bright are all, for one reason or another, disqualified. 'There remains to us Mr. Gladstone.' Trollope's objection to Gladstone is typical—he cannot give himself a straight answer to the question 'has Mr. Gladstone been honest?'

March 1868:   'About Hunting' (16 pp.). Trollope credits himself with £16. A sequel to the November article.

May 1868:   There is some difficulty in the articles for this month. Sadleir does not credit Trollope with any article in this number—yet the records show him as having been paid £13. There are two articles which Trollope could have written, 'The Irish Church Debate', (14 pp.) and

133

'Anonymous Journalism' (13½ pp.). Sadleir attributes 'Anonymous Journalism' to Stephen, which seems borne out by stylistic evidence. The Irish article is the first of a series which can plausibly be ascribed to Trollope, and it is very probable that he wrote it, although the payment does not quite fit page length. The subject discussed in the proposed disestablishment of the Irish Church.

There is a long gap in Trollope's contributions to the Magazine, accounted for by his departure for America in March on postal and copyright missions (his last work for the Post Office). He returned home in July 1868, and in November stood unsuccessfully as Liberal candidate for Beverley in the General Election.

September 1868: *'American Reconstruction' (15 pp.). Trollope credits himself with £15. Fresh from his visit to the newly united U.S., Trollope asks the English reader a question he takes to be of 'infinitely great importance'. 'Can a community of white men be made to live in subjection to a community of negroes, the numbers being, let us say equal?' According to Trollope, they can't.

November 1868: *'Clarissa' (9½ pp.). Trollope credits himself with £9 10s. One of *St. Paul's* rare reviews. Richardson's novel had been reissued, abridged and edited by E. S. Dallas and published by William Tinsley. Trollope asks 'why nobody now reads Richardson's novels'. He formulates his 'Rational Amusement' arguments, most familiar from the *Autobiography* and concludes that Richardson is 'unreadable', prolix, even when abridged. The epistolary form is 'impracticable'.

Beverley must have knocked Trollope up. He does nothing more for the magazine for three months.

February 1869:   'The New Cabinet and What it will Do For Us'
                  (14 pp.). Trollope credits himself with £14. A
                  friendly survey of the personnel in Gladstone's
                  new cabinet. He is pleased to see Bright serv-
                  ing but, anticipating Mr. Monk's resignation
                  in *Phineas Finn*, 'we cannot expect good official
                  work from him'. In this article Trollope outlines
                  his theory of Conservatism and Liberalism in
                  much the same terms (their attitude towards
                  'distance between classes') as in the *Auto-
                  biography*.

March 1869:   'President Johnson's Last Message' (13 pp.).
                  Trollope credits himself with £13. Written more
                  in sorrow than in anger, this follows the same
                  pro-Southern line as Trollope's earlier American
                  piece in September. There is some astute analy-
                  sis of the problems of a President harassed by
                  an unsympathetic Congress.

May 1869:   'Mr. Disraeli and the Mint' (6 pp.). Trollope
                  credits himself with £6. A short, savage attack
                  on the former Prime Minister for having ap-
                  pointed his private secretary to a position in
                  the Mint, over the head of an older civil servant.
                  Trollope's anger, of course, is fuelled by the fact
                  that it was just such an injustice which led to
                  him resigning from the Post Office twenty
                  months earlier.

June 1869:   Sadleir attributes 'The Irish Church Bill' to
                  Trollope. There is no entry in the business
                  papers to support this (indeed, there are no
                  more payments to Trollope recorded at all).
                  From internal evidence the attribution is quite
                  plausible.

In his *Trollope: A Bibliography*, Sadleir records that Trollope's active control of the magazine was over' by August 1869, 'although he still continued technically the editor' (p. 241). But Trollope himself did not see his 'reign' as finishing until June 1870, and published letters show him actively editing up to this date. It is hard to believe that, while busily attending to the contributions of others, Trollope did not continue to insert the occasional article himself and some supplementary attributions can be put forward.

'The Irish Church Bill in the Lords' (August 1869) follows from the earlier Irish piece, and is quite likely by Trollope. So are two other articles on Ireland (both by the same author, from internal evidence): 'What Does Ireland Want' (December 1869) and 'Mr. Gladstone's Irish Land Bill' (March 1870). Trollope took a particular interest in Ireland, and the attitudes expressed in these articles as to amnesty for Fenians, Church disestablishment (both of which are viewed favourably) and fixity of tenure (less favourably viewed) tally with Trollope's opinions.

There is firmer ground for attributing *Formosa* (October 1869) to Trollope. On the evidence of a letter to Anna C. Steele of 25 May 1870 Bradford Booth assumes that this article 'is probably by Trollope' (L. 272). The style is certainly very Trollopian, and the subject is one close to his heart at the time, namely the presentation of fallen women in literature. This, of course, was a controversial aspect of *The Vicar of Bullhampton* published in April 1870. Trollope's objection to the prostitute in Boucicault's play is oddly Shavian: the subject is not indecent but 'the character is utterly false, false to human nature and false to human life'.

The last attribution which can confidently be made to Trollope is 'Ancient Classics for English Readers' in March 1870. This puff is for Blackwood's new series, under the editorship of W. L. Collins. Although he doesn't mention it in the piece, Trollope was contracted to provide the volume on Caesar and had already seven chapters written. He makes the same points about the series as in the *Autobiography*, and finishes with a sly reference to discreet editors: 'we think that the editor of the series has chosen the best plum for himself,—as a discreet editor should do'.

Correspondence indicates that Trollope took his editorial duties seriously (perhaps too seriously for the good of the magazine, he suggests in the *Autobiography*). Dicey developed a very good imitation of his chief's manner and probably wrote to instruction. A long piece on 'The Election Petitions' (April 1869) by Dicey seems to owe a remote authorship in Trollope's experience at Beverley, and his appearance as a witness at the tribunals. Beverley is ostentatiously *not* mentioned, though other notably corrupt constituencies are. Dicey observes, as could hardly have failed to please Trollope, that candidates were generally vindicated from corrupt practice, the guilt falling on agents.

Nor can Trollope have been displeased, and he may well have solicited, a piece on 'M. Victor Hugo's England' in July 1869. (This may have been written by T. A. Trollope.) Hugo's work had ousted *The Vicar of Bullhampton* from *Good Words*, an insult which drove Trollope into explosive rage (See Sadleir's *Trollope: A Commentary*, 1927, repr. 1961, pp. 304–7). The piece in *St. Paul's* is an intemperate attack on Hugo's novel—and *St. Paul's*, it will be remembered, was to have no reviewing.

NOTES

1 References in the text to the cue-title 'A' indicate Anthony Trollope, *An Autobiography*, ed. F. Page (1950). References to the cue-title 'L' indicate *The Letters of Anthony Trollope*, ed. B. A. Booth (1951).
2 Quoted, M. Sadleir, *Trollope: A Commentary* (1927, repr. 1961) p. 205
3 Letter to Trollope dated 24 January 1867. This letter is with Trollope's business papers now in the Bodleian Library (call mark Don C 9–10*). It is from these papers that the subsequent correspondence relative to *St. Paul's* between Trollope, Virtue and Strahan is quoted.
4 References are to volume and page numbers of *St. Paul's*.
5 *A Commentary*, p. 278.
6 See his letter to Austin Dobson, 21 May 1870: 'In my endeavour to establish the Saint Pauls on what I considered to be a good literary footing, I insisted on myself naming the remuneration to be paid. It has not been very great, but it has been fairly good' (L. 270–71).
7 *A Commentary*, p. 300.
8 *The New Zealander* was published posthumously in 1972, edited and with an introduction by N. John Hall.

7

The Eustace Diamonds and Politics

by JOHN HALPERIN

Is *The Eustace Diamonds* a political novel?

It has been usual for some years to group together *Can You Forgive Her?* (1864–65), *Phineas Finn* (1867–69), *The Eustace Diamonds* (1873), *Phineas Redux* (1874), *The Prime Minister* (1875–76), and *The Duke's Children* (1879–80) under the heading of the Political or Parliamentary Novels—or, more recently, the Palliser Novels. And yet Trollope never made this grouping himself. Indeed, the promotion of these six novels into a category by themselves along the lines of the six-volume Barsetshire series occurred long after his death. In *Anthony Trollope: A Commentary* (1927), Michael Sadleir lists the six together as Political Novels. Although the division of the novels was largely his own, it derived in part from a compilation by Spencer Nichols in *The Significance of Anthony Trollope* (1925). Nichols, in turn, had accepted the classification made by Morris E. Speare, who discusses the six novels together in his book on *The Political Novel* (1924). Speare, however, refused to accept *Can You Forgive Her?* as a genuine part of the series.[1] He refers his reader to T. H. S. Escott's indispensable early biography, *Anthony Trollope: His Public Services, Private Friends and Literary Originals* (1913). Escott's book, for many years the chief source beyond the novelist's *Autobiography* (1883) of information about Trollope's life and opinions, discusses the novels together as political in tone and focus, but Escott never actually gives them any subsuming collective name. Nevertheless, Dodd, Mead and Company reissued the six novels in various editions between 1893 and 1928 with the words 'The Parliamentary Novels' on the spine. More recently, in an introduction to *Can You Forgive Her?*, Sadleir proposed that the Palliser Novels would be a more appropriate term than any of the others; the term has gained in acceptance, and in 1950 the Oxford University Press began republishing the six as 'The Palliser Novels' in the Oxford World's Classics series, re-issued in a paperback set of six in 1973 as, once again, 'The Palliser Novels'.

Whatever they are called, it is clear that these six novels are not so easily grouped together as the six novels of the Barset-shire series, in which geography and a particular cast of characters provide, through repetition and variation, a certain unity and co-herence. Even here, however, Trollope himself was equivocal, suggesting in his *Autobiography* that *The Small House at Allington* (1864) might not, after all, belong properly to the Barset series.[2] Indeed, he was so particular about how his novels ought to be categorised that, through constant self-contradiction, he wound up making very few consistent groupings at all. Nowhere does he describe the six novels we have come to call the Palliser Novels as belonging together as part of a series, and nowhere does he use the term 'Parliamentary Novels' (though he does refer often to 'The Pallisers' as the continuing focus of several of the novels). He discusses the grouping question explicitly in two places in the *Autobiography*. In the first instance: 'Who will read *Can You Forgive Her?*, *Phineas Finn*, *Phineas Redux*, and *The Prime Minister* consecutively, in order that he may understand the character of the Duke of Omnium, of Plantagenet Palliser, and Lady Glencora? Who will ever know that they should be so read?' (p. 159). Trollope was writing in the late seventies, probably before *The Duke's Children* was completed. Clearly he wanted his readers to encounter se-quentially the four novels he mentions. But what about *The Eus-tace Diamonds*, which had already appeared? Elsewhere in the *Autobiography* (p. 272) he refers to *Phineas Finn* as the novel which 'commenced a series of semi-political tales'—thus leaving out *Can You Forgive Her?*. Trollope also says that he considers the two *Phineas* novels to be one continuous and uninterrupted story despite the years and the books that separated them. He tells us in the *Autobiography* (pp. 274–75) that 'They were, in fact, but one novel, though they were brought out at a considerable interval of time and in different forms'; and he adds that their separation was due to 'much bad arrangement'. These comments suggest that he did not consider *The Eustace Diamonds*, which comes between *Phineas Finn* and *Phineas Redux*, part of the same series, and indeed modern commentators on the Palliser novels have often hesitated to include it as part of the political group.

Undoubtedly *Can You Forgive Her?*, *The Eustace Diamonds*, and *The Duke's Children* are the least political of the six novels, and of these *The Eustace Diamonds* would seem, at first glance, to have the weakest claim to inclusion. There is little more political action *per se* in it than there is in *Rachel Ray* (1863) or *The Way We Live Now* (1874–75), and certainly much less that in *Ralph the Heir* (1870–71), which recounts the story of Trollope's unsuccessful run for Parliament in 1868. The novelist himself describes the popular success of *The Eustace Diamonds*, which gave a needed lift to his declining reputation in the early seventies, as being due primarily to his 'record of a cunning little woman of pseudo-fashion, to whom, in her cunning, there comes a series of adventures, unpleasant enough in themselves, but pleasant to the reader' (*Autobiography*, pp. 295–96). There is no mention of politics or of the Pallisers, who are seen only intermittently in the novel. (Elsewhere in the *Autobiography* Trollope describes *Phineas Finn* as being a 'much better' novel than *The Eustace Diamonds*, p. 296.)

What reasons are there, then, for accepting the Sadleir grouping and continuing to list *The Eustace Diamonds* as one of the Palliser Novels? I think there are many.

In the first place, *none* of the 'Political' novels is exclusively or even more than substantially about politics. Trollope's characteristic interest is in the *social* milieu of politicians. In *The Prime Minister*, therefore, we see Plantagenet Palliser at home more often than at his office; indeed, his story takes up only half of the novel, with the Emily Wharton story occupying the other half. Even in the *Phineas* novels, the most political of the six, more attention is given to Phineas's social peregrinations and love entanglements than to his political career, and there are several other love stories thrown in as well. *Can You Forgive Her?* and *The Duke's Children* have even less to do with politics; the former focuses mainly on the emotional vacillations of Alice Vavasor, and the latter on Palliser in political retirement—as father rather than as statesman. If there is more social than political philosophy in these novels, it is because Trollope's interest in politicians, as in clergymen, centres more in their social than their professional milieux. He makes this plain in the Barset novels—in the famous apologia which concludes *The Last Chronicle of Barset* (1867), again and again in *Barchester*

Towers (1857), and elsewhere from time to time throughout the other novels in the series. So in the *Autobiography* Trollope says that he believed his readers would be bored by novels purely political in interest; he realised, as he puts it, 'that I could not make a tale pleasing chiefly, or perhaps in any part, by politics. If I wrote politics for my own sake, I must put in love and intrigue, social incidents, with perhaps a dash of sport, for the sake of my readers (p. 272). 'Love and intrigue' account for at least half the pages of each of the six novels—and in *Can You Forgive Her?*, *The Eustace Diamonds*, and *The Duke's Children* substantially more than half. Indeed, the Palliser novels place great emphasis on the social backgrounds of Parliament, and especially on the influence of women over political ambition and success, their large share of the political game. Political success anywhere depends in part on charming the social élite of the Establishment—on approval social as well as political. If in these novels politics sometimes seems 'frivolous and amateurish—women whispering to powerful politicians on behalf of handsome pleasant young men, important political decisions being made at dinner parties, personal likes and dislikes shaping public policy'—this picture nevertheless is as true for the nineteenth century as for any other, including our own. An ambitious politician must always please a peer constituency of social fashion and power.[3] It is interesting to note that a generous amount of feminine whispering and intriguing on behalf of handsome young men at dinner parties and other places also occupies many pages of Disraeli's novels—indeed, he himself refers in one of them to 'those social influences which in a public career are not less important than political ones'.[4] A political novel that deals almost exclusively with politics (*Coningsby* is a good example) tells us very little indeed about the political process if it is not also careful to place its subject in the social contexts from which, after all, it cannot really be separated. Unlike Disraeli, a professional politician who wrote what is often political propaganda under the guise of fiction in order to promulgate or elucidate a particular political creed (and attack some political enemies along the way), Trollope is a professional novelist who happens to deal in some of his books with politics, and with politicians in society. I do not mean to suggest that he has no political creed of his own[5]— only that his primary concern as novelist is less with political theses than with those human beings who are politicians. He sees

141

society and politics as inextricably linked; much political action springs from social or domestic causes, Trollope shows us, and many private actions have political causes. A power-struggle that never really ends, even in the drawing-room, private life can be intensely political. Private acts are always political when they have some effect on the balance of power between people; distinctions between public and private become artificial in this context, there being no escape possible from politics—from political motivation and political acts. Conversely, public policies often are the off-spring of the private, the psychological, idiosyncrasies of public men (for instance, decimal coinage in *The Eustace Diamonds*). If personal life is largely governed by political considerations, political life is also largely a phenomenon of personality, or per-sonalities.[6] It is in this sense that Trollope's political novels are political—presenting, as he says in the *Autobiography*, 'political characters rather than other kinds (p. 307). While he is interested in the nature of political processes, he is more interested in the nature of man-as-politician. His originality is always in character-isation rather than in ideas; like Palmerston, one of his chief political heroes, he is essentially untheoretical. Trollope was shrewd enough, Bradford A. Booth tells us, 'to see that political characters must be colourless because they are so often called upon to sub-merge their identity in group action . . . Each must put aside his personal idiosyncrasies.'[7] The political novel, to keep up interests, must range far beyond politics. *The Eustace Diamonds* is no ex-ception among the Pallisers novels in this respect.

There are other compelling reasons for declaring that the novel is no anomaly in the series. All six deal in part with politics, in part with Parliament, and in part with Pallisers, and *The Eustace Diamonds* is no exception in this either. Lord Fawn and Frank Greystock, the novel's two leading male characters, are politicians. Lizzie Eustace and her diamonds eventually become, comically enough, a hot political issue. Fawn is a member of the government. Greystock is an M.P. with political aspirations, and we are given glimpses into his parliamentary career. We also see Parliament faced with the necessity of settling some colonial problems and of respond-ing to Palliser's currency reform measure. The Pallisers themselves, while they have not that much to do in the novel, are most certainly present and accounted for—in the Duke's fascination with the Eustace affair, in Lady Glencora's entrance into the controversy, and of course in Palliser's heroic efforts in behalf of his decimal coinage bill. But only to insist that the novel is not unlike the others in the series is to argue negatively, and there are a number of more positive connections between *The Eustace Diamonds* and the Palliser novels that precede and follow it. One of the chief connections is its unflattering and cynical picture of party politics, a picture I shall examine in some detail shortly. The others are more specific and immediate.

Were we to exclude *The Eustace Diamonds* from the Palliser series we would be confronted, on moving from *Phineas Finn* (second in the series) to *Phineas Redux* (fourth), with some unanswerable questions and bewildering developments. *The Eustace Diamonds* carries forward the stories of many of the characters who are important to the plots of the other novels. Palliser, who becomes Liberal Chancellor of the Exchequer in *Phineas Finn*, 'had now for more than two years, filled [that] high place' when *The Eustace Diamonds* opens.[8] Lady Glencora, unfortunately not at her best in this novel, does little more than interfere, briefly and irrationally, in the question of the diamonds and their owner's suitors. The old Duke of Omnium, who has some importance in *Phineas Finn* and whose death in *Phineas Redux* takes Palliser out of the House of Commons and helps to make him Prime Minister in *The Prime Minister*, is seen in *The Eustace Diamonds* as a querulous invalid living on scandal. Emilius, who is introduced at the end of *The Eustace Diamonds* in time to marry Lizzie, is essential to the plot of *Phineas Redux*. There he and Lizzie are living apart from one other; Emilius's machinations to restore himself to his wife's good graces cause a murder to be committed for which Phineas Finn is tried. Lord Fawn, who first appears as a minor character in *Phineas Finn* courting Violet Effingham and then Madame Max Goesler, reappears in *Phineas Redux* as a bumbling orator in the House of Lords. He is again a minor figure in these novels, having occupied so many pages of *The Eustace Diamonds*. It is Violet Effingham's marriage to Lord Chiltern at the end of *Phineas Finn* that causes Fawn to court Lizzie Eustace in *The Eustace Diamonds*. Phineas Finn, who is in Ireland during the action of *The Eustace Diamonds*, returns in *Phineas Redux* to marry Madame Goesler. Lizzie, a minor character in *Phineas Redux*, also reappears briefly in *The Prime Minister*. Many of the characters in *The Eustace Diamonds* are also of importance in the two

Phineas novels, and much of what happens in *Phineas Redux* would be inexplicable without reference to *The Eustace Diamonds*. Here, certainly, is another important reason for including the novel as part of the political series. But *The Eustace Diamonds*, I would argue, is also a political novel in its own right, and thus qualified for inclusion on wider grounds.

Let us not, after all, under-emphasise the importance of politics in the Palliser novels. In his *Autobiography* Trollope says of these novels specifically that, having been 'debarred from expressing my opinions in the House of Commons, I took this method of declaring myself' (p. 262). Here the frustrated politician spoke to the gallery of his readers—taking, as he says himself, a 'fling at the political doings of the day' (p. 184). In his two most purely political novels, *Phineas Finn* and *Phineas Redux*, Trollope raises issues that were actually being debated in the House of Commons as he wrote.[9] And in an 1876 letter to Mary Holmes the novelist does not deny that certain identifications could be made between some of his leading political characters and some of the leading politicians of his day—specifically between Daubeny and Disraeli, and Gresham and Gladstone.[10] There is room for a great deal of speculation on the who's who question; Trollope clearly drew much of his political material for the Palliser series from contemporary goings-on—a subject I cannot consider in depth here.[11] Certainly the Palliser novels objectify to some extent his political thinking.[12] Trollope's lifelong fascination with politics is manifest everywhere—far beyond his run for Parliament in 1868—from his first published writings (articles on social and political conditions in Ireland; the *Dublin Review* asserted in 1869 that Trollope understood the Irish tenant-right question better than almost all Englishmen of his time) to his memoir of *Lord Palmerston* (1882), almost the last thing he wrote.[13] In the fifties he penned a series of essays on essentially political themes—recently published as *The New Zealander* (1972); in the fifties and sixties he was a staunch defender of Palmerston, and of Lord John Russell and his policies;[14] also in the sixties he helped to found two politically progressive journals which characteristically supported the Liberal party—the *Fortnightly Review* and *Saint Paul's Magazine* (he edited the latter); and in the seventies he sided with Gladstone and against Disraeli (whom he always detested) on the Eastern Question, reading aloud to his family and some guests Gladstone's pamphlet on *The Bulgarian Horrors and The Question of the East* in October 1876; at the end of his life he broke explosively with Gladstone over matters essentially political.[15]

Trollope's novels and his non-fiction volumes alike testify to a curious sort of double vision on the subject of politics. They testify, that is, both to his sometime reverence for the profession and to his more usual cynicism. He could say in his *Autobiography* that 'to sit in the British Parliament should be the highest object of ambition to every educated Englishman' and that so to serve 'is the grandest work that a man can do' (pp. 250–51); he could regard public life 'as, of all paths, the noblest and the manliest' (*The Eustace Diamonds*, p. 163); and he could also fill the Palliser novels with political hacks and opportunists who are never to be believed, men who regard politics as a huge game, 'an affair of expediency' from which sincerity, principle, and patriotism are almost always absent.[16] This double vision runs through the Palliser novels, though in them the focus for the most part is on the abuses, tricks and dishonesty of the average professional politician. And yet it is these novels too which chronicle the political and social life of his own favourite creation, Plantagenet Palliser, a spectacular exception in his portrait gallery of political conjurers and double-dealers. In *The Prime Minister* Palliser ultimately grows into a personification of Trollope's ideal statesman, and by contrast we see once again what the rest of the political landscape is like. In *The Eustace Diamonds*, however, Palliser has not yet advanced beyond trivial obsessions.

Trollope always had a special tenderness for these novels, describing them in his *Autobiography* as 'the best work of my life' (p. 155) and the Palliser people themselves in the letter to Mary Holmes cited above as 'the best I ever made'.

With the notable exception of Booth, who calls Lizzie Eustace 'the poor man's Becky Sharp',[17] most of the novel's readers have included *The Eustace Diamonds* among their favourite Trollope volumes. Hugh Walpole called it 'one of the best comedies in the ranks of the English novel',[18] and Michael Sadleir and others have commented on the novel's superior construction. What has not been sufficiently noted is the novel's political content, especially the way in which Trollope weaves politics through the story of Lizzie Eustace and her diamond necklace.

In *Can You Forgive Her?* we do not see much of the political world beyond the aspirations of the unscrupulous George Vavasor. *Phineas Finn* gives us the parliamentary world in much greater detail. Yet while both novels demonstrate how important it is for a rising young politician to have good connections and financial backing, to bend to party discipline and avoid having—or at least expressing—his own opinions, the picture of the political process is not nearly so black as in *Phineas Redux* and *The Prime Minister*. The political stage of *Phineas Redux* is dominated by the amoral parliamentary magician Daubeny (Disraeli), who maintains himself and his Tory party in power by virtue of having no principles to fall by. In *The Prime Minister* Plantagenet Palliser, now Duke of Omnium, falls from power because he is too honest to become involved in the social insincerity and partisan patronage required of a Premier who would stay in office. Here *The Eustace Diamonds* is transitional; it is neither so good-humoured as *Phineas Finn* nor so bitterly satirical as the later Palliser novels. It is, perhaps, a watershed work in the progression of Trollope's long perspective on the politics of his time.

If this is true, surely one explanation lies in Trollope's biography. Between *Phineas Finn* and *The Eustace Diamonds*, an important event had taken place in his life. Attempting to realise at last a lifelong ambition, Trollope in 1868 ran as a Liberal candidate for Parliament.[19] The borough of Beverley in Yorkshire, stunned by a bribeless campaign based on political principles clearly articulated, unequivocally rejected his candidacy.

The novelist's confrontation in the flesh with English democracy was an enlightening experience—one which he discusses candidly in the political chapters of *Ralph The Heir* and *The Duke's Children* and in the *Autobiography* (pp. 250–62). His tone is always bitter. The voters, he says in the *Autobiography*, 'cared nothing for my doctrines, and could not even be made to understand that I should have any . . . political cleanliness was odious to (them)' (pp. 259 and 261). 'Perhaps nothing more disagreeable, more squalid, more revolting to the senses, more opposed to personal dignity, can be conceived', he says of 'Parliamentary canvassing' in *The Duke's Children*.[20] The effect on Trollope of his electoral experience, and of his defeat, may be seen in the glumly satirical way in which he subsequently describes elections in *Ralph the Heir*, *Phineas Redux*, *The Way We Live Now*, *The Prime Minister*, and *The Duke's Children*. In these novels the difficulties encountered by unprosperous non-professionals such as George Vavasor and Phineas Finn in the earlier novels are multiplied tenfold. The voters are no better, and often worse, than the candidates, who are pictured as having to stump through a pig-sty to sit at Westminster. Trollope's unpleasant experience at Beverley resulted in a deeper cynicism and a more unequivocal perspective upon political unscrupulousness and adventuring; from *The Eustace Diamonds* on, the Palliser novels begin to articulate a thoroughly jaundiced view of the political process—a view which suggests that in the political arena cunning and dishonesty are the best allies a combatant can have. Partisanship, not principle, is what is needed; you have to vote black to be white and white to be black in order to stay in good odour with your political colleagues. The fall of Daubeny's Conservative ministry in *Phineas Redux* is brought about when the Liberals, who favour church reform, vote against Daubeny's church reform measure not because they oppose it (they do not) but because it is proposed by the other party. Daubeny, the political archfiend of the later Palliser novels, is ultimately defeated, that is to say, only by his own brand of opportunism. *The Eustace Diamonds*, perhaps in its own way as fully as *Phineas Finn*, prepares us to understand such a political climate, and in doing so it embodies a political commentary of its own.

Whether or not *The Eustace Diamonds* is a 'Palliser' or a 'Parliamentary' novel, it is genuinely a political novel—within the framework established above. Although we see Lord Fawn and Frank Greystock in a social more often than a political context, it remains true that they are the novel's leading men and that they are professional politicians. Fawn, a Liberal, is a member of the sitting government, with duties in the Colonial Office. Greystock, a barrister, is a member of the vocal Conservative opposition in the House of Commons. Between them, they account for the two major marriage interests of the novel's ubiquitous anti-heroine. *The Eustace Diamonds* resembles the other five Palliser novels by virtue of the fact that some of its leading characters are politicians, even if politics is not always the paramount focus.

Lord Fawn's story is perhaps the more entertaining of the two. An Under-Secretary of State and member of the India Board, Fawn is equally timorous as lover and politician. Indeed, he sometimes fails to distinguish between the two roles. Having 'suffered a dis-

147

appointment in love [Violet Effingham] . . . he . . . consoled himself with bluebooks, and mastered his passion by incessant atten-
dance at the India Board' (p. 23). His characteristic way of making
love is to lecture ladies on 'the nature and condition of the British
Parliament' (p. 46). He is fond of 'submitting his opinion in writing' (p. 560) on matters matrimonial as well as political. And his
courtship of Lizzie Eustace finally comes to an end when she 'accepts
his resignation' from the affair (p. 566). Indeed, one of the pre-
cipitating reasons for the termination of the relationship is his
suggestion that Lizzie ' "place the diamonds in neutral hands"—
Lord Fawn was often called upon to be neutral in reference to the
condition of outlying Indian principalities' (p. 604). His letter to
her on the subject reads like 'an Act of Parliament' (p. 607). A
peer without capital, he 'must marry money'; this, however, is a
difficult undertaking, for Fawn is 'pompous, slow, dull, and careful' (p. 24). His political career, unspectacular and unexciting,
suddenly becomes more controversial, however, when he is persuaded by the family governess, Lucy Morris, to interest himself
in the fate of the Sawab of Mygawb, a subject being debated in the
House of Commons. Lord Fawn, who does not understand India
or its political problems, submits the government reports on the
question to Lucy for her opinion, and would form his own from hers
were he allowed to do so by his political superiors. As the debate
on the Sawab takes a more partisan turn, Fawn, as a member of the
India Board, is accused by Frank Greystock of being an administrator of tyranny. Quite clearly Lord Fawn understands little of
what goes on in his office, and nothing beyond it. And yet it is said
at one point that 'the whole of our vast Indian empire . . . [hangs]
upon him' (p. 123). This indispensable administrator, however,
has a rather serious problem: 'he . . . could not think and hear at
the same time' (p. 92). Despite his responsible political position,
Fawn possesses 'no outward index of mind' (p. 59). He is considered by Lizzie Eustace stupid enough to be easily entrapped in
marriage—a plan which nearly succeeds through Fawn's social
obliviousness and his interest in Lizzie's income, about which he
is frequently cross-examined by his mother (e.g., p. 76). Despite
Lizzie's amorality and Fawn's comparative honesty, he is not
exculpated by Trollope. On the contrary: 'the one was as mercenary
as the other' (p. 89). Fawn, further, is described by Trollope as
being a moral coward—without 'strength of character' and 'as

148

weak as water'; indeed, in politics, his position notwithstanding, he 'almost disgraced [any] cause by the accidence of his adherence to it' (p. 250). And yet this man is almost a junior cabinet minister. When, inevitably, he has a falling out with his political adviser, the Tory governess, and she says some hard things to him, Lord Fawn, 'like a great child, [went] at once . . . and [told] his mother' (p. 259). The last reference to him in the novel is spoken succinctly by Lizzie Eustace: 'Lord Fawn is an idiot' (p. 666). So much for the Empire.

Lizzie herself is characterized by Lady Linlithgow as 'about as bad as anybody ever was . . . false, dishonest, heartless, cruel, irreligious, ungrateful, mean, ignorant, greedy, and vile!' (p. 308) and by Mrs. Hittaway as 'a nasty, low, scheming, ill-conducted, dishonest little wretch' (p. 602). Despite the essential truth of these assessments, Lizzie, because she is rich, is considered by her cousin Frank Greystock's relatives and some of his friends as a more suitable wife for him than Lucy Morris, who is virtuous but poor.[21] Indeed, Mrs. Greystock feels that if her son 'would only marry his cousin one might say that the woolsack was won' (p. 319). The path to political glory is not obscure. A public man needs a bank account. And so Lizzie is attended throughout much of the novel by the impoverished M.P., who does not let his engagement to Lucy stand in the way of an amorous adventure or two. Fawn, though stupid, nevertheless fears scandal enough to back away from Lizzie before she is able to catch him. No such scruples govern the behaviour of Greystock, who is simply dazzled by her beauty and covetous of her wealth. 'From the very commencement of his intimacy with her', Trollope reminds us at one point, 'he had known that she was a liar' (p. 642). Ultimately Lizzie is revealed as too bad even for Frank's sympathy, and so he returns at last to the forgiving Lucy. But he is in many ways a less appealing character than Fawn, as Trollope's Tories are so often less appealing than his Liberals; and his story, perhaps even more than Fawn's, contributes to the grim commentary on contemporary politics. The government may be dim-witted, but the opposition, in its amorality, is probably worse. Fawn is never sure, until she is finally exposed, whether or not Lizzie is actually a thief, and so he is cautious; Greystock has fewer illusions about her, yet wedges his foot in the door each time she opens it a crack to peek out at him. That is the way to the woolsack.

Greystock had run for Parliament hoping that election would improve his law practice—exactly the sort of motive always abhorred by Trollope. He complained bitterly against those who (like George Vavasor in *Can You Forgive Her?*) wished to use parliamentary careers to protect and enhance their own financial and business positions.[22] (Phineas Finn is sensibly warned by his friend Mr. Lowe to establish himself professionally before going into politics so as to be an independent member when he gets to Parliament. He should have listened; but then there would have been no novel.) Once he is elected, great glory is predicted for Frank—so long as he 'abstains from marrying a poor wife' (p. 29). The great threat is Lucy Morris. Greystock has no political principle except opportunism, and no political allies. As such he must, so everyone tells him, seek a wealthy wife—and so he does, despite his commitment to Lucy. In love as in politics, principles are encumbrances. Lucy is only 'a log round his leg'; were he to honour his commitment to her he must 'abandon Parliament altogether' (p. 164)—for to succeed a politician in this world must either be rich, or seem to be. Where political advancement is tied to social *éclat*, the appearance of wealth is essential. Thus we are reminded again and again that although Frank is doing well for himself, 'he could hardly continue to prosper unless he married money' (p. 269); though he is well on his way to becoming a great man, he 'cannot become [one] without an income' (p. 483). Lizzie has no trouble understanding what is at stake: 'what she offered him would be the making of him. With his position, his seat in Parliament, such a country house as Portray Castle, and the income which she would give him, there was nothing that he might not reach!' (p. 690). The qualities of the man mean nothing, his possessions, everything. Ultimately, of course, Lizzie is found to have behaved too badly even for Frank Greystock, and he returns to Lucy—thus ruining forever, so we are told, his prospects of becoming Lord Chancellor. Lady Glencora likens his decision to marry Lucy to deliberate and calculated suicide—'To her thinking the two actions were equivalent' (p. 682). Conduct that is morally right is often portrayed by Trollope in the Palliser novels (especially *Phineas Finn* and *The Prime Minister*) as politically disastrous—and such apparently is the case here. Greystock's fate in the subsequent novels is left obscure, suggesting at the very least that Lucy and the woolsack are incompatible after all.

Trollope concludes his portrait of Greystock with the assertion that his predicament is only symptomatic of the dilemma many other such men find themselves in. Certainly he is no better or worse, Trollope argues, than 'the majority of barristers and members of Parliament among whom he consorted' (p. 681). Money, social position, and moral flexibility are what, politically, it takes —and so Greystock's future, beyond any domestic happiness that may await him, is bleak.

Trollope's satire is even more pointed in his account of how the Fawn–Greystock love rivalry and the question of the Eustace diamonds themselves are overtaken by party politics. Is Lady Eustace actually guilty of theft? Fawn suspects that she is and retreats from his offer of marriage; Greystock, whatever he may really think, declares that she is not. The issue is debated in fashionable society.

> It was worthy of remark that [the] Lizzieites were all of them Conservatives. Frank Greystock had probably set the party on foot;—and it was natural that political opponents should believe that a noble young Under-Secretary of State on the Liberal side, —such as Lord Fawn,—had misbehaved himself. When the matter at last became of such importance as to demand leading articles in the newspapers, those journals which had devoted themselves to upholding the Conservative politicians of the day were very heavy indeed upon Lord Fawn. The whole force of the Government, however, was anti-Lizzieite; and as the controversy advanced, every good Liberal became aware that there was nothing so wicked, so rapacious, so bold, or so cunning but that Lady Eustace might have done it, or caused it to be done. . . . It [was] . . . a matter of faith with all the Liberal party that Lady Eustace had had something to do with stealing her own diamonds. That esprit de corps, which is the glorious characteristic of English statesmen, had caused the whole Government to support Lord Fawn. . . . The Attorney and Solicitor-General were dead against her. . . . But they were members of a Liberal government, and of course anti-Lizzieite. Gentlemen who were equal to them in learning, who had held offices equally high, were distinctly of a different opinion. . . . And . . . these gentlemen . . . were Lizzieites and of course Conservatives in politics. (pp. 423, 487, and 445, *passim*)

Where politics is concerned, independent judgement and objectivity are in abeyance—even in trivial matters. Indeed, the importance the Eustace controversy assumes in the political world is a direct commentary on the absurdity of the other ersatz issues of the day (such as the Sawab and the Palliser penny) that have been engaging the attention of partisans. Whatever the question, the party line must be followed and defended—except, perhaps, by those who are beyond such considerations by reason of wealth or influence. Such a one is Lady Glencora, wife of the Chancellor of the Exchequer and future Duchess of Omnium, who causes political shock waves by bucking the Liberal party line and defending Lady Eustace. Here a different sort of political comedy is enacted—for Lady Glencora's energetic apostasy makes clear, among other things, how dependent political underlings such as Lord Fawn and Mr. Bonteen are upon the good will of their social and political masters. When Glencora, perversely and irrationally, takes Lizzie's side, 'all the . . . Mr. Bonteens found themselves compelled to agree with her. She stood too high among her set to be subject to that obedience which restrained others,—too high, also, for others to resist her leading. . . . When she declared that poor Lady Eustace was a victim, others were obliged to say so too' (p. 488). Among these 'others', inevitably, is Lord Fawn, who is 'more afraid of the leaders of his own party than of any other tribunal upon earth,—or, perhaps, elsewhere' (p. 559). For poor Fawn, Glencora's interference is terrifying. He wishes to tell her to mind her own business, as indeed she should—'But Lady Glencora was the social queen of the party to which he belonged, and Mr. Palliser was Chancellor of the Exchequer, and would some day be Duke of Omnium' (p. 508). In such circumstances settled conviction goes for nothing; and so the whim of one influential woman forces Fawn, no specimen of moral bravery himself, to adhere to his well-known suit for Lizzie's hand, lest he 'give his political enemies an opportunity for calumny' (p. 142) beyond their present means. Fawn is shortly thereafter saved by the emergence of unimpeachable proof of Lizzie's guilt—but only by that.

To recognise the part politics plays in determining the outcomes of the novel's several love stories is also to see how ubiquitous the political theme is in *The Eustace Diamonds*—just as it is in *Can You Forgive Her?* and the *Phineas* novels and *The Duke's Children*, in all of which the connections between romantic and political endeavour are kept constantly before us.

Trollope's sardonic light penetrates everywhere. The silly debate in the House of Commons over the position of the Sawab of

Mygawb gives him still another opportunity to illuminate the political subject. Greystock attacks the government's position on the Sawab; Lord Fawn's chief defends it. 'We all know the meaning of such speeches', Trollope remarks. 'Had not Frank belonged to the party that was out, and had not resistance to the Sawab's claim come from the party that was in, Frank would not probably have cared much about the prince. . . . But what exertion will not a politician make with the view of getting the point of his lance within the joints of his enemies' harness?' (p. 60). Fawn later observes, correctly indeed, that Greystock 'chose to attack me because there was an opportunity'—because, that is, the situation offered him a chance to claim 'some future reward from his party'; but Lady Fawn, the Under-Secretary's mother, silences the family's indignation by reminding one and all that 'everything is considered fair in Parliament' (pp. 60–2, *passim*).

Again this is no anomaly. The Palliser novels teem with instances of partisan rhetoric spoken hotly in the House of Commons; followed by normal and even friendly discourse among the combatants immediately after adjournment beyond the eye of the gallery; and with men who consistently ignore their own convictions—if they have any—under the yoke of party discipline, the defiance of which will usually bring down upon them exclusion from place when the party is in power. No other English novelist has left on record so many vivid portraits of political hacks—not even Disraeli. In an earlier essay on the House of Commons, Trollope had written that the vast majority of politicians were men

> whose political lives had been passed in doing the work of a weathercock, turning every which way the breezes of patronage may blow, men who have always been up for sale, like some old screw well known at Tattersals. . . . If Mr. Smith out of the House states that Black is White he will lose his credit for veracity. . . . But if he merely votes Black to be White within the House, no one on that account accuses him of untruth. Did he not do so, he would be as a public man impracticable, unmanageable, useless, and utterly unfit for any public service.[28]

Unless he is financially secure, the political aspirant, forced to live among men richer than he and dependent on their patronage when in power for his own livelihood, inevitably finds himself in an equivocal, not to say helpless, position: 'There is, probably, no man who becomes naturally so hard in regard to money' (p. 74). He must do, in politics, what he is told—and the result is that 'scruples [are] regarded as follies and public truth as at best a political dream'.[24] Thus 'A peasant can marry whom he pleases' (p. 101) and retain his own political beliefs—but men like Greystock and Fawn cannot afford such luxuries. Trollope pounds away at this theme again and again in these novels. Political opposition becomes, finally, only another form of self-aggrandisement—its object being not the preservation of democracy but rather the exchange of those who are out for those who are in. To be in means solvency, and abuse leads to being in. 'Most of the young men rise now by making themselves thoroughly disagreeable', says old Lord Brentford in *Phineas Redux* (I, 414), a novel largely about the equivalent moral perils of office and opposition. The successful politician needs special attributes, but most of them are not appealing. He must be able to disregard criticism and eschew a 'too thin-skinned sensitiveness' (*The Eustace Diamonds*, p. 263); he must accept the fact that 'nobody . . . can be somebody without having to pay for that honour' (p. 290); and he must understand that a public man 'has so many things to think of . . . that he could hardly be expected to act at all times with truth and sincerity' (p. 415). He must not, in a word, be subject to attacks of conscience. Indeed, it will be better for him in his chosen profession if he is thoroughly dishonest, for honest guys finish last: 'Let two unknown men be competitors for any place, with nothing to guide the judges but their own words and . . . looks, and who can doubt but the dishonest man would be chosen. . . . Honesty goes about with a hang-dog look. . . . Dishonesty carries his eyes high' (pp. 480–81).[25]

Lizzie Eustace is the novel's central character, but by weaving so many others in and out of her story Trollope means us to see that she is only, like Becky Sharp, a product of her time—and not much worse than it is. In a passage near the end of *The Eustace Diamonds*, he explicitly links her immorality with the milieu she adorns and suggests that private peculation and public opportunism are symptoms of one another. Is Lizzie any worse than those who court her? The eminent Mr. Dove puts it this way: 'She has hankered after her bauble, and has told falsehoods in her efforts to keep it. Have you never heard of older persons, and more learned persons, and persons nearer to ourselves, who have done the same?' (p. 651). And there follows an account of political intrigues sweeping the legal profession at this time with regard to 'various positions of high honour and employment, vacant or expected to be vacant'. Trollope makes it clear that Mr. Dove 'was referring to those circumstances when he spoke of baubles and falsehoods' and that Lizzie's crimes are no worse than those committed for political motives. In politics and society both 'there existed jealousy, and some statements had been made which were not . . . strictly founded on fact' (p. 651). The 'hankering after baubles' disease is as rife among embryo Lord Chancellors, Attorneys-General, and Chief Justices as among others. Lizzie Eustace has no monopoly on mendacity and and greed. She is merely acting out in her own sphere the charade being performed around her by those in more responsible positions. If she is a social politician, they are political Lizzies. This is a revealing example of how the pressures and intrigues of society and politics tend to resemble one another in Trollope's fiction.

The political theme in *The Eustace Diamonds* is articulated, finally, in one other way. There is a sub-plot of mock-heroic proportions which details the vicissitudes of England's embattled Chancellor of the Exchequer. Palliser, a genuinely heroic figure as Prime Minister in *The Prime Minister* and again as private citizen in *The Duke's Children*, is seen here, in less flattering terms, as the victim of an eccentric fixation. The subject is decimal coinage. Palliser is energetic, patriotic, and honest, but his battle in behalf of currency reform is seen ironically by Trollope as a manifestation of political monomania and absurdity. A House of Commons forced to spend its time debating the penny and the Sawab of Mygawb can hardly be taken seriously, and Trollope refuses so to take it in *The Eustace Diamonds*. Everyone plays his own game in this parliamentary world; actually to be committed to something, no matter how trivial, inevitably invites the ridicule—a defence mechanism—of others. Palliser is committed, but his cause is trivial. Once again the welfare of the citizenry takes a back seat to a hobby-horse of the moment.

Trollope's language, as he recounts the heroic struggle of the Chancellor, invites us to see the issue of currency reform from a comic perspective—one man's folly and a joke indeed. One wonders, however, who is watching over the economic affairs of the country while Palliser struggles with his farthings.

Mr. Palliser . . . was intending to alter the value of the penny.

Unless the work should be too much for him, and he should die before he had accomplished the self-imposed task . . . the arithmetic of the whole world would be so simplified that henceforward the name of Palliser would be blessed by all schoolboys, clerks, shopkeepers, and financiers. But the difficulties were so great that Mr. Palliser's hair was already grey from toil, and his shoulders bent . . . Mr. Bonteen with two private secretaries from the Treasury . . . were near to madness under the pressure of the five-farthing penny. Mr. Bonteen had remarked . . . that those two extra farthings that could not be made to go into the shilling would put him into his cold grave before the world would know what he had done. . . . On the 13th of February Mr. Palliser made his first great statement in Parliament . . . and pledged himself to do his very best to carry [his] stupendous measure . . . in the present session. The City men who were in the House that night . . . agreed in declaring that the job in hand was too much for any one member or any one session. . . . It was . . . probable, many said, that [Mr. Palliser] might kill himself by labour which would be herculean in all but success, and that no financier after him would venture to face the task . . . the halcyon penny, which would make all future pecuniary calculations easy to the meanest British capacity, could never become the law of the land. (pp. 424–25 and 485–86, *passim*)

The absurdity of Palliser's labours is further underlined by a letter from Lady Glencora to the Duke of Omnium which describes the five-farthing-penny speech made by her husband as having been delivered, in the course of four hours, to a sleeping House: 'Plantagenet says nothing about it, but there is a do-or-die manner with him which is quite tragical' (p. 489). Having thoroughly bored everyone (even Mr. Gresham, the Liberal Prime Minister of the day, slept through the address) with his new penny, Palliser's next challenge is to find a suitable name for it: 'Should he stick by the farthing; or should he call it a fifthing, a quint, or a semi-tenth? "There's the 'Fortnightly Review' comes out but once a month," he said to . . . Mr. Bonteen, "and I'm told that it does very well"' (p. 495). Gresham suggests that the new coin be called a 'squint'. Glencora fears that it might be named after her husband: 'I shouldn't like to hear that . . . two lollypops were to cost three Palls' (p. 498). In the novel's last chapter Palliser is still at his herculean labour:

his mind was still deep in quints and semitenths. His great

measure was even now in committee. His hundred and second clause had been carried, with only nine divisions against him of any consequence. Seven of the most material clauses had . . . been postponed, and the great bone of contention as to the two super-fluous farthings still remained before him . . . he now had with him a whole bevy of secretaries, private secretaries, chief clerks, and accountants. . . . Mr. Bonteen was there . . . repeatedly declaring to all his friends that England would achieve the glories of decimal coinage by his blood and over his grave. (pp. 721–22)

Despite this civil service mobilisation in behalf of the penny, the great measure never gets passed; Palliser is called to the House of Lords before he can complete his work. When he is Prime Minister some years later, Palliser, by then Duke of Omnium, looks back to these days of struggle in the House of Commons as the happiest of his life—as the one period of his career when he was fully occupied. In the later Palliser novels he is a more complicated figure—and a more admirable one too as we see, especially in *The Prime Minister*, the kinds of degrading political pressure he is strong enough to resist. Here, however, he has not yet grown into statesmanship, serving as he does as another reminder that the world of politics is populated not only by the shallow and the unscrupulous but also, sometimes, by the obsessed.

A final note. In his *Autobiography* Trollope describes himself as 'an advanced conservative liberal' (p. 253). He ran for Parliament as a Liberal, and throughout his life usually supported the Liberal party (his two chief political heroes, Palmerston and Russell, were both Liberals). In *The Eustace Diamonds* Trollope offers us, with tongue just a bit in cheek, a whimsical but interesting de-scription of the Tory character. The Conservatives, he says,

feel among themselves that everything that is being done is bad, —even though that everything is done by their own party. It was bad to interfere with Charles, bad to endure Cromwell, bad to banish James, bad to put up with William. The House of Hanover was bad. All interference with prerogative was bad. The Reform Bill was very bad. Encroachments on the estates of the bishops was bad. Emancipation of Roman Catholics was the worst of all. Abolition of corn-laws, church-rates, and oaths and tests were all bad. The meddling with the Universities has been grievous. The treatment of the Irish Church has been Satanic. The overhauling of schools is most injurious to English education. Education bills and Irish land bills were all bad. Every step taken has been bad. (p. 33)

Despite the fact that everything is bad and getting worse, to the Tory mind 'old England is of all countries in the world the best to live in, and is not at all the less comfortable because of the changes that have been made' (p. 33). Is there contradiction, a paradox here? Not really, says Trollope; 'A huge, living, daily increasing grievance that does one no palpable harm, is the happiest possession that a man can have' (p. 33). The Tories, if 'pressed hard . . . will almost own that their so-called convictions are prejudices. But not for worlds would they be rid of them' (p. 32).

Despite the relatively good-humoured tone here, we are clearly meant to understand that those who watch and cheer from the sidelines (both sidelines, presumably) take neither themselves nor their political champions—those who play—very seriously; they enjoy the play-acting, they expect the sham. And thus it is small wonder that the participants themselves compete as if they were contestants in a vast game, fun to play but meaningless (except in a personal sense) to win, and distinguished throughout by the insincerity, cynicism, and irresponsibility of competitors and partisans alike. In the other parliamentary novels Trollope frequently describes political goings-on in terms of games or sporting contests of various kinds—cricket, football, swimming, hunting, baiting, and so on. It is this picture of politics as a game, perhaps the greatest English game of all, that *The Eustace Diamonds*, no anomaly among the Palliser novels, offers to us.

NOTES

1   See *The Political Novel* (New York, 1924), p. 185.
2   *An Autobiography* (London, 1953), p. 239. This is the Oxford World's Classics edition, from which all subsequent references are taken. The *Autobiography* was first published, posthumously, in 1883 in two volumes.

   Trollope says here: 'I have sometimes wished to see during my lifetime a combined republication of those tales which are occupied with the fictitious county of Barsetshire. These would be *The Warden, Barchester Towers, Doctor Thorne, Framley Parsonage,* and *The Last Chronicle.*'
3   See Speare, p. 200; Sadleir, p. 418; and especially Robert M. Polhemus, *The Changing World of Anthony Trollope* (Berkeley and Los Angeles,

1968), pp. 154–55, whose argument I have freely adapted to my own use here.

4 *Tancred* (1847), p. 101. I am quoting from the second edition (1877).

5 I could hardly do so. See John Halperin, *Trollope and Politics: A Study of the Palliser and Others* (London and New York, 1977).

6 See Polhemus, pp. 214, and 213, *passim*, and p. 198. My argument here is indebted to his.

7 See *Anthony Trollope: Aspects of His Life and Work* (Bloomington, Indiana, 1958), p. 98.

8 *The Eustace Diamonds* (London, 1952), p. 127. This is the Oxford World's Classics edition, reprinted in 1968 with an Introduction by Michael Sadleir. All subsequent references to the novel are to this edition.

9 E.g., parliamentary reform, the ballot, Irish tenant-right, and disestablishment. For further discussion of this, see J. R. Dinwiddy, 'Who's Who in Trollope's Political Novels,' *Nineteenth-Century Fiction*, 22 (June 1967), 33; John Halperin, 'Trollope's *Phineas Finn* and History', *English Studies*, 59, No. 2 (Spring, 1978); and Halperin, *Trollope and Politics* (n. 5, above), especially Chapters 4 and 7.

10 See *The Letters of Anthony Trollope*, ed, Bradford A. Booth (London, 1951), pp. 255–56.

11 For further discussion of this and related matters, see R. W. Chapman's brilliant statement in *Essays mainly on the Nineteenth Century presented to Sir Humphrey Milford* (London, 1948); A. O. J. Cockshut's feeble rejoinder in *Anthony Trollope: A Critical Study* (London, 1955); F. E. Robbins, 'Chronology and History in Trollope's Barset and Parliamentary Novels', *NCF*, 5 (March 1951); Blair G. Kenney, 'Trollope's Ideal Statesmen: Plantagenet Palliser and Lord John Russell', *NCF* 20 (December 1965); the essays by J. R. Dinwiddy and John Halperin cited in n. 9, above; Halperin *Trollope and Politics*, especially Chapters 4, 7, 8, and 9; and Halperin, 'Politics, Palmerston, and Trollope's Prime Minister', *Clio*, 3, No. 2 (1974).

12 Booth, *Anthony Trollope*, p. 81. For a fuller discussion of Trollope's political perspectives, see Halperin, *Trollope and Politics*, Chapter 1.

13 There has been some disagreement over the years about the date of *Lord Palmerston's* composition. See John Halperin, 'The Composition of Trollope's *Lord Palmerston*', *Notes and Queries*, 222 (October 1977).

14 See his review of R. H. Hutton's *Studies in Parliament* in the *Fortnightly Review*, 4 (April 1, 1866) and his letter to *The Examiner* (6 April 1850) defending Russell's Irish policy.

15 See 'Trollope's Irish Novels', *Dublin Review*, 65 (October 1869), 361–67; N. John Hall, 'Trollope Reading Aloud: An Unpublished Record', *N&Q* (March 1975); and P. D. Edwards, 'Trollope to Gladstone: An Unpublished Letter', *N&Q* (May 1968).

16 *The New Zealander*, ed N. John Hall (Oxford, 1972), pp. 120–21.

17 *Anthony Trollope*, p. 91.

18 See *Anthony Trollope* (New York, 1928), p. 99.

19   A detailed account of this episode in Trollope's life is given in Halperin, *Trollope and Politics*, Chapter 5.

20   See *The Duke's Children*, II, 148, in The Oxford World's Classics edition (London, 1963; two volumes in one).

21   See, for example, p. 287.

22   See Halperin, *Trollope and Politics*, Chapter 3.

23   *The New Zealander*, p. 117 and 122, *passim*.

24   *The New Zealander*, p. 117. Consider the case of poor Laurence Fitzgibbon in *Phineas Redux*, who, as a junior minister, finds himself obliged to speak in the House of Commons against a measure that he himself has researched, prepared, and recommended for adoption to his party. See *Phineas Redux*, II, 423–24 in the Oxford World's Classics edition (London, 1964; two volumes in one). Subsequent references to the novel are to this edition.

25   This theme abounds among Trollope's novels (e.g., to name just two, *The Three Clerks* and *Is He Popenjoy?*).

8

Trollope's Liberalism

by A. O. J. COCKSHUT

1

It is said that both Mr. Harold MacMillan and the late Hugh
Gaitskell, when asked for the best guide to the inner workings of
political life in this country, replied, 'It's all in Trollope'. This is
only the first of a series of paradoxes which confront us when we
consider Trollope's political novels. For these two eminent statesmen were directing attention to an outsider, a man who never sat
in Parliament, whose intimate friends were not politicians, whose
knowledge of political history was only that of the intelligent, busy
man of the world, and whose acquaintance with political philosophy
was almost nil. How often does it occur, in any complex field of
knowledge, that those best able to judge point to an ill-informed
amateur as the best guide?

The second paradox is more striking still. Trollope is invariably
praised (and occasionally denigrated) as a supreme realist; and
nowhere is this characteristic more apparent, in its most unyield-
ing form, than in the political novels. But if we read the pages of
the *Autobiography*,[1] which deal with his unlucky campaign as
Liberal candidate at Beverley in 1868, we shall be struck with two
features, both inimical to realism, an intense romantic idealisa-
tion of English political life and of the personal glory of being a
member of Parliament, and an intense personal disgust at the
practical working of the electoral system, and sense of grievance at
the way he had been treated. He speaks of his own desire to sit
in Parliament as 'almost insane'. This most shrewd and practical
of men tells us that in politics he could never have been a practical
man.

It is true that one of his reasons for wishing to enter Parliament was very characteristic. He wished to avenge himself on the dead uncle, who, long ago had told him that few clerks in the Post Office had become Members of Parliament. We are reminded of the way he wrote about floggings at Winchester and Harrow, and of the general misery of his boyhood. In some ways his whole life can be seen, as he himself partly saw it, as an attempt, breath-taking in its drive and energy, and startling in its success, to compensate for that deeply-engrained sense of inferiority to almost everybody he knew, that lasted until his marriage and modest successes as a civil servant in Ireland.

Startling in its success, I say; but, of course, politics proved to be the only exception. He was a success as a writer, as a civil servant, as a family man, as a clubman, even, despite his weight, at riding to hounds. If, as I am inclined to think, his political novels represent his most lasting achievement, it may be partly because as a politician he indubitably failed, and so here, the effort to retrieve failure in art was at its strongest.

For all his strong simplicity and directness, for all the naïvety of some of his general views, Trollope was a subtle man. He resisted the obvious temptations to take vengeance on the political world that had rejected him by satirizing it, or to paint the unattainable in the colours of romance. He took a deeper, a more satisfying compensation; he told the truth. This could be illustrated by a hundred different examples. One, in particular, seems to me revealing. Phineas Finn is an outsider like himself, or rather even more than himself. He is an Irishman, whose means of livelihood is scanty, while Trollope, however strong his personal sense of inferiority, was an English gentleman, who, by 1868, had acquired a sufficient fortune to be able to compensate retiring from the civil service. Phineas Finn, then, is almost wholly dependent on his hopes of office. Suprisingly early, his hopes are fulfilled. He receives a letter from his patron, Lord Brentford, which begins:

> You are no doubt aware that Lord Bosanquet's death has taken Mr. Mottram into the Upper House, and that as he was Under-Secretary for the Colonies, and as the Under-Secretary must be in the Lower House. . . .

Trollope interjects:

> The heart of Phineas Finn at this moment was almost in his mouth. Not only to be selected for political employment, but to

be selected at once for an office so singularly desirable! Under-Secretaries, he fancied, were paid two thousand a year. What would Mr. Low say now?[2]

When he returns to the letter Phineas Finn finds that this choice plum is to be given to Laurence Fitzgibbon, whom he knows to be a poor creature, idle, intemperate and always in debt. He himself is to replace Fitzgibbon as the Irish representative at the Treasury Board. 'There was a moment in which he thought that he would refuse to be made a junior lord.' The moment passes; he reflects that he will get a thousand a year, a considerable salary in the 1860's; he remembers that if he accepts he may be promoted further. But the real point is that he knows that the man who will occupy the higher post is both inferior in talent to himself and unfit for the work required.

The time comes, and quite soon, when Phineas is asked to take Fitzgibbon's higher place. Trollope's point here is neither a personally bitter one—that the fool is always preferred to the wise man—nor (still less) a compensation for his own failures in writing of a surrogate hero's success. Rather, Trollope is reminding us, as he constantly does, that politics is only a particular aspect of life in general, and so can only be governed by those passions which move men in private life; and, of these, *amour propre* is one of the strongest. Success is not wanted for its own sake, nor is money, but for the sake of a man's idea of himself, which he arrives at partly by comparing his own achievements with those of others.

Also Trollope shows us that politics are boring, not uniquely or peculiarly so, but in the way life in general is:

'I shall never get over it,' said Mr. Ratler to Mr. Finn, seated one terribly hot evening on a bench behind the Cabinet Ministers,—'never. I don't suppose such a session for work was ever known before. Think what it is to have to keep men together in August, with the thermometer at 81°, and the river stinking like,—like the very mischief.'[3]

The third paradox is more complex, and brings us to the heart of our subject. We know that Trollope was a Liberal; but we feel him, surely, as a mainly conservative force. Why? In attempting to answer—and there is no simple answer—we can bear in mind that his own fullest statement of his political creed includes both ideas. He called himself 'an advanced, but still a Conservative–

163

Liberal'. He also said, being over sixty at the time, that his political opinions had never undergone any change.

One explanation, tempting but facile, we can dismiss straight away. It is not merely a question of changing times, which may sometimes make opinions which seemed radical in their day appear traditional to later generations. So, for instance, contemporaries were struck with the radicalism of Lord John Russell in his speeches about Reform in 1832, while we may be more forcibly struck by his firmly anti-democratic tendency, and by the way he proclaimed the 1832 settlement to be 'final'. No; it is in comparison with his own contemporaries that Trollope so often strikes us as conservative. Mrs. Gaskell, Thackeray and Dickens were all his seniors, and in each there is a more or less powerful conservative strain, yet each will at times take a radical view which Trollope dismissed as absurd. Dickens's Sir Leicester Dedlock, though not without attractive features, is shown as a fossil of a dead age. Trollope, having described Mr. Thorne of Ullathorne, a man living even more deliberately in the past, expresses the wish that it will be long before the numbers of this type diminish. Trollope is bitterly opposed to the opening of the Civil Service to unrestricted intellectual competition, thus, apparently, putting himself on the side of the Barnacles against the castigations of the author of *Little Dorrit*. Mrs. Gaskell is not uncritical of Trade Unions, but she certainly sees more to be said for them than Trollope does for the agitators at Hiram's Hospital in *The Warden*, whose aspirations seem so moderate when compared with those of industrial workers. More striking still is the case of Disraeli, born before all the novelists just mentioned, and writing *Sybil* not long before his great speech against Peel which took the backwoods Tory gentlemen of the House of Commons by storm. If we were asked to name a work of Trollope which showed as much sympathy with radical causes as *Sybil*, we could only reply with silence.

Now in the first place Trollope writes more about the country and less about the town than any of the authors just mentioned, and more perhaps than any well-known Victorian novelist except Surtees. He does write about London, but many of his London scenes concern people who are essentially visitors to London, whose roots are in the country; and even those who are residents, like John Eames and Adolphus Crosbie, often have strong country connections. The urban working-class make very occasional appearances; Bunce, Phineas Finn's landlord, is enough of an exception to be very noticeable; and even he, receiving rent from a member of Parliament, cannot stand as typically proletarian. Despite his mother's example—she was a pioneer in the industrial novel—there is nothing in Trollope remotely comparable to the factories in *North and South*, or *Sybil*, or the description of the tailor's life in *Alton Locke*. Trollope's experience tended, perhaps, to make him see a harmony, not a conflict of classes. The poor, in his novels are, very often, those who depend directly for their livelihood on the affluent, and who feel loyal to them, butlers, gardeners, ostlers, ladies' maids. Trollope lived in a time of technical and economic change of unprecedented rapidity; and the novelists of his time, or some of them, convey the excitement and the alarm of the process. But the country changed much less rapidly than the town; and in Trollope we are usually approximating to the country pace of change which is moderate and manageable.

Trollope writes frequently and lovingly of country squires. When he writes, as he occasionally does, of a great commercial magnate, he shows him in a setting remote from the sources of his economic power. The radical politician Turnbull, we are told, makes his thirty thousand a year in business; but we see him only in Westminster and its environs. Moreover, the portrait is notably unsympathetic, almost, if we remember Trollope's wonderful, habitual balance and fairness, it might be called prejudiced. And this is not an isolated case; Mr. Bott, the Manchester business man of the political novels, Moffat, the wealthy master-tailor in *Dr. Thorne* and Neefit in *Ralph the Heir* are all, in varying degrees absurd or despicable. Often, perhaps usually, these people are politically liberal. And this only adds to the difficulty of our problem; by being a Liberal Trollope seems to be grouping himself with the people he doesn't like against the country squires and hunting men whom he does like. But against this, we need to remember that the really great country magnates, as Trollope often reminds us, were usually Whigs, who eventually became Liberals.

Are there then no great general issues where Trollope's instincts strike us as being clearly on the Liberal side? I can think of only two, and one of those is decidedly ambiguous. To take the doubtful case first, Trollope was opposed to the ballot. This was a particularly difficult and interesting issue in the 1860's, since advanced Liberals, like Mill, agreed with Conservatives and old-fashioned Whigs in opposing it, while ordinary Liberal opinion supported it, and eventually, in 1872, Gladstone's Liberal government carried it.

One of Trollope's best scenes of political conversation occurs in Chapter XXIII of *Can You Forgive Her?*, where the venerable Whig duke, St. Bungay, is being challenged on his commitment to the new liberalism by a bold young girl, Alice Vavasor:

> 'There is nothing I want so much, Miss Vavasor as to become a radical;—if I only knew how.'
> 'I think it's very easy to know how,' said Alice.
> 'Do you? I don't. I've voted for every Liberal measure that has come seriously before Parliament since I had a seat in either House, and I've not been able to get beyond Whiggery yet.'
> 'Have you voted for the ballot?' asked Alice, almost trembling at her own audacity as she put the question.
> 'Well; no, I've not. And I suppose that is the crux. But the ballot has never been seriously brought before any House in which I have sat. I hate it with so keen a private hatred, that I doubt whether I could vote for it.'
> 'But the Radicals love it,' said Alice.

The date is 1864. The point about the ballot which caused opinion about it to cross normal party divisions was this: it would diminish the influence of property. Landlords and employers often expected tenants and employees to vote as they did. Sometimes they scrupulously refrained from any such expectations, but even then their known convictions might well be influential. (Trollope shows a beautiful case of this last situation when Plantagenet Palliser attempts to renounce his traditional family privileges in the borough of Silverbridge and finds engrained habits of deference too strong for him.) The Duke of St. Bungay is influenced by the feeling, so strong in Whig noblemen, that his own class were the true friends of the people and knew better than they did themselves what was best for them. His feeling is tender and paternal; but there are cases in history of a rougher kind, as when Gladstone's first patron the Duke of Newcastle served forty of his tenants with notice to quit on account of their exercise of their parliamentary vote. The advanced Liberals arrived at the same conclusion as the Duke of St. Bungay by reasoning directly opposite. They said that no one who was not independent enough to resist all inducements and intimidations was fit to have the vote at all.

In 1884, years after the issue of the ballot had been settled for good, Gladstone, introducing a bill for the enfranchisement of rural labourers could still say: 'If he [the agricultural labourer] has a defect, it is that he is too ready, perhaps, to work with and accept the influence of his superiors—superiors, I mean, in worldly station.'[5]

Now it would seem from the language Trollope uses in attacking the ballot that his reasons for disliking it are nearer to those of the advanced Liberals than to those of the real Duke of Newcastle and the fictional Duke of St. Bungay. He writes: 'thinking it to be unworthy of a great people to free itself from the evil results of vicious conduct by unmanly restraints.'

A clearer case is provided by Trollope's attitude to what Ruskin called the 'goddess of getting on'. The great Victorian prophets, Carlyle, Ruskin and Arnold are at one in denouncing the worship of material prosperity, which they associate especially with Manchester business men (Liberals almost invariably) or what Arnold calls 'our liberal practitioners'. Here Trollope is on the common-sense, progressive, Liberal side against the old Toryism of the school of Southey's *Colloquies*, the prophetic Tory-radicalism of Ruskin, and the cultivated distaste for commercial hurry and vulgarity displayed by Arnold. And it is worth noting that he is one of very few eminent literary men on that side. Perhaps only Macaulay, among these, wholeheartedly agreed with him. Indeed, as we read our Victorian classics, from Carlyle's *Chartism*, to *Hard Times*, *Munera Pulveris* and *Culture & Anarchy*, we might be excused for wondering whether Manchester school economics is not a rather factitious Aunt Sally. Everybody seems to be against it and nobody to speak for it. The reason appears after a moment's thought. Successful businessmen and rising politicians don't usually write books, and, if they do, they seldom achieve classic status. But Trollope, like Macaulay seems perfectly convinced of the truth of the contention that by benefiting himself and his family, a man is indirectly benefiting society. The disgust felt after his death at Trollope's unblushing literary accountancy was, to some extent, unreal and even hypocritical. Others, like Dickens, had made more money and taken an equal satisfaction in success, and had simply been more reticent both about the figures and about their own feelings. At the same time, we may well feel that Trollope's satisfaction at being a self-made man, who had earned hard cash by his labours, is a little naïve, or even crude. And it smacks of the business ethos, which the Tory country squires so much distrusted. No doubt he was here, as in so many other ways, a divided man. He knew very well, in another part of himself, that there were things, even material things, that could not be reckoned up according to their cash value. He makes fun of the American senator for not understanding that this is the case about fox-hunting. And he makes one of his more worldly clerical characters, Archdeacon Grantly relent in his bitter anger against his son because the latter has shown a gentlemanly concern about the foxes of Plumstead.

Against all this, there are still more obvious points, which need not detain us long, where Trollope's convictions, habits and circumstances seem naturally to place him on the Conservative side. He was an Anglican, but was told at the Beverley by-election, that he would hardly be welcome on Sunday at the local church. He was told: 'He [the Tory candidate] goes there in a kind of official profession, and you had better not allow yourself to be seen in the same place.'[6] (We need not give too much weight to this point, since Gladstone, the Liberal leader, was a much more devout Anglican than Trollope.) He shows himself, especially in *Is He Popenjoy?*, contemptuous of the movement for woman's rights. This was not, of course, in Trollope's time a Liberal Party cause, but all those who supported it were sure to be Liberals or Radicals.

But perhaps we come nearer to Trollope's basic political philosophy when we consider his attitude to corruption. In his novels he shows himself comparatively tolerant. In *Ralph the Heir* (where the election scenes are very close to his own experience at Beverley) he allows Mr. Pile who 'hates Purity' a very fair run. He is wrong of course, but in his own perverse way he is speaking up for the traditional right of the poor man to receive something from the rich man who desires a seat in Parliament. In his eyes, purity means self-righteous parsimony, and treating means general friendliness and the lowering of class barriers. We may be a little surprised after this to find that he speaks very severely about purity in the Beverley chapter of the *Autobiography*. He says, and we well know he means it, that when he realised that his wasted money and his miserable fortnight of electioneering had contributed to getting Beverley disfranchised for corruption, 'I did flatter myself that I had done some good.' Disfranchisement, which punishes innocent and guilty together, is a very strong measure. Trollope knew how gradually old ways change and old prejudices die. His whole political series of novels may be considered from one point of view, as a history of the extreme gradualness of the effect of the Reform Bill of 1832. Yet Trollope here shows himself without hesitation on the side of his reforming contemporaries, a bustling minority working painfully against the inertia of habit and the self-interested smugness of an unregenerate mass. The fact that our ancestors approved or at least tolerated corruption is no argument at all for him.

Naturally, I am not suggesting that the question of corruption was a party one. Trollope explicitly indicates that this was not the case in showing Ratler and Roby, the opposing party managers in the House of Commons so much of one mind about the gradualness of the process of reducing it. But the issue does show us Trollope going by principle and theory, not by custom. And this is particularly impressive in a man who grasped with a fulness of understanding which few have equalled the immensely strong hold that tradition, habit and custom had on the English nation.

Another feature of Trollope's mind which may have helped him to take the Liberal side was a certain confidence in England's destiny and future. He was aware that others did not have it, and that they might have good arguments for their view. This is well illustrated by the case of Tregear in *The Duke's Children*, who influences Silverbridge, the son of the great Whig magnate, Plantaganet Palliser, Duke of Omnium, to join the Conservative side. Tregear is an intellectual and a comparatively poor gentleman. He is a stronger character altogether that Silverbridge, and he persuades him (for a time) that the great Whig magnates with their immense wealth, influences and hereditary self-confidence are digging their own graves by collaborating with Radicals in the Liberal Party, who are preparing the way for revolution. Tregear is about the only person in Trollope's novels who is aware of the Communist Manifesto, which appeared before all but the very earliest of them. In this, as in so many other ways, Trollope (we may think) was realistic. The number of his English contemporaries who concerned themselves with such things was probably infinitesimal. But the point for us is that Trollope seems clear in his own mind that Tregear's fears are chimerical, and that Plantagenet

Palliser's gradual reform shows a more far-sighted understanding of the realities of the case. Bagehot was a Liberal, too, but he shows on the whole a deeper fear of rapid change and of the consequences of popular ignorance than Trollope does.

From one point of view, perhaps, Trollope's liberal principles and his conservative sensibilities may (by a further paradox) have been allies. Tregear is afraid because he is an intellectual who knows how to reason from principles to distant conclusions. He over-rates the power of ideas. Trollope is not afraid of radical ideas just because he is so like the great unthinking mass of his countrymen in his sense of habit and tradition. England—and this applies to Liberal as well as to Conservative England—is so instinctively conservative that the danger Trollope sees is rather that ideas will have no effect at all, than what Tregear fears, that they will have too much. He was fond of imagining liberal opinion as a coachman with conservatism as the brake. The brake is so powerful that the danger that the coach will stick fast in the mud is real, the danger that it will run headlong downhill and crash is negligible. Derby and Disraeli, on the Tory side, must have made some similar calculation when they introduced the daring Reform Bill of 1867, and the event vindicated them, despite the panic of Carlyle,[7] and the more reasonable fears of men like Robert Lowe and the future Lord Salisbury. It would be possible to divide politically conscious Victorians into confident and fearful—a division that would cut right across the division between Conservative and Liberal. Trollope was one of the confident. His pessimism, which was strong, was not political or public in its character. It was more Johnsonian; it moved in the realm of the inescapable pains and limitations of human life, where not politics only but all decision and action are powerless.

Trollope's sense of the working of habit and tradition is an important presence even when his aim is to show political change occurring. A beautiful example is to be found in chapter XXIX of *Phineas Finn*, entitled 'A Cabinet Meeting'. Trollope must have been struck, as any thoughtful student of English institutions will be, by the paradoxical nature of the concept, *constitution*. The constitution is unwritten, and is far from being fixed. Yet people constantly appeal to it as a court of last resort, whose authority is beyond question. How then does it change, and how do people know when it has changed? Trollope gives his answer in dramatic form, and before examining it, we may note that in writing of a cabinet meeting, of which there was no public record, he is much more truly realistic by the power of imagination than he often was in writing of what he knew well. (*The Three Clerks* which deals with the familiar Civil Service world is one of his least convincing novels.) Mr. Mildmay's cabinet, having been defeated in the Commons are discussing resignation:

> 'You will advise her Majesty to send for Lord De Terrier,' said Mr. Gresham.
> 'Certainly;—there will be no other course open to me.'
> 'Or to her,' said Mr. Gresham. To this remark from the rising Minister of the day, no word of reply was made; but of those present in the room three or four of the most experienced servants of the Crown felt that Mr. Gresham had been impudent. The Duke, who had ever been afraid of Mr. Gresham, told Mr. Palliser afterwards that such an observation should not have been made; and Sir Henry Coldfoot pondered upon it uneasily, and Sir Marmaduke Morecambe asked Mr. Mildmay what he thought about it. 'Times change so much, and with the times the feelings of men,' said Mr. Mildmay. But I doubt whether Sir Marmaduke quite understood him.

I leave it to the constitutional historians to say when and how the change occurred. But it is clear that in the time of George III, the monarch's personal wishes were influential in the making of Prime Ministers, and in the late nineteenth century they were not. Trollope's point is not at all that a sudden change is happening now. It is rather that there is a period of latency when everybody knows that something has really happened, that some traditional force has become obsolete, and nobody wishes to say so. The first person who does say so is guilty of bad taste in the eyes of many, but is speaking too truly to be contradicted. In admitting something for the first time into their conscious minds, men are aware of regret at the ending of a venerable fiction.

The Cabinet in this case was a Liberal one; and any diminution in the power of the Crown entails an increase in the power of Ministers. Yet Liberal principles and personal ambitions combined are shown as a weaker force than a certain sentimental reverence for outmoded forms. Believing that his countrymen were like this, the instinctively conservative Trollope, we may say, could *afford* to be an advanced Liberal.

Then Trollope shows family traditions as the usual determining factor in political affiliations. In chapter XXIII of *Can You Forgive Her?* the guests at dinner in the house of one of the great Whig families, the Pallisers, are facetiously discussing a 'feminine House of Commons'. Jeffrey Palliser, an inconspicuous minor cousin, says that his cousins Iphy and Phemy would, of course, be members. Asked if they are politicians, he replies, 'Not especially. They have their tendencies, which are decidedly Liberal. There has never been a Tory Palliser known, you know.' The remark is received as a platitude; yet it is not at all obvious why a great aristocratic family should ally itself with radicals. The reasons, presumably, though Trollope doesn't mention them, go back to 1688. One has the impressions that few members of the family have thought much about the reasons. They were born Liberals just as they were born English. Later, it is true, there is an exception, which I have already mentioned, the young Lord Silverbridge. And this has all the characteristics of an exception which shows the strength of the rule. The change is only temporary. Palliser's Tory neighbours, instead of welcoming a promising recruit to their party bemoan the irresponsibility of the young in going against family tradition. One is left with the impression that a similar rebellion will be even rarer in the future.

And yet, Trollope knew that some people do have convictions of their own. Is there any essential difference, among those of his political characters who think and decide for themselves, between Conservative and Liberal types? Such a question can only receive a tentative answer, and we must be on the watch for exceptions. But in general it seems that Trollope's Conservatives may be called instinctive 'belongers', whose role in life and family position raises no question in their minds. His Liberals are often either conscious enquirers, like Monk and Phineas Finn, or people who act out a dramatic performance for the benefit of the public, like Turnbull or the old Duke of Omnium, or enthusiasts like Ontario Moggs in *Ralph the Heir*. There are exceptions, of whom the most obvious is the Conservative leader, Daubeney, who is certainly one of those who act a dramatic part with an eye to effect. If, however, I am right in thinking that the exceptions are rare enough to make this generalisation worth while, then we have another reason why Trollope was a Liberal. As the *Autobiography* so poignantly shows, Trollope never took his position in the world for granted. He was bewildered by misery and failure in early years, and surprised by success later. His class position he felt to be anomalous; he felt estranged from his contemporaries at Winchester and Harrow, and, when success came to him, his failure as a politician left him still unsatisfied. But we must remember that his Liberal politicians are simply more various and interesting than his Conservative ones, since he chose to present so much of his political material through the experience of two Liberal politicians of very different background and character, Phineas Finn and Plantagenet Palliser. Also, during Trollope's productive middle years, from 1846 to 1874, a Whig or Liberal government was the norm and a Conservative one the exception. Trollope's practical nature was likely to find the problems of government more stimulating to the imagination than those of opposition.

2

I turn now, in the second part of this essay, from Trollope's own liberalism to his portrayal of the Liberal party and its members. It is a curious amalgam. Apart from the mere careerists and placemen, like Bonteen, who perhaps do not differ very much from the corresponding people in the Conservative party, we may find the following particularly interesting and representative; Barrington Erle, the Duke of St. Bungay, Plantagenet Palliser, Mr. Monk, and Mr. Turnbull.

Barrington Erle is the least complex, and might be thought hardly worth special mention. But Trollope is fond of bringing him on to the stage at the beginning of every new phase of political life, because he never changes, and so, like a milestone, he enables us to gauge the speed at which others are moving. He is a minor member of the Whig aristocracy, a relative of Lord Brentford, Phineas Finn's patron, and his daughter Lady Laura Kennedy. His idea of politics is simply loyalty to the party, which means for him especially the person of revered leaders like Mr. Mildmay. A vote against one's own party is something he cannot understand except as an inexplicable aberration. A party to him is a kind of extended family. Many of the members are actually related by blood. The new men, like Phineas Finn, ought to be particularly careful to behave as if they were. Political measures are of no importance to such a man, except as they show or fail to show the harmonious collaboration of this extended family. Just as a man might decide to go on a family holiday to Devonshire or to Switzerland, but would think it crazy to be so much set upon either as to go alone or with strangers to the place not selected by the family's other members, so with political measures. And just as many a father of a family has wished that there needn't be a holiday at all, and wanted to stay at home all the year, so do people like Erle incline to wish that government could go on smoothly without legislation or debates or votes. But he knows that this is asking too much of the collective good sense of mankind. Let us, then, get through these necessary evils with as little fuss, dissension and ill-temper as possible. Trollope, the administrator who yearned to be a politician, reserves a kindly smile for this type, but hardly conceals his opinion that it is a dull and unheroic one.

The Duke of St. Bungay, whom we have already seen objecting to the ballot, is similar in some ways. He is older than the others and wiser through experience; his memory is often long enough to remember as charming girls the mothers of the men with whom he is working now. More than Erle, he realises that things do change and that ideas do play a part in political life. Though he says that the most important requisite for a Prime Minister is a thick skin, we sense that he is fascinated by the restless sensitiveness, and proud self-criticism of the younger duke, Plantagenet Palliser, to whom he acts as mentor. Even as he shakes his head over the other's over-principled vagaries, we are aware that he inwardly salutes him as one made of finer clay than himself. He may mutter nostalgically about the days when Prime Ministers opened the letters from their gamekeepers before dealing with official business, but we doubt whether he really believes those days were better. In any case he is enough of a realist to know that they cannot return. Two moments in his story are particularly significant. One is the time of the resignation from the cabinet of Finespun, a character who makes only a brief appearance[8] in a book which is only intermittently political. In offering his place as Chancellor of the Exchequer to his friend, Palliser, he says:

> He must have gone, or I must have done so . . . I admire his character and genius, but I think him the most dangerous man in England as a statesman. He has high principles,—the very highest; but they are so high as to be out of sight to ordinary eyes . . . he may probably know how England ought to be governed three

centuries hence better than any man living, but of the proper way to govern it now, I think he knows less.

Here we have something that Erle does not contemplate, the demon of progress. The recognition is grudging, but unquestionably sincere. And the implication is that the Whig governing class do not regard themselves as a permanent ruling clique, but as guardians and schoolmasters to the well-meaning but inexperienced people. Finespun's mistake in St. Bungay's eyes is more one of timing than of substance. He has, as it were, mistaken the schoolboy stage for the under-graduate stage, in looking at the political state of the common people. We get an interesting early hint here of what will be a main theme later in the series, a hint of an answer to the question, 'How is it that the Whig aristocracy, the most exclusive ruling clique in the world, allied themselves with popular causes?' But as far as St. Bungay is concerned they will do so only with extreme caution and gradualness.

The other notable moment in St. Bungay's career comes when his young friend Palliser is Prime Minister and has in his gift a knighthood of the Garter. In St. Bungay's eyes to give it to a philanthropic and hard-working Conservative peer is quixotic, while to give it to a useless and immoral Whig magnate, who is not even an active politician, is mere common sense. Governments cannot subsist without patronage, which must be exercised to win or retain political support. St. Bungay, who is himself an upright and conscientious public servant, regards it as irrelevant that he is rejecting a man whose conduct he approves and admires, and recommending one he almost despises. It does not worry him that there should be two different standards for public and private use. It is one of the great points of contrast between him and Palliser. Palliser is always troubled by his own effort to make a consistent synthesis of all his principles.

Plantagenet Palliser is perhaps Trollope's fullest and subtlest portrayal of a human being; and there are important aspects that do not concern us here. For our purposes, the main question is: what light does the portrayal of him throw on the transformation of the Whig oligarchy into the Liberal Party? First we notice that he is immensely industrious; and in this he is prophetic of a race of aristocrats (Salisbury and Curzon are notable examples) who combine a keen sense of their aristocratic traditions with a sincere deference to middle-class values of work, effort, merit. Nobody knew better than Trollope that the English dearly loved a lord; and, as is indicated by the deference shown to that arrogant and idle consumer of wealth who preceded Palliser as Duke of Omnium, many still judge them by different standards as if they were exempt from moral obligations. But the times are changing. Mme. Goesler, who had been fond of the old duke in her way, reflects at the time of his death that no one should dare to live idly as he has done. Part of Plantagenet Palliser's strength is that he loves work; he does not have to be persuaded to imitate the industrious middle classes.

Palliser's attitude to his high rank and immense wealth is complex. In one way it gives him the confidence to care more for the work to be done than for advancement. The death of his uncle forces him to give up being Chancellor of the Exchequer (since the holder of that office must be in the Commons) but he cares more about giving up the work of the office than the office itself. So, later, he suggests to the Prime Minister that he take the much inferior office of the Board of Trade in succession to the hack, Bonteen, who has been murdered. Trollope seems to suggest that it is just because a Whig aristocrat is so completely certain of his position in the country that he can afford to be so surprisingly careless of his status in political life. In caring for measures more than for office he is the direct opposite of Barrington Erle, and decidedly different from his mentor, St. Bungay. Yet, when he eventually becomes Prime Minister, there seems to be a contradiction. He spends long hours brooding on the possibility that only his rank and wealth have won him the office, and desperately hoping that it is not so.

The contradiction is only apparent. Deep as is his instinctive sense of the traditional privileges of his family, his reverence for political institutions is deeper still. A duke can afford to be careless about office, but his reverence for the constitution is too strong for him to be able to bear to think that a man became Prime Minister because he was a duke. As he says to an American visitor, in a most revealing phrase, 'A prime minister can make a duke'. It is not so much his own sense of himself as his sense of the dignity and glory of the premier's office that would be diminished if his fears about the reasons for his advancement to premier proved justified. Hence, in part, his resentment against his wife's over-lavish entertaining. It gives colour to suspicions that his social position was more necessary than his political gifts.

There is another side to his dislike of his wife's social extravagances. There is a certain Roman dignity, a patrician simplicity, a pride wrapped in the appearance of modesty. Extravagance is assertive and shows a lingering doubt; 'do people really know who I am without reminding?' He always expects his position to be recognised without the need for any overt claim. Two particular moments in his history are especially revealing. The first[9] shows him in Switzerland, a most unwilling exile for family reasons from the joys and ardours of politics. News of a General Election has arrived, and Palliser is completely absorbed in the newspapers just arrived from England.

When his wife says she hears he is returned for Silverbridge

> 'Who? I! yes; I'm returned,' said Mr. Palliser, speaking with something like disdain in his voice as to the possibility of anybody having stood with a chance of success against him in his own family borough. For a full appreciation of the advantages of a private seat in the House of Commons let us always go to those great Whig families who were mainly instrumental in carrying the Reform Bill . . . The Pallisers and the other great Whig families have been right in this. They have kept in their hands, as rewards for their own services to the country, no more than the country is manifestly willing to give them.

The point about this confidence is that it is too deeply rooted to be arrogant. It flourishes below the level of consciousness, so that the incongruity of combining it with radical causes is not felt. This unconsciousness, Trollope suggests, is one of England's great political strengths. However inconsistent they are, the Whig aristocrats are transparently sincere in their belief that the continuation of their hereditary privileges is a means to the reduction of inequality. Much later in his career, when he is Duke and Prime Minister, we see the other side of the coin.[10]

Talking to Phineas Finn he says:

> 'Don't you go and tell Ramsden and Drummond that I have been preaching equality, or we shall have a pretty mess. I don't know that it would serve me with my dear friend, the Duke [of St. Bungay].
>
> 'I will be discretion itself.'
>
> 'Equality is a dream. But sometimes one likes to dream,—

especially as there is no danger that Matching [his family house] will fly from me in a dream. I doubt whether I could bear the test that has been attempted in other countries.'

'That poor ploughman would hardly get his share, Duke.'

'No;—that's where it is. We can only do a little and a little to bring it nearer to us;—so little that it won't touch Matching in our day. . . .

The chapter ends with the other duke contemplating a reform of suffrage forced upon the government by Mr. Monk and others:

There must surely have been a shade of melancholy on that old man's mind as, year after year, he assisted in pulling down institutions which he in truth regarded as the safeguards of the nation;—but which he knew that, as a Liberal, he was bound to assist in destroying.

The two dukes differ, as we have seen, but it is only a matter of degree. We see Trollope here at his most perceptive and prophetic. The time was coming when the danger that 'Matching would fly away' would become real. It was never to be reached in Trollope's narrative or in his lifetime. He died four years before Gladstone's first attempt at Irish Home Rule. But Trollope appears to foresee not this particular measure but a coming state of affairs in which aristocrats would really have to choose between fighting for their position and property and supporting radical causes; and he seems to give a hint, in Palliser's words to Finn, that when that time comes, they will choose their family interests and thus be lost to the Liberal Party. High Whig radicalism, Trollope suggests, is a passing phase, though the phase covers two or three generations and is both impressive and useful to the country. While such people are in charge there cannot be a revolution, and for this Trollope is thankful.

The second reve:ling moment occurs when he expels from his house an unfortunate political aspirant, who solicits his influence in getting into Parliament. He does it with an altogether surprising brusqueness. Why? The intrusive major has touched him on one of his secret fears. He has been clinging to his theory that hospitality is a private matter, while his more realistic wife has seen it as a lever of political power. The inept Major Pountney has unwittingly confirmed his wife's view, and thus caused him to feel degraded in his own eyes, no longer a free agent, used by his political friends. And another secret fear is touched at the same time. He feels guilty about the brazenness of the political influence wielded by his ancestors; he himself is determined to renounce this in large part, and to use what remains for the public good. But here is a man who, in his excitement, he takes to be addressing him in the coarse language of eighteenth-century jobbery. He reacts with violence because he is struck with inner doubts about the sincerity of his love of progress and his modified yearning for equality, or at least he is driven to wonder whether others doubt it. The very insignificance of the man before him makes the matter worse; if he thinks so, thousands of other ordinary people will think the same. For a moment, he is tempted to see his whole industrious well-meaning career in a distorting glass as a monstrous confidence trick, with privilege pretending to serve the common good but really still serving sectional interests and selfish ends. His anger suggests that his conscience is not quite clear. Above all, he is a self-questioner, and this makes it easier for us to accept without irritation a hero who has been endowed with so many of the world's goods.

Monk is a self-questioner too, it is a neat example of Trollope's technical skill that we see Monk generally not in the company of Palliser, but in that of Turnbull, who is so much his opposite in this. The eighteenth chapter of *Phineas Finn*, in which Monk is host at dinner to both Finn and Turnbull is particularly important in determining the reader's attitudes to these two radical leaders, and to much of the long political narrative that follows through several volumes. Monk and Turnbull are contrasted from the first. Monk is courteous, Turnbull rude. Monk is poor, Turnbull rich. Both are effective orators, but Monk through his questioning intelligence and wit, Turnbull through the skills of the demagogue. Yet both are advanced liberals; they agree about many public causes. What Trollope is doing here is what so many writers on politics neglect to do. He is stressing the inwardness of politics. No one knew better than he the crudity of most political arguments, the superficial character of most slogans, the ineffectiveness of most policies. But at the same time he is ever true to his principle that politics, being only an aspect of life in general, does obscurely touch the nuances of character and the deep places of the heart. The dislike that politicians often have for their colleagues, their sympathy for some of their opponents, is much more to Trollope than a mere illustration of the looseness of the party ties in his time. People instinctively recognise the presence or the absence of a sincerity answering to their own. Finn feels it in Monk, feels its absence in Turnbull, just as Palliser feels it in his Tory country neighbour Mr. Upjohn. Later, Finn will feel its absence in his colleague, Bonteen. The party conflict cuts across an invisible line that divides men of good will from careerists, and those who mean what they say from those who are drunk with their own rhetoric.

Monk may surprise a little, in the pages of the ever-practical Trollope, by being so theoretical, even philosophical, a politician. Finn, who combines something of the rawness of the student debating society with a quick-learning worldly tact and charm, instinctively turns to him as a mentor. Monk is the idealist without illusions, a type Trollope valued particularly because he thought it so rare. His advice to Finn is often on the side of caution and prudence; yet Finn is always able to feel that it comes from a moral insight higher than his own. The young political aspirant may often be tempted to wonder whether there is any bridge between impractical theories and base ambitions. Monk's steadying presence deprives such reflections of their sting.

One of the things we notice at once at this dinner-table is that Monk understands unspoken thoughts as well as the nuances of tone while Turnbull is aware only of words, and sometimes barely stops even to listen to them. So it is fitting that while Monk's political creed cannot be easily formulated, Turnbull's is given us right from the start:

> Progressive reform in the franchise, of which manhood suffrage should be the acknowledged and not far distant end, equal electoral districts, ballot, tenant right for England as well as Ireland, reduction of the standing army till there should be no standing army to reduce, utter disregard of all political movements in Europe, and almost idolatrous admiration for all political movements in America, free trade in everything except malt, and an absolute extinction of a State Church. . . .

Trollope is not so much concerned with the question, how many of these things are good? Rather he asks us to note the shallowness of the manner of holding them. 'Free trade in everything except malt' with its hint of militant teetotalism is a reminder of the way those who live by slogans frequently keep them in compartments and are unaware of contradictions. At the same time Trollope's obvious admiration for Monk enables him to hold the balance and to avoid any philistine contempt for abstract principles.

Trollope's political world depends on a large degree of consensus. How far that is because he saw such a consensus in the political world of his time, and how far it was a deeper-rooted temperamental assumption may be a question. We may be tempted to wonder whether he would have been so successful describing a deeply divided society, where people denied a hearing to each other's fundamental assumptions. Yet the violence and irrationality of human nature was no stranger to his thoughts, as we can see in books like *He Knew He Was Right*. Even in the political novels themselves, we find in *Phineas Redux* a crazy murder and an innocent man very nearly convicted of it. If we are tempted to think that he could not have written so well about France in the 1790's or England in the 1970's, that may only be because we are unable to guess how his genius would have adapted itself to new challenges. It is at least a reasonable presumption that he would have adapted himself. One reason, I would guess, for the tributes from Macmillan and Gaitskell, with which I began, was this: Trollope was always ready for the unexpected.

NOTES

1 *Autobiography*, Chapter XVI.
2 *Phineas Finn*, Chapter XLIII.
3 *Phineas Finn*, Chapter XLVII.
4 *Autobiography*, Chapter XVI.
5 See C. S. Emden (ed.), *Selected Speeches on the Constitution*. Vol. II, p. 194.
6 *Autobiography*, Chapter XVI.
7 See Carlyle, *Shooting Niagara*.
8 *Can You Forgive Her?*, Chapter LIX.
9 *Can You Forgive Her?*, Chapter LXIX.
10 *The Prime Minister*, Chapter LXVIII.

9

A Lesser Thackeray? Trollope and the Victorian Novel

by ROBIN GILMOUR

1

'It may seem rather hard that critics should read Mr. Trollope's novels and enjoy them,' the *Saturday Review* observed in 1863, 'and then abuse them for being what they are. But this is, we believe, the exact combination of feelings which they would awaken in many minds.'[1] Things have not changed much since then. Trollope's novels are still widely read and enjoyed—more widely today, I suspect, than Thackeray's—but the critical verdict remains rather grudging. Despite some excellent recent criticism, his reputation continues to be haunted by the old ghost from the *Autobiography*, with its portrait of the artist as the genial and prolific servant of the literary market-place. Was that legendary productivity—which even the fecund Henry James found 'gross' and 'importunate'[2]—compatible with a serious conception of the novelist's task? Did Trollope struggle enough with the materials and conventions of his art? Can an *oeuvre* which in its even professionalism seems to offer no agreed defining masterpiece, no *Vanity Fair* or *Middlemarch*, justifiably be called major? The fact that these questions are still being asked is evidence of a continuing Trollope problem.

Most of the reluctance to admit Trollope to the company of the unquestionably great Victorian novelists boils down to a suspicion that he acquiesced rather too easily in the conventions of mid-Victorian realism, and therefore in the social and moral assumptions those conventions express—a suspicion that only rarely, as James put it, has he 'dared to be thoroughly logical' and 'not sacrificed to conventional optimism . . . not been afraid of a misery which should be too much like life.'[6] 'Can You Forgive Him?' George Levine wittily asks in the most persuasive recent re-statement of the old critical reluctance about Trollope, and concludes that on the whole you can't.[4] Levine sees Trollope as 'for better or worse, a conventional artist—that is, a writer who unquestioningly accepted the conventions he inherited'. But he is an interesting writer because the logic of his presentation continually promises a break with the formal conventions he usually ends by accepting:

> Trollope, who invites us in Can You Forgive Her? to see well beyond the hypocrisies and irrationalities of social conventions, to understand the brutality of society's treatment of women, the hypocrisies of respectable society, the viciousness of the money game, the centrality of money to power, invites us as well to accept the necessity of accommodation. Strong enough to show us the incompleteness of the relation between his protagonists, he requires that we take as beautiful and satisfying the impossible accommodations they try to make to each other.

In other words Trollope is a tease: he gives an airing to the frustrations of Alice Vavasor and the rebelliousness of Lady Glencora, yet resolves these potentially disruptive conflicts by showing both characters accommodating to the demands of conventional marriage. 'Trollope's is an act of acceptance,' Levine concludes, 'an act which will not struggle with its materials. Can You Forgive Her? takes in on the edges of its vision the possibility of other realities, but it circles three times around them and dismisses those possibilities with a pat on the head.'[5] Levine does not invoke Thackeray (his heroes are George Eliot, Hardy, and Henry James) yet his essay is in effect a sophisticated modern re-formulation of the old judgement that Trollope is a 'lesser Thackeray'. Trollope's contemporaries were prone to compare his 'common sense' unfavourably with the 'profound philosophy' of Thackeray, and although it is no longer fashionable to find Thackeray profound the implication remains the same: where Thackeray or Dickens or George Eliot were bold enough to push beyond the conventional boundaries of the novel form, Trollope (in James's words again) 'accepted all the common restrictions, and found that even within the barriers there was plenty of material'.[6]

A notorious example is Doctor Thorne (1858), an earlier and

on the face of it much simpler novel than *Can You Forgive Her?*
Here Trollope created an action that explores and seems to call in
question many of the characteristic assumptions of landed society,
notably those relating to birth, heredity, money and 'trade', professional status, and the self-made man. Frank Gresham, heir to
the impoverished Greshamsbury estate, is in love with Mary Thorne,
the illegitimate niece of the local doctor. Frank must marry money,
and Trollope shows up the hypocrisy of Gresham family attitudes:
they do not care about the social origins of Frank's future wife
provided she brings money with her, but cold-shoulder Mary for
her poverty and low birth although she has been a constant
visitor to the house since childhood. In Chapter 39 ('What the
World says about Blood') Mr. Gresham explains to Frank that were
Mary an heiress '"the world would forgive her birth on account
of her wealth"'——

> 'The world is very complaisant, sir.'
> 'You must take it as you find it, Frank. I only say that such is
> the fact. If Porlock were to marry the daughter of a shoeblack,
> without a farthing, he would make a *mésalliance*; but if the
> daughter of the shoeblack had half a million of money, nobody
> would dream of saying so. I am stating no opinion of my own: I
> am only giving you the world's opinion.'
> 'I don't care a straw for the world.'
> 'That is a mistake, my boy; you do care for it, and would be
> very foolish if you did not. . . .'

In a sense this is Trollope's position too, at least in *Doctor Thorne.*
He is not a novelist to challenge 'the world' although he is moralist enough to point out its follies and hypocrisies, and in this novel
he manages to have it both ways. The moralist portrays sympath-
etically Mary's sufferings under the cruel ostracism of the
Greshamsbury parents, and Frank's patience and loyalty, and he
shows that each has been able to overcome the pressures of 'the
world'. But the basic conflict inherent in their respective social
predicament is never pushed to its logical conclusion, with all the
pain and readjustment it would necessarily involve—for Mary too
is sensitive to the needs of the Greshamsbury estate and the values
it ideally represents: 'she did think of the old name, and the old
Gresham pride; she did think of the squire and his deep distress:
it was true that she had lived among them long enough to understand these things, and to know that it was not possible that this

marriage should take place without deep family sorrow' (42). But the kind of readjustment to a life of useful work and modest hopes that Fred Vincy and Mary Garth make in *Middlemarch* after Fred loses his expectations from old Featherstone does not take place in *Doctor Thorne*. All is resolved by a convenient legacy from Mary's other, 'low', uncle, Sir Roger Scatcherd, a drunken *parvenu* who has made his fortune building railways. (It is worth noting in passing how characteristic of Trollope's kind of realism it is that he should make virtually nothing of the symbolic potential in this blood transfusion from trade to rank, especially when one compares it with what Dickens does with the convict's legacy in *Great Expectations*.) The money enables Frank to redeem the estate and marry Mary, the pain of family rejection is forgiven and forgotten, and Lady Arabella has the grand society wedding of her dreams, graced by the Duke of Omnium, the De Courcy family, the Bishop of Barchester, and so on. 'And thus Frank married money,' the novel blandly concludes, 'and became a great man' (47).

It is difficult to know what to make of the ending of *Doctor Thorne*, and of the novelist who can offer it as a satisfactory resolution of what has gone before: that, in miniature, is the Trollope problem. Is it not a simple case of a novelist capitulating to convention and the expectations of his readers? Trollope's admirers have had, broadly speaking, two different answers to make to questions and objections like these. One has been to argue that Trollope is in fact much more self-conscious than we tend to assume in his handling of fictional conventions, and that he is continually manipulating his reader to subtle questionings of, and disengagements from the conventional while keeping within a basically comic form which presupposes a romantic resolution of conflict. In this view, which has been convincingly argued by James Kincaid in what is perhaps the best recent study of Trollope, Trollope's adherence to the framework of comic form is even an enabling device, providing the sanction for adventurous and sometimes radical explorations within the frame: 'By thus suspending action and making the comic resolution so certain and so clear in all its details very early on, Trollope provides a cover that allows the comic form to contain much real darkness'.[7] The other answer has been to concede that the early novels like *Doctor Thorne* are indeed conventional and unsatisfactory, and to stress in their place Trollope's progress to pessimism (the phrase is Mr. Cockshut's), pointing to the disenchanted vision of later novels like *The Eustace Diamonds* (1873), *The Way We Live Now* (1875), and *Mr. Scarborough's Family* (1883). There, it is argued, one can see a far from complacent and conventional novelist—a castigator of sham, hypocrisy, and greed, whose 'sombre vision' of a corrupt society displays an 'honesty and clarity of vision that places Trollope with the greatest social novelists of the nineteenth century, with Dickens, Thackeray, and George Eliot'.[8]

This has been a seductive view, not least because it has enabled Trollope to be brought in on the same tide that landed a 'dark' Dickens and a self-divided Tennyson. Freed from his Barsetshire associations Trollope could be rehabilitated along with other Victorian writers in terms of their 'alienation' from what was seen to be a corruptly materialistic society. If this approach to the Victorians now seems a little dated and many of its assumptions questionable, it nonetheless performed the useful service of locating some interesting areas of disenchantment in Trollope's fiction. *The Way We Live Now*, in particular, has been beneficiary of this approach. Now widely considered to be Trollope's satirical masterpiece, it is perhaps the one single work outside the Barset and Palliser series that many Trollopians would put forward in answer to the charges of compromise and conventionality which Levine and others have made. Masterpiece or not, it is certainly a novel in which Trollope's central values and assumptions are put under an unusual, perhaps unique, degree of pressure, and for this reason I should like to take it as a test-case for exploring the question of his relation to his world and to the inherited conventions of his art. It may be argued that *The Way Live Now* is a little off-centre in Trollope's fiction as a whole, that it is untypically dark and satiric, and that his more characteristic achievements lie elsewhere—with all these qualifications I would tend to agree. But this huge novel is also arguably his most ambitious attempt to imagine the forces in the contemporary world which threatened the foundation of his own values, and as such is a remarkable extension of his art into territory normally associated with Dickens and Thackeray. In making the comparison it prompts with *Little Dorrit* and *The Newcomes*, I want to argue that the true measure of Trollope's relationship to his world is to be taken not by stressing the satirist's antagonism to society, for which he had only a limited capacity, but by uncovering the ambivalence in his attitude to the social and moral assumptions underlying the fictional conventions he employs. What will emerge, I hope, are some tentative conclusions about Trollope and the conventions of realism which have a wider bearing for his work as a whole.

2

The Way We Live Now has been so widely admired and written about, I suspect, because it seems to lend itself readily to the kind of moral and thematic analysis with which modern criticism is most at home. Here is one Trollope novel at least with a unifying theme, which can be talked about as Dickens's later novels are talked about, in terms of comprehensiveness of social vision and 'modern significance'.[9] The critic fresh from explicating the prison symbolism in *Little Dorrit* is able to settle with relief to unpacking the implications of Trollope's generalising title, and his expectations of another fictional anatomy of society are not disappointed. The prominence of the corrupt financier Melmotte, and the collapse of standards which his rise portends, can be traced through what is (for Trollope) an unusual concentration of analogical effects. Melmotte is both cause and symptom, symbol and victim, of a social malaise which has reached into almost every area of contemporary life. Corruption and the knowing betrayal of traditional values are seen to be at work in the aristocracy, among the gentry, in the City, in political life, even in the gentleman's club and the literary world. Mined from within by greed and hypocrisy, English society is portrayed as vulnerable to predatory outsiders like Melmotte himself and the two Americans, Hamilton Fisker and Mrs. Hurtle. Against this widespread corruption is set the resolute Englishness of Roger Carbury, the embattled squire (Carbury Manor is appropriately circled by a moat) who is almost alone in speaking out against the voices of the age. There is hardly a character in the novel, it can be argued, who is not affected by the social changes Melmotte's rise brings into focus.

Put like this, *The Way We Live Now* can be made to seem an impressively unified work, with a thematic coherence and satirical power not unworthy of comparison with the great satires of Dickens and Thackeray; and of course there is a good deal of evidence to support such a reading. The trouble with it is the trouble with most 'thematic' readings of novels, that it knits a net with so wide a mesh that much of what is most interesting in the novel slips through. My own impression of *The Way We Live Now* is rather different: as a satire it seems to me powerful, certainly, but in many ways less original, more traditional and even conventional than it has been made out to be; it becomes interesting at those points where the simpler oppositions of satire give way to a deeper disquiet which satire cannot adequately express. Perhaps this is only to make the familiar observation that satire was not Trollope's forte. But to explore the limits of his satire, to see where the satirical impulse breaks down or gives way to something else, and why, may help to reveal something of Trollope's true relationship to his world. There are three related aspects of the novel which I should like to examine from this point of view: the tone and stance of the narrator, the treatment of the two alien invaders, Melmotte and Mrs. Hurtle, and the interplay between convention and social pessimism, loneliness and marriage celebration, at the end of the book.

To begin with the narrator. The 'we' of the title seems to be inclusive, but one cannot read very far in the novel without realising that the community it presupposes has in fact certain important but undefined social limits. Douglas Hewitt, in his excellent essay on the novel, has spoken of the 'partnership in mediocrity' between reader and narrator in *The Way We Live Now*, arguing that 'the tendency of the whole book, however, is to explore and to modify the assumptions and standards which are assumed as shared between the writer and the reader.[10] The inital assumptions and standards are, specifically, those of gentlemen: the way we live now is the way gentlemen, who ought to know better, have come to behave, and this contributes not only a definite tone but also a strongly implied—and sometimes explicit—system of values to the satire. At the start it can even take the form of blunt indignation, the outrage of the decent man, as in this early comment on Lady Carbury:

> Detestably false as had been her letters to the editors, absolutely and abominably foul as was the entire system by which she was endeavouring to achieve success, far away from honour and honesty as she had been carried by her ready subserviency to the dirty things among which she had lately fallen, nevertheless her statements about herself were substantially true. . . .(2)

The expression here is perhaps uncharacteristically extreme; it smacks of the moral absolutism of Roger Carbury, just as the vocabulary ('false', 'foul', 'honour', 'dirty things') suggests the moral code of the traditional gentleman, which Roger is. But then much of the narrator's commentary does indeed sound like a rather more intelligent Roger Carbury, and this despite the fact that Trollope attempts to distance himself from Roger, as in Chapter 55 where the Bishop of Elmham's easygoing meliorism is wheeled in to 'place' his host's excessive pessimism. Consider, for example, this passage describing Melmotte's growing arrogance under success:

> Six months since he had been a humble man to a Lord,—but now he scolded Earls and snubbed Dukes, and yet did it in a manner which showed how proud he was of connecting himself with their social pre-eminence, and how ignorant of the manner in which such pre-eminence affects English gentlemen generally. The more arrogant he became the more vulgar he was, till even Lord Alfred would almost be tempted to rush away to impecuniosity and freedom. Perhaps there were some with whom this conduct has a salutary effect. No doubt arrogance will produce submission; and there are men who take other men at the price those other men put upon themselves. Such persons could not refrain from thinking Melmotte to be mighty because he swaggered; and gave their hinder parts to be kicked merely because he put up his toe. We all know men of this calibre,—and how they seem to grow in number. . . .(54)

The 'we' here is not ironic and there is no attempt to discriminate within the category of 'English gentlemen' between those who honour the rank and those, like Lord Alfred Grendall, who are gentlemen only in name and by their conduct disgrace it. The comment that Melmotte was 'ignorant of the manner in which such pre-eminence affects English gentlemen generally', looks out on him from within the security of the rank he cannot hope to enter, and pronounces him to be 'vulgar'. The adjective appears again a couple of pages later, when we are told that 'Melmotte was not the first vulgar man whom the Conservatives had taken by the hand, and patted on the back, and told that he was a god'. How close the narrator's valuation here is to Roger Carbury's can be seen in the following chapter, where Roger pronounces on Melmotte:

> 'You think Melmotte will turn out a failure.'
> 'A failure! Of course he's a failure, whether rich or poor;—a

miserable imposition, a hollow vulgar fraud from beginning to end,—too insignificant for you and me to talk of, were it not that his position is a sign of the degeneracy of the age. What are we coming to when such as he is an honoured guest at our tables?' (55)

Fortunately for the novel, as we shall see, Trollope is capable of looking further round the values of gentlemanliness than Roger does here, or than the narrator does in the preceding passage. In so far as *The Way We Live Now* is a satire, however, the code of gentlemanliness is what it offers as an opposition to Melmotte and all he represents. Soured and pessimistic though he may be, Roger speaks out for the values and standards that are being violated:

No one pretends to think that he is a gentleman. There is a consciousness among all who speak of him that he amasses his money not by honest trade, but by unknown tricks,—as does a card-sharper. He is one whom we would not admit into our kitchens, much less to our tables, on the score of his own merits. But because he has learned the art of making money, we not only put up with him, but settle upon his carcase as so many birds of prey. (15)

What is bluntly explicit in Roger is often implicit in the narrative and in the narrator's tone. His comparison of Melmotte with a card-sharper is made at large in the novel in the analogy between the Beargarden Club, where fashionable young men gamble with I.O.U.s, and the Stock Exchange where their elders scramble to get in on Melmotte's paper speculations. It is the solidity of land, too—which 'Squire' Roger pre-eminently represents—that in the end pricks the bubble of Melmotte's credit when he attempts to forge the title-deeds of Pickering Park. The narrator comes before us as a man who shares these traditional values—instinctively distrustful of the new club run by a single proprietor where 'there were to to be no morning papers taken, no library, no morning-room' (3); a little suspicious of foreigners, especially those with Jewish connections: Samuel Cohenlupe, one of Melmotte's directors, is kept at arm's length by being described as 'a gentleman of the Jewish persuasion' (9); a man for whom epithets like 'vulgar' and 'manly' seem to have unequivocal force. It is enough for him to say of Roger that 'a more manly man to the eye was never seen' (6), or that Sir Felix failed in 'manly conduct' (20) when the occasion required it, for a whole dimension of social and moral judgement to be invoked. Even the rhythms of the prose sometimes suggest the denizen of the gentleman's club:

> Melmotte himself was a large man, with bushy whiskers and rough thick hair, with heavy eyebrows, and a wonderful look of power about his mouth and chin. This was so strong as to redeem his face from vulgarity; but the countenance and appearance of the man were on the whole unpleasant, and, I may say, untrustworthy. He looked as though he were purseproud and a bully. . . . (4)

It is the novelist in Trollope (if one can make such a distinction) who notices the 'wonderful look of power about his mouth and chin', but this neutral observation immediately gives way to the blunt judgement that the appearance of 'the man' was 'on the whole unpleasant, and, I may say, untrustworthy'. That 'I may say' has all the deliberation of the gentleman who realises the gravity of the charge he is making against 'the man'.

These examples come from the first half of the novel, mostly from the opening chapters. It is all the more remarkable, then, that Trollope should move in the course of the book from this rather bluff conservative position to the point where he can concede of Melmotte in his ruin that 'there was a certain manliness about him . . .' (81), but by then much of the original satirical impulse has spent itself and the simpler oppositions with which the novel opened have become considerably, and interestingly, complicated and qualified. My immediate point, however, is that the reader coming to *The Way We Live Now* and expecting to find it Trollope's *Little Dorrit* is likely to be struck not only by the obvious differences he would expect—the slow and even pace of the narrative, patiently moving from group to group, the absence of spectacular stylistic effects such as symbolism—but also by the traditional nature of the satire itself. Promised a novel with 'modern significance', he will soon become aware how old-fashioned its message is, and indeed how little capable Trollope is of transcending his world, of finding access to values outwith the frame of reference of the society he observes and comments upon. Within that frame Trollope has some powerful things to say about the marriage market, the betrayal of moral standards by those who should know better, the growth of a credit economy, the decline of the gentry, but this criticism is phrased in the social and moral

191

vocabulary of the gentry class whose decline, or impotence, he regretfully records.

Trollope is too deeply a part of the world he satirises for his satire to achieve the radical bite of, say, Thackeray's, similar as the two novelists may look at a distance. *The Newcomes* is obviously a large presence in the background of *The Way We Live Now*, and of Trollope's fiction generally: the interplay of rank and trade in the marriage market is a Thackerayan subject he took over early in his career and made very much his own, and like Thackeray he is continually drawn to contemplate the image of the gentleman as both victim and critic of a materialistic society. But Thackeray had a capacity for moral and historical detachment from his world which gives his satire a real purchase upon early Victorian England. In *The Newcomes* he shows an impressive command of a whole phase of English social history, tracing the fortunes of the Newcome family back to their origins in trade and Evangelical Christianity, and then forward on the familiar path from 'serious' religion to City respectability and fashionable life. It is because Thackeray understands this process of social evolution that he can make Colonel Newcome such an effective embodiment of the values he admires and sees as vulnerable and threatened in the modern world; for the Colonel belongs to an alternative tradition of gentility associated with the Army and India and through these with the eighteenth-century's most robust and open-hearted chivalry, which City respectability cannot understand and which in the novel is linked with the fictional archetype of Don Quixote. Thackeray's long perspective makes Colonel Newcome at once historically credible and yet a timeless figure, an enduring image of a certain kind of human integrity and faithfulness by which a greedy society can be judged. Trollope, it is true, is writing about a later stage of Victorian social development, but his inability to distance himself from and transcend his material comes, I believe partly from a deficiency of the historical imagination which Thackeray possessed. He stands too close to what he observes to achieve the satirist's detachment; in this respect he is indeed a 'lesser Thackeray'.

3

If the social analysis of *The Way We Live Now* recalls *The New-comes*, then the figure of Melmotte equally obviously recalls Mr. Merdle in Dickens's *Little Dorrit*, a novel Trollope read and may conceivably have been influenced by. And here, it seems to me, we can see where the rather conventional satire gives way to something much more interesting. As R. B. Martin has shown, both Melmotte and Merdle were probably based in part on George Hudson, the Railway King, whose spectacular rise and fall in the eighteen-forties and -fifties is one of the exemplary histories of Victorian capitalism.[11] Trollope's memories of Hudson may have been awakened by reading obituary notices of the Railway King in 1871, and the conception of Melmotte may also have been influenced by recent reading of Robert Bell's novel, *The Ladder of Gold: An English Story* (1850), which as Martin points out contains a fictional portrait of Hudson as well as a Lady Carbury figure who plots to marry her worthless son to the great financier's daughter. To recognise these possible sources may lead to the conclusion that in Melmotte Trollope was drawing upon a convention, a cultural stereotype, for Hudson passed quickly into contemporary mythology as a symbol of the over-reaching commercial Colossus of the new industry. This is true but ignores what Trollope is doing with the convention, the way Melmotte grows in his creator's hands beyond the satirical frame into a stoic loneliness that is not only moving in itself but also causes us to question and modify the earlier easy judgement that 'the man' is not one of 'us'. Dickens's Merdle, by contrast, is of course a much more brilliant creation, but it is the brilliance of an imprisoning rhetoric which will not release the character from Dickens's conviction of his utter nullity. The irony works continually to contrast the profane worship Merdle attracts with the mean reality of the man himself, and his suicide becomes the occasion for a triumphant display of Dickens's indignation:

> For by that time it was known that the late Mr. Merdle's complaint had been simply Forgery and Robbery. He, the uncouth object of such wide-spread adulation, the sitter at great men's feasts, the roc's egg of great ladies' assemblies, the subduer of exclusiveness, the leveller of pride, the patron of patrons . . . he, the shining

wonder, the new constellation to be followed by the wise men bringing gifts, until it stopped over a certain carrion at the bottom of a bath and disappeared—was simply the greatest Forger and the greatest Thief that ever cheated the gallows. (II, 25)

Dickens's 'simply' is the *q.e.d.* at the end of a successful moral theorem; for Trollope there is no 'simply' about Melmotte. As the novel progresses Trollope's sympathy for his creation starts to loosen the simpler absolutisms of satire. At the outset we see him very much as Roger Carbury does, as an alien invader whose presence at 'our' tables is a sign of national degeneracy; by the end we are looking through his eyes at the society which has cast him out. In the process deeper questions about the way we live now are released than any that satire can ask.

The turning-point is the dinner Melmotte stages for the Emperor of China. This is the climax of his social fortunes and the beginning of his ruin, for the rumour that he has been guilty of forgery is about and many of his fashionable guests have decided at the last minute to stay away. As Melmotte stares round apprehensively at the empty spaces at his banquet, like some Victorian Macbeth, Trollope's treatment of him moves inward and we start to share Melmotte's own view of things, his fears, doubts, self-reproach for mistakes made, but above all his courage in shaking off his panic and resolving to shoulder the burden of the isolation he knows he must carry from now on:

> He had not far to go, round through Berkeley Square into Bruton Street, but he stood for a few moments looking up at the bright stars. If he could be there, in one of those unknown distant worlds, with all his present intellect and none of his present burdens, he would, he thought, do better than he had done here on earth. If he could even now put himself down nameless, fameless, and without possessions in some distant corner of the world, he could, he thought, do better. But he was Augustus Melmotte, and he must bear his burdens, whatever they were, to the end. He could reach no place so distant but that he would be known and traced. (62)

It is at moments like these that we come up against a central paradox of Trollope's fiction—that of all Victorian novelists he has the most intimate knowledge of, and respect for, the norms that hold society together, and yet is drawn again and again to the creation of characters who flout and transgress these norms. The loneliness of the outsider deeply interests him, and he is often at his best when writing about it. Thus we are likely to take away from the novel an impression of Melmotte considerably modified from the earlier satirical anathematising: the vulgar entepreneur is a stock figure who can easily be judged and dismissed, but when Melmotte forges Dolly Longestaffe's signature on the Pickering title deeds he breaks one of the cardinal rules of Trollope's world and for that reason becomes a source of fascination to its creator. The contrast with Dickens's Merdle ('simply the greatest Forger and the greatest Thief that ever cheated the gallows') shows the difficulty Trollope has in maintaining the pressure of satiric indignation, how naturally he moves to sympathise with the character who violates the rules. One of the most memorable chapters in the novel is the account of Melmotte's last visit to the House of Commons, when he is a ruined man and his titled friends have all deserted him; cold-shouldered by the members, he eats his dinner alone, drinks too much, falls drunkenly in attempting to make a speech, and then goes home to commit suicide. Parliament is the highest court of gentlemen in Trollope, and it is characteristic of him to bring the outsider and his jury together and yet leave us with a dominant impression of the outsider's strength and courage, even dignity, in braving the hostile gathering. And in Melmotte's deepening isolation and suicide the 'we' of the title widens to include the man who has violated 'our' standards, linking his case to that of all unendurable suffering in a hard world: 'He had assured himself long ago . . . that he would brave it all like a man. But we none of us know what load we can bear, and what would break our backs' (88).

4

Trollope's handling of Melmotte shows his ability to depart from satiric convention and in doing so to bring his reader round to the point where, briefly, he looks through the outsider's eyes at the insider's world and can feel its powers of rejection and repudiation. A more direct challenge to fictional conventions and the normative values they embody is provided by another outsider, the American woman Mrs. Hurtle, who pursues the nominal hero, Paul Montague, back to England. In a schematic reading of *The Way We Live Now* she figures with the ruthless American businessman

Hamilton Fisker as one of the alien invaders of English society, her passion and rootlessness a challenge to the rooted, squire-archical Englishness of Roger Carbury and the narrator. Her admiration for Melmotte as a Napoleon of commerce—' "Such a man rises above honesty . . . as a great general rises above humanity when he sacrifices an army to conquer a nation" ' (26)—seems to put her on the side of the amoral characters, and her love for Paul Montague brings her domineering passionateness into unfavourable comparison with the sweet passiveness of the conventional heroine, Hetta Carbury. Initially at least, the opposition seems a familiar and conventional one, especially as Mrs. Hurtle attracts the disapproval of the spokesman for English pastoral values, Roger Carbury, who cannot accept that she is a 'lady' (87). As with Melmotte, Trollope begins by seeming to share Roger's prejudiced view of her as a dangerously independent creature: she is beautiful, wild, is rumoured to have 'shot a man through the head somewhere in Oregon' (26); to Paul she seems to have 'the breeding of the wild cat' (38), and she herself invokes Medea, declaring that there is ' "a dash of the savage princess" ' about most women (27). In all these respects, and most of all in her Americanness, she appears to be another portent of the way we live now. But again the semi-cliché of the cosmopolitan wild-cat is soon modified by Trollope's fascination for a character who has become an outsider by virtue of the intensity of her feelings and her inability to subdue them as decorum requires. Her loneliness and self-division emerge at Lowestoft, when after their weekend together Paul attempts to break off their relationship:

> Was this to be the end of it? Should she never know rest;—never have one draught of cool water between her lips? Was there to be no end to the storms and turmoil and misery of her life? In almost all that she had said she had spoken the truth, though doubtless not all the truth,—as which among us would in giving the story of his life? She had endured violence, and had been violent. She had been schemed against, and had schemed. She had fitted herself to the life which had befallen her. But in regard to money, she had been honest and she had been loving of heart. With her heart of hearts she had loved this young Englishman;—and now, after all her scheming, all her daring, with all her charms, this was to be the end of it! Oh, what a journey would this be which she must now make back to her own country, all alone! (47)

Trollope shows how in her loneliness she is divided against herself,
drawn to desire the English placidity and respectability she also
despises (and not simply out of jealousy because in the person of
Hetta they have won her lover's heart):

> With all the little ridicule she was wont to exercise in speaking
> of the old country there was ever mixed, as is so often the case in
> the minds of American men and women, an almost envious
> admiration of English excellence. To have been allowed to forget
> the past and to live the life of an English lady would have been
> heaven to her. But she, who was sometimes scorned and some-
> times feared in the eastern cities of her own country, whose name
> had become almost a proverb for violence out in the far West,—
> how could she dare to hope that her lot should be so changed for
> her? (47)

There are blemishes in the portrait—the reference here to 'English
excellence', the playing upon the melodramatic detail of her pro-
verbial violence, the utterly improbable role she is called upon to
play at the end as match-maker to Ruby Ruggles and John Crumb.
But Mrs. Hurtle is a powerful and moving creation, because she
is a woman and not a girl (as she tells Hetta), and a woman at a
crisis of her life when the issue is too important for conventional
maidenly modesty—though that is what wins Paul—or for turning her face to the wall: to the end she is reproaching and challenging him, reminding him of the intensity of her love and loss:

> 'Every word you say is a dagger.'
> 'You know where to go for salve for such skin-deep scratches
> as I make. Where am I to find a surgeon who can put together
> my crushed bones? Daggers, indeed! Do you not suppose that
> in thinking of you I have often thought of daggers? Why have
> I not thrust one into your heart, so that I might rescue you from
> the arms of this puny, spiritless English girl?' All this time she
> was still seated, looking at him, leaning forward towards him
> with her hands upon her brow. 'But, Paul, I spit out my words
> to you, like any common woman, not because they will hurt you,
> but because I know I may take that comfort, such as it is, without
> hurting you. You are uneasy for a moment while you are here,
> and I have a cruel pleasure in thinking that you cannot answer
> me. But you will go from me to her, and then will you not be
> happy? When you are sitting with your arm round her waist, and
> when she is playing with your smiles, will the memory of my

words interfere with your joy then? Ask yourself whether the prick will last longer than the moment. But where am I to go for happiness and joy? Can you understand what it is to have to live only on retrospects?' (97)

As Douglas Hewitt says, 'she impresses us because she speaks with the note of real loss, of uncompromising pain, which convinces us of an intensity of feeling which is so lacking in most of the personages in the book, which is, in a sense, what is lacking in the whole society which rejects those who intrude into it'.[12] Her tragedy is that she is so much more vital and human than the 'sweetness' of the 'English manners' that defeat her:

> She loved Paul Montague with all her heart, and she despised herself for loving him. How weak he was;—how inefficient; how unable to seize glorious opportunities; how swathed and swaddled by scruples and prejudices;—how unlike her own countrymen in quickness of apprehension and readiness of action! But yet she loved him for his very faults, telling herself that there was something sweeter in his English manners than in all the smart intelligence of her own land. . . .(97)

It could be argued, and perhaps the thematic structure of the book supports such a reading, that the defeat and exile of Mrs. Hurtle, and the marriage of Hetta and Paul under the aegis of Roger Carbury, represents a muted resurrection of English pastoral values once the poison of the alien invaders has run its course through English society. If that is the pattern, however, then the novel Trollope actually wrote continually challenges and complicates it. Mrs. Hurtle bites back at the conventions which exile her. Her story sounds a note of loss and homeless feeling which reverberates through all the concluding marriage settlements that attempt to muffle it.

This is most obvious in the case of Hetta Carbury. She is such an insipid character that it is difficult to believe Trollope is not challenging convention here and inviting us to share Mrs. Hurtle's verdict on this ' "puny, spiritless English girl" '. Hetta is totally pliant to convention, including the convention of maidenly passivity, and her reactions are invariably proper, sometimes comically so, as when she learns from Paul about her rival:

> 'Is she a widow?'—He did not answer this at once. 'I suppose she must be a widow if you were going to marry her.'

'Yes;—she is a widow. She was divorced.'
'Oh, Paul! And she is an American?'
'Yes.'
'And you loved her?' (76)

Her favourite epithets are 'nice' and 'horrid'. It seems clear that
Trollope means her to show up poorly in comparison with Mrs.
Hurtle, for the two characters are compared throughout the book
and meet at last in Chapter 91, 'The Rivals'. Having 'trusted herself all alone to the mysteries of the Marylebone underground
railway' (this to visit a woman who has come from California!),
Hetta arrives at Mrs. Hurtle's Islington lodgings and finds her
very different from what she had imagined: 'She had thought that
the woman would be coarse and big, with fine eyes and a bright
colour. As it was they were both of the same complexion, both
dark, with hair nearly black, with eyes of the same colour.' The
parallel is deliberate, as is what it suggests: that Hetta has won
because she is younger:

> 'He has preferred you to me, and as far as I am concerned there
> is an end of it. You are a girl, whereas I am a woman,—and he
> likes your youth. I have undergone the cruel roughness of the
> world, which has not yet touched you; and therefore you are
> softer to the touch. I do not know that you are very superior in
> other attractions; but that has sufficed, and you are the victor. I
> am strong enough to acknowledge that I have nothing to forgive
> in you;—and am weak enough to forgive all his treachery.' Hetta
> was now holding the woman by the hand, and was weeping, she
> knew not why. . . .

After this it is difficult to take as seriously meant the conventional
maidenly hopes Hetta indulges in when she leaves Islington, confident that Paul is now hers: 'No other man had ever touched her
lips, or been allowed to press her hand, or to look into her eyes
with unrebuked admiration. It was her pride to give herself to the
man she loved after this fashion, pure and white as snow on which
no foot has trodden.' The hurt in Mrs. Hurtle has been too powerfully registered for this sort of thing to carry any conviction at all.
   Indeed, there is something muted, even half-hearted, about the
ending of *The Way We Live Now*, as if Trollope had become too
much involved in the loneliness of his outsiders to feel much
enthusiasm for the conventional winding-up. Mrs. Hurtle loses

but the criticism she leaves behind her ('"this puny, spiritless English girl"') sticks. Roger Carbury's pastoral, gentry world, which at the outset provided the values by which the way we live now was judged, appears enervated by the end—no less a source of value perhaps, but lacking vital force. It is only in the tedious John Crumb–Ruby Ruggles sub-plot that the marriage celebrations have any vigour: the Paul–Hetta wedding is overshadowed by our awareness that Roger has no true heir, and that he has swallowed his disappointment about Hetta by becoming the conventional 'father' to the young couple. And disappointment makes strange bedfellows, for although Roger is Mrs. Hurtle's implacable opponent they both owe the loneliness of their lives to Paul's marriage. The conventions point to the restoration of community, but the impression at the end is of how much that is humanly valuable has been left out of the the restored community.

5

'"One becomes so absorbed in one's plot and one's characters!"', Lady Carbury says gushingly of the novel she has just finished. '"One loves the loveable so intensely, and hates with such fixed aversion those who are intended to be hated. . . ."' (89). Trollope's own fiction is rather different, as I have tried to show; by becoming absorbed in his characters he tends to move away from the simple loves and hates of conventional fiction, though not far enough perhaps for his sterner critics. *The Way We Live Now* turns out to be the exception which proves the rule. The novel begins with the strong oppositions of satire voiced in the sometimes gruff tones of an honest gentleman who doesn't like the way things are going, but as it develops Trollope and his reader become involved in the sympathetic understanding of those very outsiders who seem to offer the most dramatic threat to what one senses to be his own values. This suggests concluding observations. One is that Trollope's imagination did not run naturally to the satirical social anatomy of the *Little Dorrit* or *Newcomes* kind, and that to argue it does is finally to do him a disservice: from this point of view he is bound to seem a 'lesser Thackeray'. The moral absolutism of satire, and the detachment it requires from communal norms, was foreign to the habit of his mind. Another is that Trollope's novels are a more or less disconcerting mixture of the predictable and the surprising, of conventional and unconventional elements, and are likely to be most interesting at those points where conventional valuations are being probed and tested. In *The Way We Live Now*, for example, the meal-dealer John Crumb, and the bad baronet Felix Carbury, belong entirely to stereotype; but stereotype is challenged by the 'good' Jew Brehgert, who counters the hints of prejudice in the presentation of Mr. Cohenlupe ('a gentleman of the Jewish persuasion'), and much more radically, as we have seen, in Melmotte and Mrs. Hurtle.

But what of Trollope's attitude to fictional convention? Is he in the last analysis, as Levine argues, a novelist who flirts with other possibilities only to rope his characters in at the end to marriage and similar accommodations to a comfortable bourgeois sense of what is 'real'? Here *The Way We Live Now* may suggest the beginnings of an answer. I have argued that the central paradox of Trollope's fiction is the co-presence of an intimate awareness of and respect for social and moral norms, and a fascination with characters who trangress those norms. The unease which informs *The Way We Live Now*, and which the satire only partly expresses, comes from a sense of enervation about the roots which sustain the norms, a suspicion that the human circle ringed by the Carbury moat lacks vitality and purpose; and it is the outsiders who make us aware of this. The novel is a pessimistic example of a general tendency in Trollope's work, his remarkable capacity for pushing his explorations of character and motive against the grain of his prejudices. He is drawn to his outsiders, drawn to imagine their challenge to values he also shares.

The important point, however, is that this challenge would not be as powerfully felt as it is in his best novels, his lonely or alienated characters would not be as good as they nearly always are, if Trollope did not see something valuable in the norms which the fictional conventions express. It is the complexity of his commitment to the binding sanctions of his world—marriage, inheritance, the code of the gentleman, the responsibilities of land—which leads him to understand the moral and psychological strain they put upon individuals, and draws him to the outsiders who break them. His real position is that of a much more intelligently troubled Roger Carbury. The fashionable view of Trollope as a moral relativist, proponent of 'situation ethics', ignores the bedrock of ethical conviction in his work and its basis in land and the

responsibilities of inheritance. Roger Carbury speaks for that bedrock on the penultimate page of *The Way We Live Now*:

> The disposition of a family property, even though it be one so
> small as mine, is, to my thinking, a matter which a man should
> not make in accordance with his own caprices,—or even with his
> own affections. He owes a duty to those who live on his land, and
> he owes a duty to his country, And, though it may seem fantastic
> to say so, I think he owes a duty to those who have been before
> him, and who have manifestly wished that the property should
> be continued in the hands of their descendants. These things are
> to me very holy. . . . (100)

These things were also holy to Trollope, I believe, although he was
not a squire himself and was too subtle a man and novelist to make
them quite as explicit as Roger does here. Land as the source of
stability, inheritance as a responsibility that ensured continuity
through the generations—these are at the heart of what Paul Elmer
More called Trollope's 'feeling for the vast integrity of civilisation'.[13] That feeling could find expression through the themes and
conventions of the novel of manners he inherited from Jane Austen
(a more important predecessor than Thackeray in this respect).
Marriage settlements, the problems of inheritance, the struggles
between parents and children over money and land, the interplay
of rank and trade: the resolution of such conflicts, to which his
novels so often tend, has at least an ideal relationship to the values
which feed his fiction, and Trollope's resort to them is not necessarily cynical or opportunistic. Resolution promises a precious
continuity, while the accommodations it requires are sometimes
painful and even maiming: it is Trollope's awareness of these often
contradictory possibilities that gives his fiction its life.

NOTES

The place of publication is London unless otherwise stated. All references
are by chapter number to the 'World's Classics' (Oxford) edition of Trollope's
novels.

1 *Trollope: The Critical Heritage*, ed. Donald Smalley, 1969, p. 187.
2 'Anthony Trollope', *Partial Portraits* (1888); repr. *Trollope: Critical
   Heritage*, pp. 525–45; 525.
3 *Trollope: The Critical Heritage*, p. 543.
4 'Can You Forgive Him? Trollope's *Can You Forgive Her?* and the Myth

of Realism', *Victorian Studies*, XVIII (1974), 5–30.

5   *loc. cit.*, pp. 5, 7, 30.

6   *Trollope: The Critical Heritage*, p. 540. The statement that Trollope is 'a lesser Thackeray' can be found in G. K. Chesterton, *The Victorian Age in Literature*, 1913, p. 130.

7   *The Novels of Anthony Trollope*, Oxford, 1977, p. 115.

8   Stephen Gill and John Sutherland, Introduction to the Penguin English Library edition of *The Eustace Diamonds*, Harmondsworth, Middlesex, 1969, p. 30.

9   See, e.g., Tony Tanner, 'Trollope's *The Way We Live Now*: Its Modern Significance', *Critical Quarterly*, IX (1967), 256–71.

10 *The Approach to Fiction*, 1972, p. 17. I am generally indebted to Mr. Hewitt's chapter on Trollope, which illuminated many areas of the novel for me.

11 Robert Bernard Martin, *Enter Rumour: Four Early Victorian Scandals*, 1962, pp. 187–241. See also Grahame and Angela Smith, 'Dickens as a Popular Artist', *Dickensian*, lxvii (1971), 131–44.

12 *The Approach to Fiction*, p. 30.

13 *The Demon of the Absolute*, Princeton, 1928, p. 124.

Index